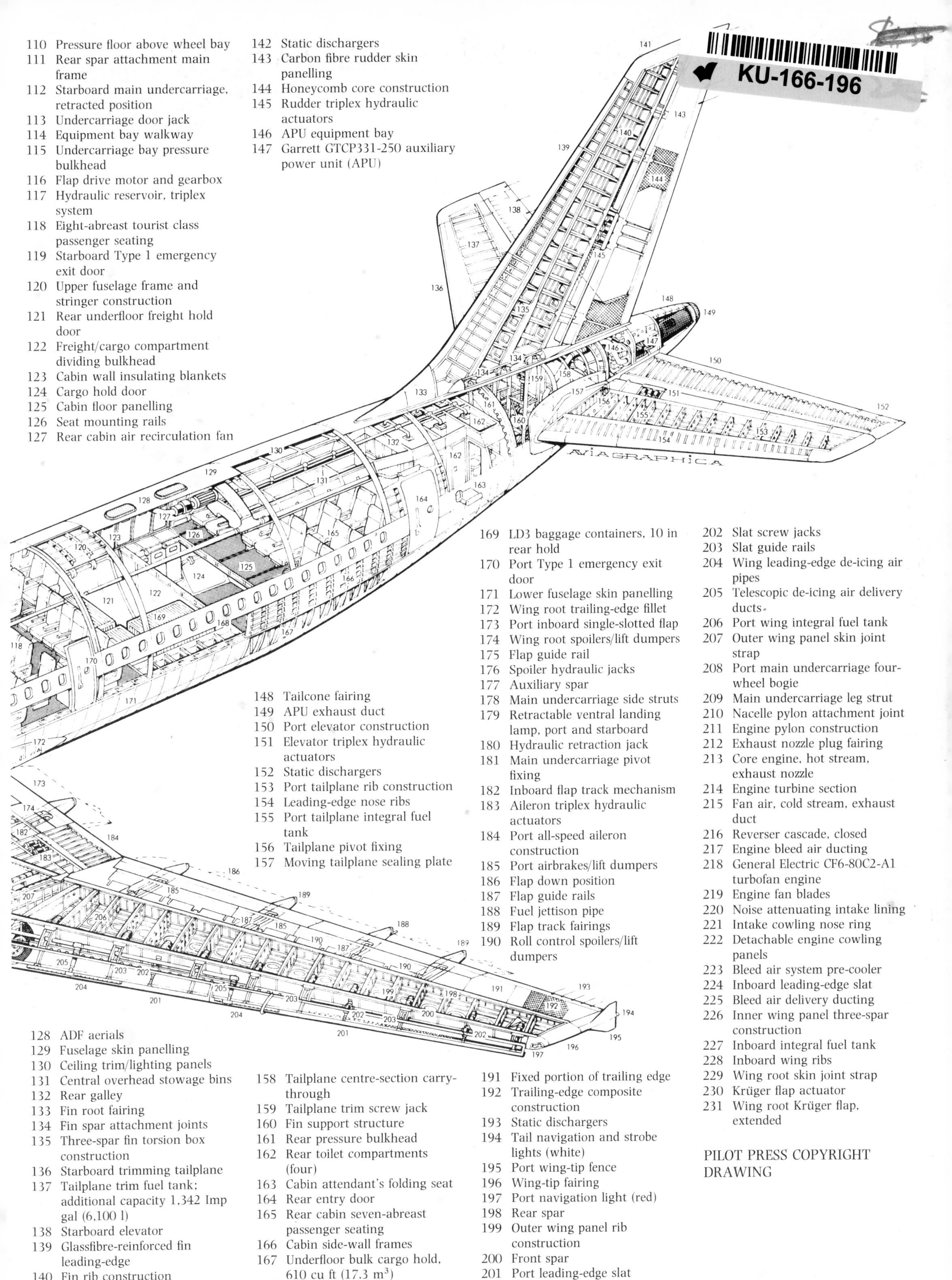
110 Pressure floor above wheel bay
111 Rear spar attachment main frame
112 Starboard main undercarriage, retracted position
113 Undercarriage door jack
114 Equipment bay walkway
115 Undercarriage bay pressure bulkhead
116 Flap drive motor and gearbox
117 Hydraulic reservoir, triplex system
118 Eight-abreast tourist class passenger seating
119 Starboard Type 1 emergency exit door
120 Upper fuselage frame and stringer construction
121 Rear underfloor freight hold door
122 Freight/cargo compartment dividing bulkhead
123 Cabin wall insulating blankets
124 Cargo hold door
125 Cabin floor panelling
126 Seat mounting rails
127 Rear cabin air recirculation fan
128 ADF aerials
129 Fuselage skin panelling
130 Ceiling trim/lighting panels
131 Central overhead stowage bins
132 Rear galley
133 Fin root fairing
134 Fin spar attachment joints
135 Three-spar fin torsion box construction
136 Starboard trimming tailplane
137 Tailplane trim fuel tank; additional capacity 1,342 Imp gal (6,100 l)
138 Starboard elevator
139 Glassfibre-reinforced fin leading-edge
140 Fin rib construction
141 Fin tip fairing
142 Static dischargers
143 Carbon fibre rudder skin panelling
144 Honeycomb core construction
145 Rudder triplex hydraulic actuators
146 APU equipment bay
147 Garrett GTCP331-250 auxiliary power unit (APU)
148 Tailcone fairing
149 APU exhaust duct
150 Port elevator construction
151 Elevator triplex hydraulic actuators
152 Static dischargers
153 Port tailplane rib construction
154 Leading-edge nose ribs
155 Port tailplane integral fuel tank
156 Tailplane pivot fixing
157 Moving tailplane sealing plate
158 Tailplane centre-section carry-through
159 Tailplane trim screw jack
160 Fin support structure
161 Rear pressure bulkhead
162 Rear toilet compartments (four)
163 Cabin attendant's folding seat
164 Rear entry door
165 Rear cabin seven-abreast passenger seating
166 Cabin side-wall frames
167 Underfloor bulk cargo hold, 610 cu ft (17.3 m³)
168 Cabin window panels
169 LD3 baggage containers, 10 in rear hold
170 Port Type 1 emergency exit door
171 Lower fuselage skin panelling
172 Wing root trailing-edge fillet
173 Port inboard single-slotted flap
174 Wing root spoilers/lift dumpers
175 Flap guide rail
176 Spoiler hydraulic jacks
177 Auxiliary spar
178 Main undercarriage side struts
179 Retractable ventral landing lamp, port and starboard
180 Hydraulic retraction jack
181 Main undercarriage pivot fixing
182 Inboard flap track mechanism
183 Aileron triplex hydraulic actuators
184 Port all-speed aileron construction
185 Port airbrakes/lift dumpers
186 Flap down position
187 Flap guide rails
188 Fuel jettison pipe
189 Flap track fairings
190 Roll control spoilers/lift dumpers
191 Fixed portion of trailing edge
192 Trailing-edge composite construction
193 Static dischargers
194 Tail navigation and strobe lights (white)
195 Port wing-tip fence
196 Wing-tip fairing
197 Port navigation light (red)
198 Rear spar
199 Outer wing panel rib construction
200 Front spar
201 Port leading-edge slat segments
202 Slat screw jacks
203 Slat guide rails
204 Wing leading-edge de-icing air pipes
205 Telescopic de-icing air delivery ducts
206 Port wing integral fuel tank
207 Outer wing panel skin joint strap
208 Port main undercarriage four-wheel bogie
209 Main undercarriage leg strut
210 Nacelle pylon attachment joint
211 Engine pylon construction
212 Exhaust nozzle plug fairing
213 Core engine, hot stream, exhaust nozzle
214 Engine turbine section
215 Fan air, cold stream, exhaust duct
216 Reverser cascade, closed
217 Engine bleed air ducting
218 General Electric CF6-80C2-A1 turbofan engine
219 Engine fan blades
220 Noise attenuating intake lining
221 Intake cowling nose ring
222 Detachable engine cowling panels
223 Bleed air system pre-cooler
224 Inboard leading-edge slat
225 Bleed air delivery ducting
226 Inner wing panel three-spar construction
227 Inboard integral fuel tank
228 Inboard wing ribs
229 Wing root skin joint strap
230 Krüger flap actuator
231 Wing root Krüger flap, extended
AVIAGRAPHICA
PILOT PRESS COPYRIGHT DRAWING

AIRBUS

OSPREY
Lufthansa
Airbus A300

AIRBUS

BILL GUNSTON

Published in 1988 by Osprey Publishing Limited
27A Floral Street, London WC2E 9DP
Member company of the George Philip Group

Sole distributors for the USA

British Library Cataloguing in Publication Data

Gunston, Bill
Airbus.
1. Airbus Industrie
I. Title
338.7'62913334'094 HD9711.E884A4

ISBN 0-85045-820-X

Editor Dennis Baldry
Designed by Roger Walker

Filmset in Great Britain by Tameside Filmsetting Limited, Ashton-under-Lyne, Lancashire, and printed by BAS Printers Limited, Over Wallop, Hampshire

Title page *After initially being very cool towards the Airbus the flag carrier of the Federal German Republic at last stuck one toe in with an order for three A300B2s, plus nine options which many in the airline thought would never be taken up. Here the first Lufthansa B2 is seen at Frankfurt in 1976. Today the airline has a big fleet of 300s and 310s, and has ordered the 320 and 340*
(Illustrations courtesy Airbus Industrie unless otherwise credited)

Contents

Introduction

THIS BOOK TELLS THE STORY of a company—or, more correctly, a GIE (*groupement d'intérêt economique*, or a group formed to exploit a common interest). This happens to be a French term, but Airbus Industrie is not, as is commonly thought, French. It is a truly international partnership. The basic shareholders are companies in France, Federal Germany, Spain and the UK, and other countries deeply involved are Belgium, the Netherlands, Italy, Australia and, to a very large extent indeed, the USA, which plays a major role in the engines, avionics and high-cost systems.

AI started out with a single product, called the A300B. The designation meant 'Airbus, 300 seats, second version', and as it was sized for around 250 seats it ought to have been restyled the A250. At that time, in the late 1960s, various companies in the USA had provided the technology for a new 'size plateau' in commercial jets pioneered by the 747 Jumbo Jet. This was planned as a monster long-range transport with four of the new high-bypass-ratio turbofan engines. Such engines made possible the mass movement of people and cargo in vehicles much bigger than ever before, with far better fuel economy and about one-hundredth as much environmental disturbance. It was one of the giant advances of mankind.

The aircraft builders of Western Europe reasoned that it made sense to build a vehicle almost as big as a 747 but matched to shorter airline sectors—where there is far more traffic—and thus needing much less fuel per trip and so able to fly on just two of the new engines. At first a few people questioned the wisdom of carrying so many people on just two engines, but this was never really an issue. The British government, in one of its perpetual flashes of idiocy which characterize its attitude towards aerospace, pulled right out. It apparently believed that a vehicle which offered a wholly new standard of comfort, fuel economy, direct operating cost and quietness was an undesirable development unlikely to appeal to the airlines. For the first ten years it looked as if they were right. In this period sales of the rival 727, 737 and DC-9 went way beyond the 3,000 mark despite the fact that they have narrow cabins, guzzle fuel and make a thunderous din. Total sales of the A300B amounted to just 20, plus one aircraft leased.

Back in the 1950s the widespread introduction of jets to the world's airlines led a highly respected British aviation writer to pen a major pontification entitled 'An Industry Gone Mad' (he couldn't have been more wrong). In the 1970s I beat my head against the wall, convinced that on this occasion the industry really had gone mad. Airlines vied with each other to think up ever more fatuous reasons why the very idea of an Airbus was some kind of sick joke. I quote a few at the start of the opening chapter. But in the world of aerospace, and big commercial jets in particular, if you really do have it right then, sooner or later, even the airlines will recognize the fact. Unfortunately, it is usually later—unless you happen to have a high established reputation, in which case the airlines will actually listen to what you have to say.

Today AI (Airbus Industrie) has established a reputation that stands right on a par with Boeing and probably ahead of everyone else. Its products have consistently set records for quality, high technology, reliability, operating economy and safety. It would be very unwise to make too much of this last point, but in millions of hours there are thousands of opportunities for having accidents. All the other big jets have suffered a long succession of major accidents in service, but Airbus has never had one. Apart from a spectacular hijack to Entebbe the only time an Airbus has hit the headlines has been when a terrorist bomb nearly blew the tail off, and it speaks volumes for AI's design engineers that nobody was sucked out and the aircraft made a normal landing. That's a record without parallel.

This kind of thing never happens by chance, and in the field of commercial jets there are ample opportunities for getting it wrong. For a start, it costs billions to launch the programme. It takes maybe five years to fly the first off the line, seven years to get into revenue operation and—if you take nothing but right decisions and have a lot of good luck—12 years to break even and begin making a profit on the billions put in at the start. Of course by this time inflation and about 200 almost unpredictable variables have mucked up your original detailed calculations. The airlines have a history of generally sustained growth, but they are incredibly sensitive to all sorts of economic winds of fortune which blow unpredictably. Wars, fuel crises, economic slumps, trade 'wars', interest rates, cold feet by the banks, the emergence of giant leasing companies, cheap secondhand aircraft, and the purely political decisions of government agencies can all have a profound effect on the world market for big jetliners, and who builds them.

The results are also influenced by the planemakers' own management. But what a business to be in! One of the author's favourite quotations was a comment by Sir Robert Watson Watt, the 'father of radar', in 1935. Before he came along the only kind of air-defence detection system the British government could think of was the sound mirror: gigantic concrete walls curved to focus the sound of the approaching bombers on a microphone. Of course, if the bombers came from a different country the colossal edifice failed to work, and Wattie's comment was, 'Reinforced concrete is rudely uncompliant to the winds of diplomacy'. I love the quote because it applies to so many of man's enterprises. Aluminium is almost as uncompliant as concrete, and if you bend it the wrong shape in a jetliner your rival picks up all the business. How can a design engineer take the right decisions in year X in order to ensure an overall profit on the operation in year X+12? Anything can have happened in that time. People keep inventing new wing profiles, new ultra-fan engines, new all-electric systems and a dozen other things to render the exercise almost impossibly difficult.

So far AI has hardly put a foot wrong. Of course, one vital factor has been the fact that, contrary to what used to happen in Britain, AI has never been forced to design for a particular national airline, which is the absolute guarantee of marketing limitations if not of total global unacceptance. Today AI has a track record that can only be described as fabulous. You only have to read the book to appreciate this. But AI is an international conglomerate, and it speaks with the collective voice of many nations. Indeed, the author was once at the Toulouse headquarters when, not entirely as a fun diversion, the number of different nationalities actually working there for AI or its suppliers was totted up and the total came to 39. These folk are all proud to wear an AI cap, but they don't have a powerful political lobby such as is enjoyed by the industry of the United States. The leader of the Western democracies operates roughly half the big jetliners in the world. It used to build virtually all the jetliners for the non-Communist world, and its own airlines always represented an almost captive market. There had been the occasional penetration of that market by such aircraft as the Viscount, Caravelle and One-Eleven, but these were very limited and very much the exception.

Today AI has changed the situation. Already five of the biggest and most respected US airlines are major AI customers, and this has caused a lot of people in Washington to jump up and down—or, as one US trade official put it, to 'ricochet off the walls'. Americans love competition, provided they win. In the past there hasn't been any foreign competition. Even today, with such operators as British Airways, the feeling lingers that they will buy any airliners they like so long as they are American. There were very good reasons for this. Not only have US products been superior, but that nation's gigantic financial and political involvement with its major markets has virtually made the result of a so-called 'competition' a foregone conclusion.

Those days have now gone. From now on the US commercial jet industry has to sell on merit: on its ability to equal AI's proven standard of excellence across the board. This can only be a good thing, for the US industry as much as for that of the rest of the world, and especially for the world's airlines.

Bill Gunston
Haslemere
Surrey
September 1987

1

GETTING THE ACT TOGETHER

AVIATION IS A GREAT BUSINESS to be in, provided you have limitless money at your disposal, limitless confidence in your ability to get everything right first time, and limitless resolve and iron nerve. There really are such people, and many of them created the giant enterprise recorded in this book. But they were almost defeated in their efforts by the European airlines (especially the British), the European governments (especially the British) and even the European media, all of whom might have been expected to be enthusiastic. With friends like these, Airbus didn't really need the enemies on the US West Coast.

Memories seem to be short, whereas aviation is very much a long-term business. Today Airbus Industrie has at last—by actually having the money, the ability, the resolve and the nerve—begun to reap the rewards of its labours, and established itself as the world's No 2 builder of big passenger jets. Its competitors respect and fear it, and its friends are now numerous and ready to stand up and be counted. But the author's memory is long enough to recall the time, not so many years since, when nobody appeared to take this European group seriously. Here are some quotes from the author's personal notebooks:

'*The A300B? You know what they say about the camel: a horse designed by a committee*'. Vice-president of a West Coast planemaker, 1975.

'*We're just not interested in the Airbus. It will never sell, and certainly never rival the numbers we see in partnership with the US industry*'. Leader of a famous aero-engine company, 1976.

'*Yes, you certainly could say we are cool towards the Airbus*'. Chief technical executive of the national airline of a major Airbus partner-country, 1967.

'*I don't want the Airbus*'. Chairman of a major British airline, 1967.

'*If we are to get anywhere in civil planemaking we must look to the USA, and we hope Boeing will be our partner*'. President of one of the two original Airbus partners, 1976.

'*I can't take the risk of buying such an aircraft. Can you ever see it selling, say, 200 or 300?*' Chairman of a famous Middle East airline, 1977.

There are many more, but these are enough to give a flavour of the scene in the lean years when Airbus appeared to be getting nowhere. This book could easily be written as a mere sales puff, stuffed with ever more impressive facts and figures showing that there's nobody else in the same league. But the author has had intimate contact not only with Airbus Industrie since its formation but also with the companies which formed it, and with their predecessors, and cannot forget the clashing disparity of viewpoints, the magnitude of the political, financial and parametric stumbling-blocks that often threatened to negate the whole enterprise, nor the stature of AI's leaders who overcame every obstacle and created in Europe the germ of what has already become a vast and vital industry. Nothing quite like AI existed previously, and in future chapters some attention will be paid to Airbus's people, drawn from 39 nations including Afghanistan (from before the Soviet invasion), and to the management and facilities where, within the partner companies alone, 23,000 people help build Airbuses. For the moment, however, we must take a trip back in time to the early 1960s when the seemingly obvious idea of an 'airbus' began to take a tangible form.

In the early 1960s it was 'all systems go' on the world's airlines. Despite the fact that, by modern standards, the new jets were profligate guzzlers of fuel, unacceptably uneconomic and excruciatingly noisy, they so packed in the passengers that traffic forecasts predicted annual gains upwards of 15 per cent, equivalent to a doubling of traffic every five years. This was broadly true for all routes, but the strongest growth appeared to be in the short-haul sectors, roughly defined as 1,000 miles or less. The newest equipment on these routes were all relatively small aircraft, ranging from the One-Eleven of about 70 seats to the 727 with over 100. It was gradually appreciated that seat-mile cost, first really identified in the early 1950s but somewhat overlooked in an era of cheap fuel, could exert a major influence on traffic growth and thus on the growth of the market for passenger transports.

Builders, and would-be builders, of such aircraft intensified their studies of what might make sense for the future. Apart from the basic rule of all transport, that to get down the unit cost you move the payload in bigger packages, there was not much unanimity of opinion. Jets, even inefficient ones, were all the rage. Turboprops were distinctly *passé*, and nobody appeared to have any difficulty ignoring all the arithmetic which suggested that perhaps they offered the lowest costs of all. A few bold spirits drew giant turboprop people-movers, with anything upwards of 200 seats, and Shorts even offered airbus derivatives of the RAF's cavernous Belfast, which promised rock-bottom costs by eliminating most of the bill for research and development. Airlines showed hardly the slightest interest in the things with propellers, but were prepared to co-operate in the studies for the high-capacity jets.

How should an early-1960s project team plan a future airbus, to carry anything from 180 to 300 passengers over sectors of about 1,000 miles? Almost the only features taken for granted were that it should have turbofan engines and a swept wing, but everything else was in the melting pot. The supercritical wing, then known as a 'rooftop' or 'aft-loaded profile', was just dawning on the drawing boards at Hatfield, and the HBPR (high bypass ratio) turbofan was just dawning at GE, Pratt & Whitney and Rolls-Royce. The radical HBPR concept, in which a giant fan handles from five to eight times as much air as goes through the rest of the engine (the so-called core), generating almost all of the thrust, was sparked off chiefly by the USAF's far-seeing Project Forecast of 1962, which in turn led to the C-5 Galaxy and, indirectly, the 747 Jumbo Jet. These, however, were long-haulers, and one was a freighter. The short-haul passenger jet was less obvious.

Apart from the fact that the wing could be mounted in the high, mid or low position, the engines be hung on the wing, or under the wing or on the rear fuselage, and the tailplane be on top of the fin (the so-called T-tail) or on the fuselage, the biggest problem concerned the fuselage itself. To accomodate 200 or more passengers you have either to have an incredibly long body, which suffers severe nodding and bending loads and becomes very heavy, or an extremely fat fuselage, which probably has high drag and looks ungainly. Moreover, jets have to be pressurized in order to fly high enough for the engines to work efficiently in very cold air, and this means the cabin has to be more or less circular in cross-section. A circular body with a diameter of 20 ft (6.1 m) makes very poor use of the available space. If the floor is below the mid-point the cabin is enormous, with far more headroom than is needed and with vast pressurized and heated volumes that are unwanted. If the floor is at mid-height there is far too much underfloor space for the likely amount of cargo. Of course, the underfloor area could be used for passengers as well, taking to its ultimate the 'lower deck' idea pioneered by the largest flying boats and by the cocktail lounge of most Stratocruisers.

Most designers of passenger jets will say that the most difficult variable to pin down is the cross-section of the fuselage. Once it has been fixed, it is the most difficult thing to change. Thus we find that the cabin width of 11 ft 7 in (3.53 m) established with the Boeing 707 over 35 years ago is continued to this day in the 720, 727, 737 and 757. These are all simple 'narrow body' aircraft, but what the designers were looking for in the early 1960s was something much bigger. As already noted, one can make a bigger cabin by making it longer or by increasing its diameter, but both have many drawbacks. In many ways a better answer is to make a twin-tube fuselage. This is not uncommon when the tubes are superimposed. Neither of the tubes is a complete circle, because they share a common chord in the main passenger floor. Usually these 'double-bubble' arrangements have a bigger circle intersecting a smaller one below, and to reduce drag the re-entrant joints along the sides are skinned over to give a pear shape. The original 707 has such a section, but in the short-haul 737 the underfloor region is shallower and the section more nearly a single circle.

In seeking a 1960s airbus, designers were bolder and tried putting two equal tubes above each other to give a figure-8 section. They also put them side-by-side, giving a fuselage normal in side view but grotesquely wide when seen from above or below. The left and right cabins could be completely enclosed in pressurized tubes, or they could be open to each other and separated only by a close row of strong vertical ties, looking like pillars, to stop the enormous roof from blowing off upwards under the pressurization load of perhaps 20,000 tons. The feeling of spaciousness in such a cabin could be impressive, and the only real problem seemed to be that it had not been done before.

Rather surprisingly the major airlines did not get together or draw up specifications, but merely showed mild interest in what the manufacturers were suggesting. There was only one *ad hoc* committee, and that was in Britain where The Lighthill Committee was charged with studying 'short-range minimum-cost air transport'. It accomplished little beyond setting down a lot of obvious ideas on paper. The British planemakers were still in a state of shock after an incredible series of shotgun weddings had merged 12 proud companies into just two, who were also told there would be no more manned military aircraft. At one new grouping, BAC, the numbed designers studied a double-bubble 264-seat derivative of the VC10, powered by the projected Rolls-Royce RB.178, and not unreasonably called it the DB.264. At Hatfield a team that still thought of itself as de Havilland rather than Hawker Siddeley planned various stretched versions of the Trident, again with RB.178s but with two engines instead of four; these were designated as HS.132s.

In November 1962 the governments of Britain and France had reached an agreement to develop an SST (supersonic transport) on a 50/50 basis, but nobody in the two governments or industries did anything about collaboration on an airbus. This was extraordinary. Anyone who spent a few seconds considering the problem could not have failed to conclude that, while the SST had to remain an exotic vehicle matched to only very few routes and priced to cream off the top few per cent of traffic, the airbus was bound to become the mass-market carrier that would in due course handle the other 95 + per cent on SST routes and 100 per cent on the others. Instead, while ministers became enchanted with the SST, they ignored the important vehicle that virtually all the world's major airlines were going to need. Hindsight is not an impressive kind of wisdom, but in 1962–63 the author almost lost friends through drawing attention to this argument in print.

Sud-Aviation, the French SST partner, had established a viable product in its Caravelle, flown in 1955. As the first short-haul jet to be sold, and the first airliner with engines hung on the rear fuselage, it had an uphill struggle at first but by the 1960s was well established and eventually sold 280 all over the world. Sud recognized the need to build on success, but the Caravelle's narrow body had already been stretched to the limit and there seemed no alternative to a wholly new design. The group's predecessors had much earlier used the name Grosse Julie (fat Julie) for certain portly aircraft, and it resurrected this for a series of project studies characterized by bodies fatter than anything seen previously; diameter eventually grew to 6.1 m (20 ft). Two, three or four engines were hung in every way possible, and a decision looked far off.

French rival Breguet had earlier built a piston-engined airliner with the same engines as a DC-6B but in effect with two DC-6B fuselages one above the other. Not unnaturally called the Deux Ponts (two decks), it established the idea as viable, and by 1963 it was being studied for airbuses. By 1965 these had crystallized into the Br.124 with two twin-engine pods hung below a wing passing between the decks. With up to 264 passengers the 124 seemed a bit marginal on the 46,000 lb thrust of four Rolls-Royce Speys.

Another French rival, Nord-Aviation (soon to merge with Sud to form Aérospatiale), boldly selected the previously unattempted side-by-side double-bubble concept in its Nord 600, first drawn in 1964. Most of the specification of the 600 read like a carbon copy of the Br.124, but it looked utterly different with a low wing supporting an amazingly broad fuselage with four Spey engines inside the rear end, under a T-tail. Late in 1965 the French government voted to finance continued studies by the three firms, while at that year's Paris airshow leaders of French and German aircraft companies held two informal meetings to consider a joint programme. Within days, on 2 July, all the major German companies—ATG Siebelwerke, Bölkow, Dornier, Flugzeug-union Süd, HFB, Messerschmitt and VFW—formed *Studiengruppe Airbus*, the first time the name was used formally, to co-ordinate their proposals.

In October 1965 eight European national airlines met in London to discuss what they wanted, but there was no unanamity of ideas and no enthusiasm. Again, even at the time this seemed odd. The airlines were being offered a new species of short-hauler with a much more efficient wing, dramatically more efficient engines, about 100 times less noise, unprecedented economy and the ability to move people in bigger numbers in fewer flights, yet all they could do was explain why they wanted something different. The one tangible outcome was that an Anglo-French Working Party was set up to try to write a specification meeting most of the airlines' needs. In November 1965 this emerged, calling for 200–225 seats at 34-in pitch, with DOC* 30 per cent lower than that of the 727-100 over a range of 810 nautical miles (1500 km). Later this was refined to 225 seats over the increased range of 1,200 nm with reserves, the suggested engines being two Pratt & Whitney JT9D of 41,000 lb thrust or Rolls-Royce RB.178 of 44,000 lb.

By this time the British and French manufacturers had realized they had to collaborate. First off the mark was the HBN group formed by Hawker Siddeley Aviation of Britain and France's Breguet and Nord. The British team was based at Hatfield, and it was here that fundamental work was already being done on a possible

*Direct operating cost.

wing. The de Havilland team had designed wings for the 121 (Trident) and 125 whose section profile had a flatter top than usual, bluffer front and downturned trailing edge. As a result the lift was spread more evenly across the wing from front to rear, and peak suction (and thus peak airspeed) was considerably reduced. The idea was taken further in the HS.681 STOL transport (cancelled by the British government in late 1964) and for the HBN studies it was taken further still, with assistance from the National Physical Laboratory and the Aircraft Research Association at Bedford. The new group studied five configurations, HBN.100 to 104.

What happened was that Air Commodore Rod Banks, Hawker Siddeley Chief Executive at Hatfield, accompanied by Monty Norman, the European Marketing Manager, went to Paris to see what kind of deal could be sewn together. They had a lunch date with Louis Giusta, *Directeur-Général* of Sud-Aviation. The meal was fantastic, but Sud was so tied up with rival BAC on the Concorde that Giusta said he could not get involved. At 3 pm the Brits had an appointment with Henri Ziegler, top man of Breguet. Here the response was 100 per cent positive, and an 'accord' was struck within minutes, leading to the two-nation, three-company HBN.100. But Breguet was about to become restructured as part of Dassault, and the French government decreed that the French partner on the 'airbus' had to be Sud. A little later Ziegler moved across to Sud-Aviation as PDG (*Président Directeur-Général*) and nobody looked back.

Analysing the configurations, and further studying engine prospects, took the first quarter of 1966. In addition to the obvious requirements of safety, sales appeal, development and manufacturing costs, growth potential and similar factors, the HBN team sought commonality with the Boeing 747, the first of what became known as the 'widebody' transports, details of which were announced on 13 April 1966. Thus the HBN.100, always regarded as the favoured baseline proposal, was given a fuselage of 20-ft diameter, with underfloor cargo/baggage containers similar to those of the 747. It was also soon apparent that no arrangement with three or four engines could come within 6.3 per cent of the DOC of the best twin, and this in turn meant using 747 type engines. PanAm had not then chosen between the JT9D and RB.178, but the only firm brochure figures applied to the American engine and so this was used in the HBN studies.

Meanwhile, on 23 December 1965 the German *Studiengruppe* was formally reconstituted as the *Arbeitsgemeinschaft* (abbreviated to Arge) *Airbus*, to serve as a single national partner in any future programme for what was by this time universally called an airbus. Not to be left out, Sud had earlier refined its Grosse Julie into a project called the Galion, and in late 1965 it revised this to meet the Anglo-French specification. Having achieved what looked like a Guppy version of the 737, it then joined forces with Dassault and announced a further improved specification, almost identical to the HBN.100, on 16 February 1966. Three weeks previously the

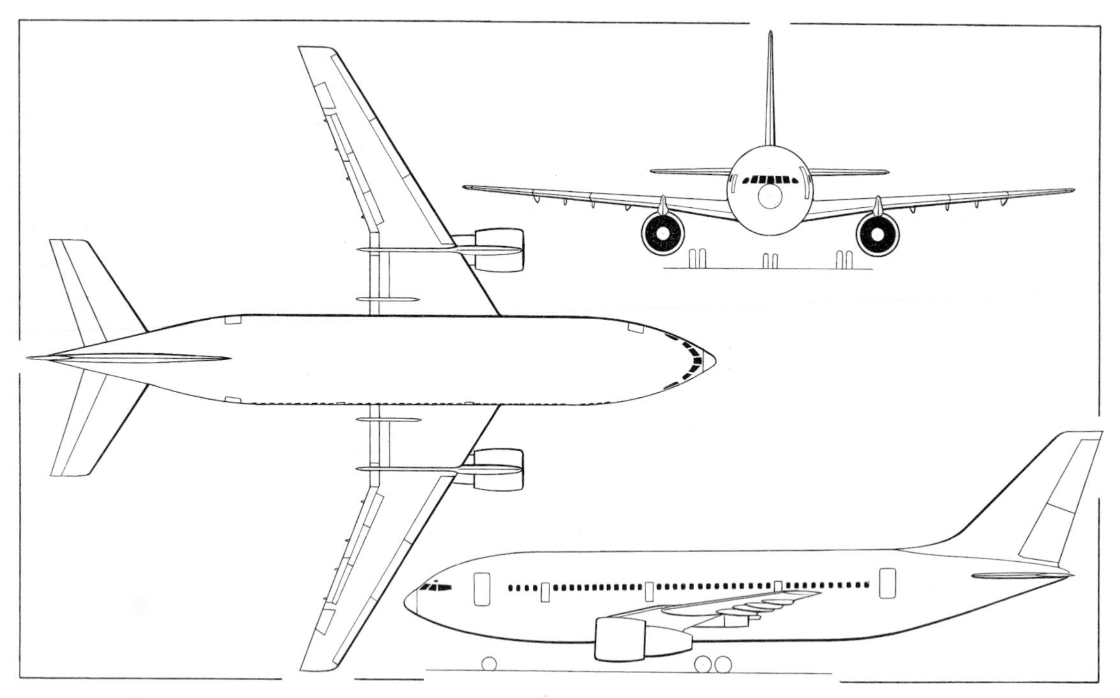

The HBN.100 was the direct ancestor of the A300 (Pilot Press)

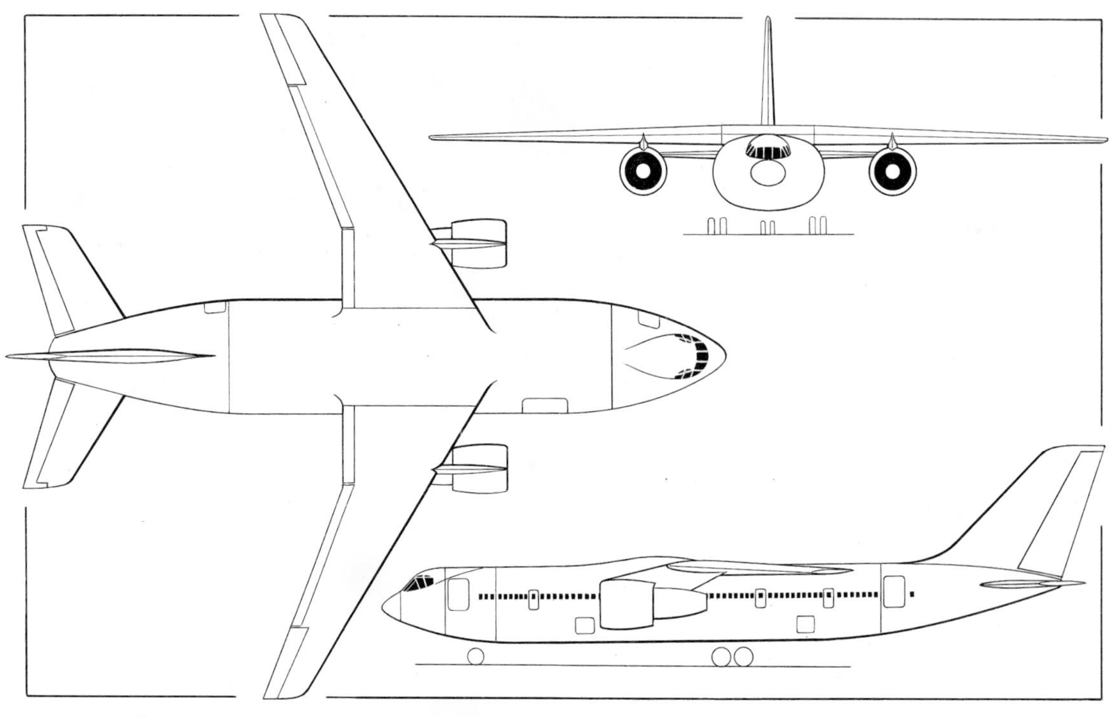

The HBN.101 was an attempt to use the lateral double-bubble configuration, with a very wide cabin formed from left and right circular arcs. The HBN.100 was preferable on almost every count (Pilot Press)

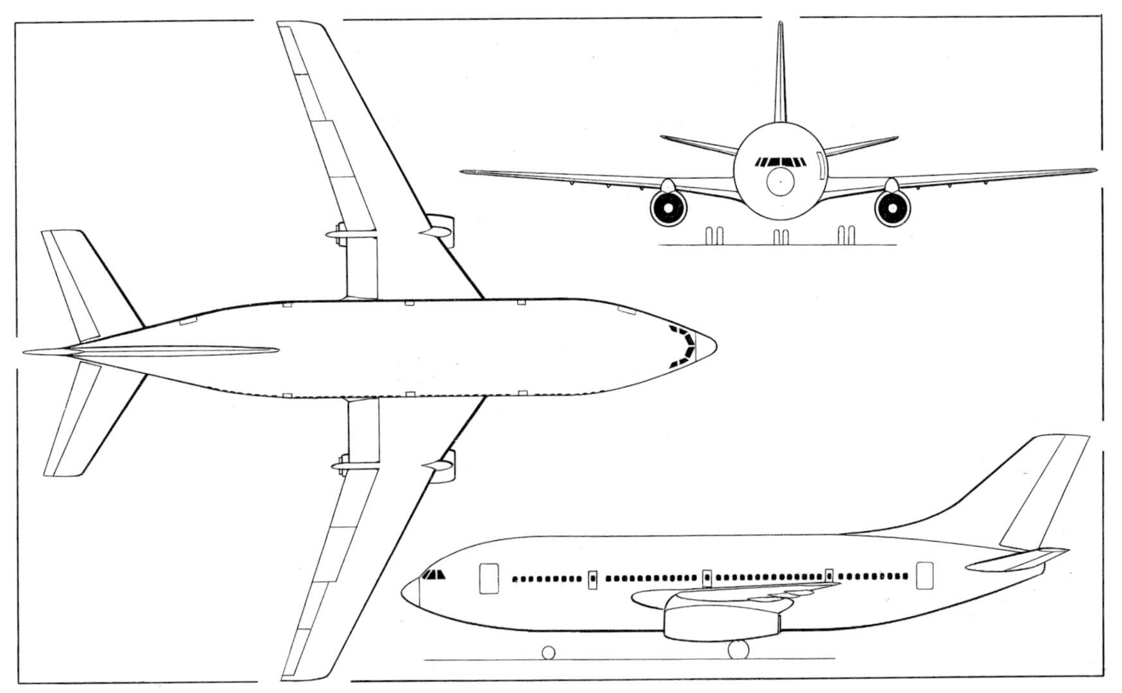

The Sud-Aviation Galion; data are on page 206
(Pilot Press)

The architect: Roger Béteille (centre) was the executive leader of the team which toiled through the desert years and at last, in April 1985, handed over a prosperous organization to Johann Schäffler (left) and Jean Pierson (right)

first meeting of government officials from Britain, France and Germany took place, at which the national partners were announced as: Hawker Siddeley, Sud-Aviation and Arge Airbus. At the same time the HBN.100 was picked as the favoured design; this was actually the genesis of the Airbus, but few people believed anything would really be built. Within a year Breguet had become largely owned by Dassault, later losing its identity, while on 1 January 1970 Nord vanished into the mighty Sud-based Aérospatiale group. In fact, several key Breguet and Nord engineers came across to Sud with the HBN.100 design.

To a very considerable degree the HBN.100 was the original design of the Airbus. When one considers the great pressure under which it was designed I feel that great credit is due to all concerned, especially to Chief Designer Guy Webb and to the leader of the wing design team Jock Macadam. Macadam attended the first meeting involving the Germans, and a white-haired gentleman got up and said he was unhappy about the wing's fatigue life. The British designer whispered 'Who's that?' and was told 'That is the great Dr Willy Messerschmitt'. Jock rose to his feet and said 'Herr Messerschmitt, I believe the fatigue life of the Bf 109 was about 50 hours—providing it didn't meet a Spitfire!' This fortunately was treated as a joke; Germans can be terribly serious.

February 1966 also saw the start of continuing meetings between the chosen partner companies, these dealing almost exclusively with market studies conducted with a growing number of major airlines. The first formal meeting at company board level took place in September 1966, and on 15 October a request for financial support was made to the three governments, accompanied by the first definitive brochure describing an aircraft renamed A300, from Airbus 300 seats, though the design had only changed in detail.

In summer 1966 PanAm had picked the JT9D-3, at 43,000 lb, to power its 747s. This left the RB.178 unwanted, and Rolls-Royce, at this time in an aggressive mood, instantly invented a newer and bigger three-shaft engine known as the RB.207, with a promised thrust of 47,500 lb. The Derby company was absolutely determined to 'get aboard the Airbus' (as the papers put it), and began a massive lobbying campaign which proved it had more political clout than the British aircraft industry, seriously distorted and delayed the Airbus programme and then, when a US market emerged, saw Rolls transfer its blandishments across the Atlantic. Suddenly it was disinterested in the European aircraft, but in 1966 things were very different. When it looked as if the European A300 partners might pick the Pratt & Whitney JT9D—an eminently sensible choice, both for commonality with the 747 and because it existed and the RB.207 did not—produced by a consortium which included Bristol Siddeley of Britain and SNECMA of France, Rolls-Royce did more than merely offer competition: it drew £63.6 million from the bank and simply bought Bristol Siddeley, stopping the rivals in their tracks.

Whereas Rolls-Royce was a large and powerful company looked upon with total favour by the British government, the rationalized and merged British aircraft industry had had its morale shattered, and was even regarded as something (said the Labour government elected in 1964) 'we would be much better off without'. British planning in aerospace had always been conspicuously absent. Where big passenger jets were concerned the procedure had always been for the national airlines, BOAC and BEA, to tell the industry *precisely* what they wanted. Aubrey Burke, managing director of de Havilland Aircraft at Hatfield, even issued an edict forbidding his technical sales staff to speak to any foreign airline until the D.H.121 (later the Hawker Siddeley Trident) had been designed exactly to BEA's requirements!! The D.H.121 was planned as a 111-seater with three engines of 13,790 lb thrust, giving a range of 2,070 miles. This would have been a fine aircraft, able to offer severe competition to the later 727. But a year into the programme, in 1959, BEA had instructed de Havilland and Rolls-Royce to tear up all they had done and start again on a 97-seater with 9,850-lb engines and a range of only 932 miles. The Hatfield team were appalled, but had to do as they were told. As a result BEA spent the next ten years desperately trying to make the Trident bigger and longer-ranged again, and the Hatfield aircraft sold a total of 117, making no impact on the world scene whatever, while the 727 sold 1,832.

While BAC, in the shape of the former Vickers team at Weybridge, strove to interest BOAC in the DB.264 and other VC10 derivatives, the Hatfield designers studied a succession of HS.132 projects as already noted, even getting up to 219 seats with a fuselage not much shorter than Concorde, before finally abandoning rear-mounted engines. By 1965 the HS.134 had been drawn, with specification and appearance virtually identical to today's Boeing 757. The author had long discussions with Phil Smith, later Deputy Managing Director of the BAe Hatfield-Chester Division but at the time in charge of all aircraft design, and he bitterly regretted the fact that, while Hatfield was forced to build the Trident, the HS.134 'fell on deaf ears'. The only good thing was that the sheer technical effort by Hatfield really paid off in knowledge of the very latest structures, aerodynamics, propulsion and systems, and especially in what later became known as the supercritical wing. This is discussed in more detail in the next chapter. Without wishing to detract from the solid achievements of the French and German partners, the author has no hesitation in stating that the HBN.100 and its successor, the A300, had their genesis principally at Hatfield. The experience of the Hatfield engineers, starting with the world's first jetliner immediately after World War 2, was of inestimable value to the sure and almost faultless development of the European aircraft.

In the first quarter of 1967 the A300 grew significantly in size. This was not because of pressure from the growing number of airlines with whom the three principals were talking, but because there was inevitably a basic belief that 'big is good'. The airlines naturally tended to prefer the JT9D engine, which Pratt & Whitney had promised to develop to 47,500 lb by 1975, but Rolls—having in the RB.207 a pure 'paper engine'—could promise any thrust that appeared to be wanted. In a matter of weeks the RB.207-03 was being offered at 50,000 lb, and the A300 was pumped up to a fuselage diameter of 21 ft (6.4 m), wider even than the 747. The basic notion of a gigantic 'airbus' carrying hundreds of passengers with the operating economy of two advanced fan engines was so exciting that there was clearly a tendency to overlook the fact that this was to be a vehicle meeting the requirements of real customers. It was extremely surprising, and rather sad, that virtually none of these customers recognized the concept for what it was.

What it was, was the obvious next-generation vehicle on all the world's short/medium trunk routes. Whereas in 1958 there was in Europe just one city-pair (London–Paris) with more than 1,000 passengers per day, by 1968 there were 16 such routes, and the projection for 1978 was for 56! It should have been blindingly obvious that to cut back the Trident to 97 seats was nonsense, and that by no amount of stretching could any future Trident be matched to the busiest routes of the 1970s. In the USA the situation was even more acute, and American Airlines was about to issue a specification for an 'airbus type' vehicle to fly out of New York La Guardia (with short runways), or fly Chicago–LA, carrying 270 to 345 passengers over all the airline's trunk-route sectors. It is significant that American envisaged this aircraft as having two large fan engines. It became known as The Kolk Machine, from American's Frank Kolk, and would have been a formidable competitor. In Europe, however, most of the big national airlines had curiously warped ideas about the big-twin airbus. Hardly any recognized it as obvious, and if they did they vied with each other to emphasize that they would not want it for many years, 1975 being typical (one airline said 1980). Not one major carrier said 'Your proposal is clearly the logical vehicle for all the world's busiest short/medium sectors on which most of the world's traffic is carried. It is vital that we sit down to get the specification as right as possible as soon as possible'.

Instead they took a lukewarm and detached view, while the media—if they thought about it at all—merely expressed horror at carrying 300 people on two engines. Worse, but perhaps predictably, this was an era when ignorant people in positions of power attached the greatest importance to something called 'design leadership'. This concept appeared to indicate that the recipient nation or company was superior to its partners in the enterprise, and in particular that the 'leader' could impose its will on the others. Today we know that for any partner to behave like this would be highly damaging to the project in almost every way; thorny points simply have to be talked through until all are agreed on the best choice. In 1965, however, it was France which, just as in so many other international programmes, demanded 'design leadership on the airframe'. It must be emphasized that this demand did not stem from such men as Sud-Aviation's Henri Ziegler, Pierre Satre or Lucien Servanty, but from the politicians. In reply it was the British politicians who agreed to the French demand, provided that the RB.207 was the chosen engine. Such decisions help politicians believe that they are important.

This was the position at the first meeting at minister level, which took place in Paris on 9 May 1967. Signatories to the decision to 'proceed rapidly with a joint project definition study of the best aircraft capable of being built around two such [RB.207] engines' were British Minister of State for Technology John Stonehouse, French Minister of State for Foreign Affairs André Bettencourt and West German State Secretary at the Economics Ministry Dr Johann Schollhorn. A final decision on the go-ahead was deferred pending receipt of the study, but important new decisions and figures were announced. It was stated that airframe research and development would cost £190 million, shared 37.5 per cent by Britain (Hawker Siddeley), 37.5 per cent by France (Sud-Aviation) and 25 per cent by Germany (Arge Airbus). Corresponding R&D for the RB.207 engine would be £60 million (had this engine gone ahead the actual cost would have been about 20 times this estimate), shared 75 per cent by Britain (Rolls-Royce), 12.5 per cent by France (SNECMA) and 12.5 per cent by Germany (MAN). The market was estimated at about 250 aircraft, but that a firm basis of sales had to be provided by orders from the three national airlines, BEA, Air France and Lufthansa.

The A300 Study was ready in mid-July 1967, leading to the crucial go-ahead meeting at Lancaster House, London, on the 25th of that month. Ministers were Stonehouse and Schollhorn, plus French Transport Minister Jean Chamant. They endorsed previous decisions, except that, amazingly, the airframe R&D bill had now been reduced to £130 million. The formal Memorandum of Understanding was not signed until 26 September (postponed from the 15th of that month because three-language documents were not ready), when it was stated that the A300 would be designed by June 1968. At that time a go-ahead on prototype construction would be sanctioned, provided the three national airlines had by that time placed orders for a total of 75 aircraft. Britain, unlike her partners, was insistent upon this point, which was in due course to prove a most unfortunate stipulation.

Spurred on by ever-greater promises of thrust from Derby, the A300 grew and grew, while the airlines expressed increasing disbelief. No publicity was given to the efforts of the engineering teams at Hatfield, Toulouse and in several locations in Germany, though this was to provide the bedrock on which the whole future enterprise was to be based. On the other hand, the media made much of many kinds of problem that conspired to harm the project. One was that, despite cutting back fuselage diameter to 19 ft 7 in (5.97 m), the aircraft still kept growing, overall length increasing from 159 ft 10 in (48.7 m) in July 1967 to 176 ft 11 in (53.92 m) a year later. Another problem was that the American Airlines specification of April 1966 for a

Kolk Machine had by late 1967 undergone a strange metamorphosis and gained a third engine. This third engine was considered justified for such reasons as dispatch reliability, en route cruising height after climbout from Denver and similar high airports, and the ability to ferry with one engine inoperative. Time was to show none of these to be valid reasons, and it was frankly admitted that they incurred a penalty in direct operating cost of 5–12 per cent compared with a big twin.

More seriously, the trijet specification led to the DC-10 and L-1011 TriStar, which in turn led to a frantic effort by Rolls-Royce to sell—history would say, oversell—a further new engine in the 40,000-lb class, the RB.211. In the case of the TriStar this effort was successful, and almost overnight David Huddie and his team at Derby pushed the European airbus into their No 2 spot. They could see glittering prizes selling RB.211s into hundreds of TriStars, an American aircraft launched on the basis of 144 so-called firm orders—including 50 placed speculatively by a British financial group—with hundreds more expected to come. In contrast, the faltering European airbus reached its decision point of July 1968 with not one order, let alone the 75 demanded by Britain. Worse, with Rolls striving day and night to design and develop the RB.211 for Lockheed, nothing much was happening to the RB.207. True to form, the optimists at Derby began to promise Lockheed ever-greater power from the RB.211. Starting with the RB.211-23 at 38,300 lb, Rolls offered the RB.211-28 at 48,000 lb, the Dash-51 at 49,000 (specifically for the airbus) and the Dash-61 at 53,000 lb. What still lay hidden deep in the Derby works was that even the very first version of the RB.211 was a technical disaster, which would come out weighing 50 per cent more than the estimate, 20 per cent down on power and, because it could not get certificated, unsaleable. With no money coming in, Rolls went bankrupt in February 1971, but by that time it had long since ceased to have any connection with the European airbus.

Just to muddy the waters further, Hawker Siddeley's rival British group, BAC, designed an aircraft in the A300 class called the Two-Eleven. It had a T-tail and aft-mounted RB.211 engines, and BEA Chairman Anthony Milward thought it was just what he wanted. His enthusiasm for the Two-Eleven could not be explained on any rational grounds. Several times the author discussed the Two-Eleven with him, and the bigger Three-Eleven which succeeded it, and formed the view that BEA wanted them because they were a possible alternative to the European airbus, which the airline heartily disliked because it was 'European'—whatever that meant. Be that as it may, the author collected 280 column-inches from the aviation press and major newspapers explaining that BEA did not want the A300 but did want the Two-Eleven/Three-Eleven, without at any time offering the slightest valid reason.

As the summer of 1968 faded into autumn, so did the European airbus partners gradually realize that the RB.207 was just not going to happen. Huddie & Co continued to radiate confidence, but the deeper the A300 engineers investigated, the worse the situation looked. Almost in secret, Béteille and his engineers worked on an A300 scaled down to suit available, developed versions of available, and hence proven engines: the JT9D, CF6-50 or 'if it ever happens' the RB.211-51. In November–December 1968 the A300 was replaced by what should have been the A250, because that number was a typical mixed-class passenger capacity, but which was actually called the A300B. Fuselage diameter was reduced to 18 ft 2 in (5.54 m) (later this was slightly increased again to 18 ft 6 in, 5.64 m), and overall length cut back to 158 ft 6 in (48.3 m). More than 25 *tonnes* was lopped off gross weight, to 275,500 lb (125 *tonnes*). At last the European aircraft began to look wholly viable and matched to engines that, in the USA, actually existed. It ought to have been a smash hit from the start, but instead all the operators that might have been expected to be its most ardent supporters found all sorts of reasons for doubting it, or at least avoiding saying anything that might have appeared in the slightest degree encouraging.

Thus, as 1969 dawned, the A300B entered its final phase of detail design, though continuing to be hamstrung in a vital area by uncertainty over the engine. It was at this time that the author first met the man who, more than any other, was to be the architect of the A300B. As Director, Airbus Programme, Roger Béteille of Sud-Aviation bore a crushing workload and tremendous responsibility. In his view, the best thing about the programme was the aircraft itself. He said 'It sets entirely new standards. It makes no technical or economic concession to political expediency. The spirit of unison that pervades the design teams is tremendous, and bodes well for the future of the project, around which a very large part of the aircraft industry of Western Europe must be based.' But he further said 'We are at last being forced to believe that Rolls-Royce will fail to produce an engine to meet our requirements, though the ball has been squarely in that company's court for more than two years'.

At 1 January 1969 about 3,700 hours had been logged in testing more than 30 models of various kinds in wind tunnels, paying particular attention to slat and flap systems, precise wing profiles, wing/pylon/pod interactions and, above all, basic stability and control. Though the aircraft as finally built is described in the next chapter, this is the place to comment on the overall configuration. The rival Two-Eleven and Three-Eleven proposed by BAC both featured rear-mounted engines and a T-tail. This configuration is still used successfully in such aircraft as the MD-80 series and Fokker 100, which are derivations of aircraft designed in the early 1960s, but back in the days of the HBN studies it was inescapably evident that it lost at least as much as it gained. Though such drawbacks can be overcome, all the rear-engine arrangements suffered from imperfect weight distribution about the centre of gravity, with excessive body length in front of the wing and, in most cases, excessive sweep on the wing. Hawker Siddeley were able to demonstrate that, with the new rear-loaded 'supercritical' wing the optimum sweep angle could be as little as 28 degrees or even 25 degrees at the quarter-chord line, and to reap full advantage of this there was nowhere for the engines to go but under the wings. This also naturally had the advantage of alleviating the wing bending moments, putting the engines in undisturbed air instead of (in some conditions) wing downwash, and restricting the fuel system to the wing. Subsequent prolonged tunnel testing resulted in many important further advantages. Compared with the corresponding trijet the A300B was able to fly at similar loads and speeds with less sweep and with a much smaller tail. Tunnel testing in 1968 led to an important lengthening of the rear fuselage, not to increase passenger capacity but in order to increase the moment arm of the tail. This made possible significant further reduction in the size of the tail, much more than compensating for the extra weight of slim rear fuselage, which in turn resulted in lower trim and yaw drag and a major improvement in flight performance.

As in several European programmes, the A300B made rapid and successful progress at the engineering level, while on the political front things went from bad to worse. In 1966 Anthony Wedgwood Benn had been appointed Minister of Technology in Britain, and it was soon apparent that his decisions were often, to put it politely, curious. He came to the job with an admitted passionate antipathy for what he called 'technomania', and this applied with particular vehemence to anything emanating from the aircraft industry (unless it was the American aircraft industry). The A300B was singled out for special dislike because it was a collaborative project with Europe. One day in Millbank Tower he told the author 'You tell me the Airbus project should be continued. I cannot see one factor in its favour. We have proved unable to cancel Concorde, but I am determined we shall have no more costly and pointless projects like this, where we are not even masters in our own house. My advisors tell me it will not sell. . . . .'

The author ventured the opinion that the A300B was the most logical vehicle in the entire history of air transport, but Benn replied 'I fear you are gullible. We have to take the broad view, to consider what kind of country we want to live in, how we can best spend our money. We have no intention of spending it on Airbuses'. And of course he reflected the view of the current government.

After this interview the author still had not the slightest inkling that the British government really would 'get off the airbus'. Such a decision seemed utterly inconceivable. If the A300B did not make sense, then what aircraft did? Certainly, the French and German governments appeared to include people able to add 2 and 2 and make 4, and in March 1969, following several sad and often acrimonious meetings with their British partners, these two countries formally declared their intention of funding the construction of a prototype 'with or without the participation of the UK'. One of the most powerful reasons for the lack of enthusiasm on the part of the British was that their ill-conceived fixation on the engine could now be seen to be leading nowhere. Gradually Rolls-Royce were forced to admit that they could not even produce their contractually committed RB.211 for the TriStar, let alone a more powerful engine for the A300B. Thanks to Britain's politicians, France had been handed so-called 'airframe leadership' on a plate, for nothing. By March 1969 Béteille told the author 'There seems little doubt we shall first fly with the CF6. After all, we have to bolt a real engine on each pylon'.

On 28 May 1969 French Minister Chamant and German Minister Schiller signed formal articles to go ahead with the hardware programme, for the first time taking them into the great and exciting area of big money and real risk. To the author the risk seemed minimal. The basic conception of the A300B was clearly just about perfect. There was not one unconventional or problematical feature in the entire aircraft, and the galaxy of subcontractors and suppliers, fully half of the latter being across the Atlantic and often with systems commonality with the DC-10, seemed to provide all the industrial muscle the programme could need. At the same time, it was a fairly agonizing period for Hawker Siddeley Aviation. This great group had not yet quite got its own act together. It still had about 92 chief designers and about the same number of chief test pilots, and the chaps at Hatfield did not take kindly to removal of the hallowed name 'de Havilland' from the main office block. In the group's HQ at 18 St James's Square, London, the crucial decision had to be taken: what to do? The company had entered into the 'European airbus' partnership fully expecting the project to be backed by all the participating governments. That's what collaborative programmes on this scale are all about. Little had been said about just how the supposed £130 million airframe development bill would be split between governments and industry, but most companies expected to have to find much less than half. Now, rather suddenly, Hawker Siddeley found itself out on a limb. It had essentially completed the design—and a very outstanding design it was—of the wing, the most crucial single part of the whole aircraft. In one extremely serious talk, Hawker Chairman Sir Arnold Hall was told by Benn that what he had most feared was true: Britain was pulling out.

This was certainly the low point in the entire programme. The author still finds it hard to believe that this particular episode actually happened. The one thing Britain most needed, and indeed most needs, is new hi-tech industry to help replace the gigantic old labour-intensive industries such as the spinning and weaving of cotton and wool, shipbuilding and heavy engineering, coalmining and the supply of land transport vehicles to the world. The aircraft industry is almost ideal for Britain, because the market is large and expanding, the value added in the final product is extremely high—in other words, the price of the product is many times the price of the raw materials—and rising all the time, the technology involved is right at the 'leading edge' where Britain and only two or three other countries have a total capability, and each aircraft sold can mean profitable ongoing support for up to 40 years. Yet the British Labour Party had won the 1964 General Election partly on a campaign directed against Britain having an aircraft industry, which was held up as the ultimate example of antisocial spendthrift waste.

The root cause of this campaign was in fact the almost total mismanagement of British aircraft procurement by the politicians. We have already had a taste of this in the ludicrously inept self-centred procurement of the British national airlines, but what really alienated the Labour politicians was the procurement of military aircraft. In a crescendo of what outwardly amounted to hate, the new government cancelled all the new British military aircraft and replaced them with purchases from the USA. It tried to cancel Concorde but was thwarted by France. The Airbus, however, was still vulnerable, because Britain had decreed that a go-ahead should be contingent upon the orders for 75 aircraft being placed by the airlines of the partner countries. In any normal country, at any normal time, politically dictated rules of this kind are not necessary. Aircraft are no different from newspapers, toothpaste or packaged holidays; they are products which are designed to meet a market need. The politicians may not be able to assess how well each new aircraft project will meet the needs of the market, but they can have the advice of experts. Even if the latter had a vested interest in the project going ahead, they would never be so foolish as to say that a doubtful conception was a sure-fire success. Planemakers have no wish to create white elephants.

Harping on the British theme a little while longer, for ten years after World War 2 Britain somehow contrived to build and fly more than 30 types of civil transport that never made money for anyone. Some smaller ones were the result of misguided optimism by the manufacturer, but the bigger and more costly ones were in every case built to government order. The trouble is, the customer was a government department and not an operator of aircraft. It gradually became almost routine to see giant prototypes being scrapped or put into Cocoons, while aircraft that had got into production—such as the Marathon and Comet 2—were simply shunted off into the RAF. There was thus a tragic history of muddle and waste in the building of even the biggest and costliest aircraft, and in the Labour administration of 1964 the aircraft industry rather suddenly found itself Public Enemy No 1. Back in the 1950s the media were full of famous test pilots, fantastic new aircraft and something called 'Britain's lead' in aviation. A decade later it was different. In 1969 some of the heat was being taken off, but the media had by this time been fully conditioned to regard planemaking as a thoroughly undesirable exercise. The situation had not been helped by a giant military project known as the AFVG (Anglo-French variable-geometry), which after making acrimonious headlines for more than a year collapsed on 29 June 1967 when the French simply pulled out.

Thus, when in March 1969 Britain announced it was withdrawing from the A300B programme there was hardly a murmur of dissent. The general feeling, as the author recalls it, was 'At last we've got a sensible government that pulls out in time, and doesn't get landed with these dreadful aircraft projects'. Any attempt to view the A300B on its merits was conspicuously absent in both the government and the media.

The author feels he has rather belaboured this darkest chapter in the Airbus story without actually explaining how it came about. In fact, it is incapable of rational explanation. Perhaps the following sentences can be offered, culled from private letters written at the time or soon afterwards by eminent people involved whose opinions were sought by the author:

'It all hinged upon the fact that customers had proved slow to come forward, though this in no way reflected upon the obvious saleability of the A300B once it could be seen to be supported by a reputable long-term organization'.

'The root cause was surely the failure of Rolls-Royce, the apple of the government's eye, to produce an engine; the government never seemed to think of the A300B as anything more than a peg on which to hang British engines.'

'It would seem to have been a purely political decision made by Wedgwood Benn . . . because of his dislike of collaboration with Europe.'

'A lot of it was childish sour grapes. We had given away programme leadership, and somehow felt our prestige could be restored by refusing to play'.

The colossal impact of this ill-considered withdrawal on almost every part of the British aircraft industry has never received the attention it deserves. Of course, the most immediately obvious impact was on Hawker Siddeley Aviation, which had masterminded the entire design of the aircraft's very special wing and was expecting to manufacture the complete wing structure, with all movable surfaces, for all production aircraft. The task was a daunting one, even with full government backing. The A300B wing was in several respects the biggest ever produced in quantity in Britain. Its manufacture demanded larger and very much more expensive machines than any seen previously on British airframes, with a precise supercritical profile generated in skins with thicknesses up to 1.25 in (31.75 mm), machined from plate as thick as one's thigh. Total investment in plant and equipment was estimated at £35 million. Every penny now had to be found from Hawker's own resources, yet no Airbus had been sold and the British government had chickened out.

On the much more nebulous credit side was the fact that a single pair of A300B wings (a pair being the left and right wings for one aircraft) would sell for about £2 million. The potential market was large, and there was no sign of a rival, apart from the big American trijets which were bigger and much more costly to buy and operate. Moreover, Hawker had really achieved something in the A300B wing, and it was loath to hand it all over to a rival company on the Continent. The HS group's main board discussed the alternatives in great detail and fully recognized the risks it was taking. For financial reasons it was unable to consider retaining responsibility for complete finished wings, and realized it would have to give up the secondary structure and movable surfaces. Finally, it showed more courage and better commercial judgement than its own government, and in July 1969 signed binding contracts with Sud-Aviation and Deutsche Airbus for the supply of main structural wing boxes for the prototypes, an option on all future wing-sets, and continuing responsibility for wing design and further development. It also agreed to fulfil a consultancy role. But it had to find almost all the money itself, not only for its own activity but also to pay a share of the sales and support costs in which it would have no executive power. Its role was purely that of a subcontractor.

The aviation technical press did comment on Hawker's courage in paying its own way to stay in the programme, even at a reduced level of activity, but hardly any comment was made on the bigger and more diverse impacts the British withdrawal had on the rest of the British industry. Instead of being a tripartite programme the A300B had become a bilateral one, run by Sud-Aviation of France and Deutsche Airbus. All the management decisions were vested in these two companies, pending the creation of a special organization which would in turn be controlled by the same two companies. Sud-Aviation and Deutsche Airbus had the immediate task of selecting management personnel, technical sales and engineering staff, and, by no means least, equipment suppliers. It was in their interest to pick the best, from wherever they could be found, and in every case Britain lost out through having no say in the decisions. This had three crucial and highly damaging effects on Britain:

It resulted in a large and sustained flow of the very best British engineering and sales talent to the A300B management centres, initially in Paris and Munich and later at Toulouse.

It resulted in the British aircraft industry progressively losing contact with the world's major airlines, to the point where, until the launch of the smaller BAe 146, there was no contact in the field of civil jetliners between any British planemaker and any major operator.

It resulted in a massive expansion of the French and German equipment and accessory industry, in almost every case duplicating products which could have been obtained from Britain. Once established on the A300B, the French and German companies were in an almost unassailable position on future developments both of that aircraft and on derived designs, to the point where by the 1980s British firms were taking a considered decision no longer to try to offer alternative sources of supply. The money involved is in the order of billions of pounds sterling.

The point should also be made that the French and German principals in the programme greatly regretted the absence of their British colleagues. At that time the disparity in strength and experience between the British industry and those of France and West Germany, particularly in civil jets, was very large indeed. The only way the A300B could make use of this talent was by enticing individuals away from their original British employer and put them to work in what became the Airbus programme.

In the earliest period in 1967–69 the design and engineering team was located at Sud-Aviation's expanding factory complex at Toulouse, in south-west France. Here, among the Concordes, were a growing team (typically growing from 15 to 80 over this period) with Sud's M P Ducasse and, until the British withdrawal, Phil Smith as chief engineers. Hawker Siddeley's initially big staff was led by A G Peters and Guy Webb, many of whom stayed after the withdrawal by leaving their UK employment, while the top DA (Deutsche Airbus) men were H Wocke and F Hoffert. All sales and contract negotiation was handled by a small group called Airbus International SA, headed by Sud-Aviation sales director Jean de Lagarde, operating from Sud's Paris headquarters at 37 Boulevard Montmorency.

On 1 January 1970 Sud-Aviation joined with other groups to form the giant called Aérospatiale. In the course of 1970, while detail design of the A300B went ahead apace, and tunnel models were tested along with full-scale structural test specimens, the new French group and Deutsche Airbus thrashed out the definitive management structure. At the start of 1970 the funding had of necessity been 50/50 between France and Germany, and a further small setback was that one of the DA companies, Dornier, withdrew as soon as it was asked to contribute any of its own money. Thus by 1970 the original seven German companies had been whittled down to two, MBB and VFW-Fokker. To make things more complicated again, VFW-Fokker was the German part of a Dutch company, Fokker-VFW; and on 28 December 1970, to regularize this position, the Dutch government took a 6.6 per cent shareholding in the A300B programme, cutting the French and German shares from 50 to 46.7 per cent each. This was the situation on 18 December 1970 when the new management company was formally set up with offices at 160 Avenue de Versailles in Paris.

The organization was called Airbus Industrie, a name which can be regarded as either French or German. AI was and remains a GIE, a *Groupement d'Intérêt Economique*, a unique and flexible structure permitted under French law which AI used for the first time in a major international venture and which, unlike the Concorde management structure, has proved ideal for its purposes. A GIE can assume many forms, interfaces easily with the laws of other nations, and is flexible in operation. It can have employees; AI had the smallest possible number, about 1,200 at the time of writing. It can have share capital; AI has none. It can own buildings and equipment; AI owns nothing but its HQ building, today an impressive structure on Avenue Lucien Servanty (named for Sud's former chief engineer) just outside Toulouse-Blagnac airport. But the crucial feature of every GIE is that each partner company accepts full liability not only for its own contribution but also for the entire corporate operations of the entire group. Thus, should any partner default, those remaining continue to be individually responsible for the entire share of that defaulting partner.

Once the concept of the GIE had been explained to the world's airlines—who seem to have taken an extraordinarily long time taking it in—there was no longer any reason for them to say 'I've never heard of Airbus Industrie, how do I know they'll look after me'? Every AI customer has always enjoyed the full legal obligation of total support from every one of the AI partners, and on 23 December 1971 a new partner, CASA of Spain, joined with a 4.2 per cent share, cutting the French and German shareholdings to 47.9 per cent each. With CASA, by the start of 1972 every nut and bolt sold by AI had 120,000 people behind it, with assets of £752 million. Very gradually, customers began to edge forward, reluctantly realizing that AI was not just a viable outfit that was here to stay but a viable outfit with colossal clout behind it. But the amazing reluctance lasted a further six years!

As hinted by Béteille earlier, the Franco-German partners were forced to look to the USA for an engine, and the increasing European sales of the DC-10-30 provided a compelling reason for choosing the General Electric CF6-50A engine, then rated at 49,000 lb thrust. Aérospatiale designed the pod to be broadly similar to the underwing pod of the DC-10-30, and with McDonnell Douglas actually supplying major parts of the nacelle. General Electric agreed to 40 per cent of the value of each engine being made in France/Germany, and the actual split in the mid-1970s was: SNECMA, 22 per cent share of parts-manufacture, plus 5.7 per cent accounted for by assembly at Corbeil and testing at Villaroche; MTU, 11 per cent of parts-manufacture (HP turbine); GE, 61.3 per cent. Both the European engine companies also won the right to supply parts for engines for the DC-10-30, shipped in the form of kits to GE. Today the work-split has been adjusted, SNECMA having 27 per cent overall, MTU 12 per cent and GE 61 per cent. As noted later, fresh agreements have been signed covering the improved CF6-80 engines, for newer types of Airbus.

Curiously, though the first tangible evidence of the Airbus seen in Britain was a mockup section of passenger cabin at the 1970 Farnborough show, these parts have from the start been the responsibility of Deutsche Airbus, which manufactures and equips the forward fuselage from cockpit to wing box, the upper centre fuselage above the wing, the rear fuselage, and the fin and rudder. Hawker Siddeley Aviation, and from 1 January 1978 British Aerospace, has always been responsible for the complete wing box, which forms the structural heart of the wing and also contains the fuel. Aérospatiale manufactures the nose and cockpit, the lower centre fuselage under the wing and the engine pylons, and also handles the assembly. Fokker-VFW, from 11 February 1980 just Fokker, makes the wing moving surfaces comprising flaps, slats, inboard Krüger flaps, spoilers and ailerons, as well as the wingtips, though the complete wings are actually assembled by MBB, a Deutsche Airbus company. CASA in Spain makes the tailplane and elevators, left and right forward passenger doors and landing-gear doors.

Main and nose landing gears were designed by Dowty Rotol in Britain but subsequently built by Messier-Hispano-Bugatti, a subsidiary of SNECMA in France.

As for the thousands of major bought-out equipment items, these tended to be of American design and often were similar or identical to corresponding items on the DC-10, but a high proportion were assembled, and often at least partly made, by affiliate companies in France or Germany. As noted earlier, the Airbus programme gave a tremendous boost to the aircraft equipment industries of those countries. Though this did not initially extend to design capability, the expanded size and prosperity of the companies concerned inevitably made it possible for them to open up flourishing design organizations. These have already flexed their muscles in later Airbus aircraft, gaining important hi-tech business which would have come to Britain.

As the formative years of the programme emphasized, the absence of any clear-cut requirement or specification, and even of much useful airline input, made it extremely hard to fix the design at the optimum size, weight and general capability. Following the rather traumatic ups and downs in size in the 'paper' stage, the design seemed fairly settled by late 1968, and even then a late decision to make the underfloor holds compatible with the newly developed LD3 cargo/baggage container, standard on the US widebody jets, resulted in a last-minute increase in fuselage diameter of 4 in (101.6 mm) in mid-1969, to 18 ft 6 in (5.64 m). But the designers were naturally anxious to retain as much flexibility as possible. The engine manufacturers were all promising a wide range of thrusts for the future, making possible a large spread of MTOWs (maximum takeoff weights), which in turn could be translated into different passenger capacities and ranges.

At this point the author must stress one unquestionably beneficial result of the British withdrawal at government level: it eliminated British Ministry influence on the design. The powerful officials at what that particular week was known as the Ministry of Technology decreed that the Airbus was a short-range aircraft, and that therefore it must not have the capability of flying longer missions. This was the same disastrous argument of the Trident 1 all over again, but on a bigger scale of size. Had Britain remained a full partner they might have had their way, but fortunately their removal made it possible to provide various increased fuel capacities. This has opened the way first to continental ranges and finally to transoceanic ranges, vastly expanding the market and the number of aircraft sold.

Indeed, from before the start of prototype construction there had been plans for a family of A300B variants each tailored to a different market segment. The original standard, to which the first two aircraft were built, was known as the A300B1, with an overall length of 167 ft 2.3 in (50.97 m), CF6-50A engines and MTOW of 291,000 lb (132 *tonnes*). By 1971 it had been decided that all subsequent aircraft would be lengthened to 175 ft 9 in (later 177 ft 5 in) by inserting plugs ahead of and behind the wings. Powered by the 51,000-lb CF6-50C engine, this could weigh 302,000 lb (136,985 kg) and carry 281 instead of 257 mixed-class passengers over slightly longer ranges. This version was called the A300B2. The B3 was to have a higher MTOW (148.5 *tonnes*), but was not built. The B4 was to have a centre-section tank, increasing MTOW to 330,700 lb (150 *tonnes*), and this was later built as the B4-100 and also as the B4-200 with a strengthened structure and other changes permitting MTOW to rise to 363,760 lb (165 *tonnes*). Unbuilt variants were the B5 freighter, B6 stretched freighter, B7 with slight stretch and a proposed RB.211-61 engine, various lightened B8s for the North American market, and rather vague B9s with considerable stretch which, as explained in the final chapter, were to come to fruition 20 years later!

At the start the designation B1 was not used, and the first A300B had its engines hung in April 1972, and made a very successful first flight on 28 October of that year. Registered F-WUAB (later F-OCAZ) it was painted white with a gold-edged orange cheat line, with the AI emblem in orange on the vertical tail. The second set of airframe components were used to make the static-test specimen assembled at CEAT (*Centre d'Essais Aéronautiques de Toulouse*), so it was the third airframe set that made the No 2 aircraft, F-WUAC, flown on 5 February 1973. The fourth set was sent to MBB in West Germany for fatigue testing. The fifth and sixth airframe sets made the first two production type (B2) aircraft, F-WUAD and WUAA, respectively flown on 28 June and 20 November 1973. These four flying prototypes completed the certification programme in 1,580 hours with an almost total absence of bother. French (DGAC) and German (LBA) certification was awarded on 15 March 1974. The first production aircraft, for Air France, had flown on 15 April 1974, and this entered service on Paris–London on 23 May, carrying 25 First- and 225 Economy-class passengers. The author, who frequented the route, noticed the delighted surprise of the passengers who had expected a 727. An amazing number asked what the aircraft was, to be told 'Eet ees an Airbus, a French aircraft'. No point in arguing!

FAA certification followed on 30 May 1974, but interest in the big twin by US operators was almost nil, in a remarkable case of emotion obliterating reason. For a long time Air France was the only real customer, signing for six B2s. Service entry was accompanied by an almost total absence of pomp and publicity, and the first aircraft simply got on with its job of moving people and cargo—an amazing amount of cargo, which seemed to take Air France by surprise—and soon showed that it was the most trouble-free aircraft in the Air France fleet, even in its most immature state. Back in May 1973 WUAC had begun automatic landing certification, and Cat IIIA (no decision height, runway visual range 700 ft, 200 m) was granted on 30 September 1974.

At entry to service the entire programme was on time and on cost. Staggeringly, the A300B still had no competitor, though McDonnell Douglas tried to launch a most unattractive DC-10 Twin. The one thing the Airbus partners had most feared from the beginning, a 'clean sheet of paper' big twin from Boeing, was still only on the drawing board. Following years of 7X7 and 7N7 studies the 767 finally got the go-ahead in July 1978, and it predictably looked to the untutored eye just like an A300B. Significant differences were a narrower body and bigger wing. The latter was demanded by United, the lead customer, who wished to climb out of difficult high-altitude airports and go straight to Flight Level 400 (40,000 ft). The big wing was also sized to fit future 767 versions with much greater weights, but it compromised the basic aircraft. As for the narrower (16 ft 6 in, 5.03 m) fuselage, this offered lower drag at the cost of a less-spacious interior and the need to invent a new non-standard cargo/baggage container. Ever since, Boeing has claimed the seven-abreast 767 cabin to be superior to an eight-abreast Airbus, to which AI naturally retort that the passenger-appeal of an Airbus furnished seven-abreast would be even greater. Naturally the 767 gained massive orders from the giant US airlines, but came a poor second elsewhere in the world to the new A310 (described in a later chapter), which AI rightly claim 'carries more passengers and more cargo than the bigger and heavier 767'.

Thus, the head-on rival never happened until more than ten years after the launch of the Airbus. Unfortunately for the Europeans, for most of those years their splendid product was viewed with a strange disbelief which to the author ignored all the facts. For example in 1976, a year in which the A300B2 was the most profitable and most reliable aircraft in the Air France fleet, the total number of aircraft sold by AI was one! This was unexpectedly tough, not only on AI and its sponsors but also on the operators who foolishly passed up the chance to buy the world's best short/medium trunk-route vehicle at bargain prices of around £19 million.

Mention of the sponsors, who made it all possible, leads to the comment that, as soon as AI began to offer real competition, the US industry ran true to form and cried 'Foul!' No potential customer has been left in any doubt that the European aircraft has sold not on its merits but on 'predatory financing' (Boeing), 'Financial deals clinched by European governments that our private-enterprise system cannot match' (Boeing), 'giveaway terms' (*Time* magazine), 'We can compete with Airbus on technical merits, but we cannot compete with the national treasuries of France and Germany, or expect "foreign aid" cocktails to assist our sales programs abroad' (Boeing), and 'My guess is that the Airbus consortium is selling a $40-million product for $25 million' ("one US aerospace executive", quoted by *Fortune*). Less publicity has been accorded the more considered statements by Airbus people, who have pointed out that the 'national treasuries' have never given money to the European consortium but have lent it under commercial rules 'at least as severe as those governing large loans from banks'. Indeed, a substantial proportion of the German funds did come from banks, in 'arrangements strictly comparable with the bank loans made to US companies'. As for selling at below cost, this would make it hard for the banks and governments to recover a return on their investment. All figures are published—by 1986 the total accumulated funding for AI from all sources was $2.36 billion—but they appear in the accounts of the partner companies.

Later attention will be paid to the massive problems of designing, building and supporting in service a multinational aircraft whose manufacturers speak five totally different national languages (not including Welsh, Flemish and several others) and who, despite the EEC, still operate under different national laws. At the start of the programme it was agreed that there should be only one source for each part, and one final assembly line at Toulouse. Sud-Aviation and Deutsche Airbus further agreed that, should demand exceed four aircraft per month, a second assembly line should be set up in Germany. For the first ten years the demand never came anywhere near four per month, and extremely slow production rates inevitably meant higher costs. From 1978, however, the customers at last began to wake up—almost entirely because of a sale to Eastern of the USA—and the monthly production rate began to climb, at first to three and finally to five big twins per month. As explained later, the plant and facilities have been progressively improved, but there has never been a need for a second assembly line.

By 1974 AI was studying a tenth variant, the B10, with a shorter fuselage. Initially planned as a vehicle for the RB.211 engine, the B10 gradually became a completely new and very efficient aircraft in the 210/250-seat class. Redesignated the A310, it went ahead on 7 July 1978 and is the subject of a later chapter.

By this time the much-buffeted British industry had spent more than a year trying to chart some kind of course for the future in civil transports. In 1977 another Labour administration had passed an act nationalizing Hawker Siddeley Aviation and other companies into a single government conglomerate called British Aerospace. This act took effect on 1 January 1978, and the often very heated arguments were then transferred from 'nationalization' to the question of whether to rejoin Airbus Industrie or link up with US manufacturers. There were many powerful advocates for a link with Boeing, under the terms of which BAe would have been responsible for the wing of the projected 757. Among those who argued for this American subcontractor role were British Airways—which is almost an all-American operator and, unlike almost every other European flag-carrier, has never bought an Airbus—and Rolls-Royce Ltd, successor to the original company which went bankrupt in February 1971, which sold a smaller version of the RB.211 into the 757.

The arguments in favour of becoming a junior partner in a Boeing programme were based on hypothetical finances which would not have been borne out in practice. For once, the sterile accountants did not carry the day, but it took a long year of complex and carefully balanced arguments before, on 18 August 1978, an agreement at the industrial level was initialled between the AI partners—Aérospatiale, Deutsche Airbus and CASA—and BAe. This agreement was ratified by the governments on 27 October 1978. The intervening period was spent trying to

Tunnel tests took place in Britain, France, Germany and the Netherlands. Here an early A300B model is being prepared in the big Low-Speed Tunnel at the British Royal Aircraft Establishment at Bedford

The first three Airbuses, pictured on the day No 3 (left) first flew, 28 June 1973. Times were hard; Lufthansa had shown no inclination to place an order, despite No 3's livery, and Iberia, in whose markings No 2 was painted, was to cancel its order a year later. The Nos 1 and 2 aircraft bear Paris airshow numbers 155 and 156; registrations were F-OCAZ (originally F-WUAB) and F-WUAC, respectively

convince the AI partners that Britain really did want to be part of Europe, a task hardly made easier by massive purchases by British Airways of 737s and 757s. It was also apparent that there must be a conflict of British interest between future Airbus sales and competing American aircraft with Rolls-Royce engines. To guard against this, BAe and the British government agreed in any such conflict situation to forego BAe's full voting rights where the A300B2 and B4 were concerned. The restriction was to be in force until delivery of aircraft No 150 or mid-1981, whichever came first, and was to be automatically eliminated by any letter of intent to purchase A300s or A310s on the part of British Airways.

The agreement, which at least gave the once-great British industry a full partnership in the manufacture of big jetliners, came into force on 1 January 1979. Since that date the shareholding in AI by the various partners has been: Aérospatiale, 37.9 per cent; MBB (through Deutsche Airbus) 37.9 per cent; BAe, 20 per cent; and CASA, 4.2 per cent. Fokker of the Netherlands is an associate on these programmes, making wing moving surfaces, composite parts and A310 hinge and leg fairing doors. A Belgian group, Belairbus, formed by SABCA and SONACA, is an associate on the A310, making leading-edge movables and detail parts. Some of the Deutsche Airbus work on the A300/310 is subcontracted to the Italian industry, notably SIAI-Marchetti, and on the A300-600/310 to the German company Dornier. Part of BAe's work on the A300/310 programmes is subcontracted to Hawker de Havilland in Australia. Shareholdings and work-splits on the A320 are outlined in a later chapter.

2
THE A300B

As EXPLAINED EARLIER, the A300B was planned as the best possible large passenger jetliner for use on sectors of up to 1,200 nm (1,382 miles, 2,224 km), carrying a nominal 250 passengers. The basic design was a refinement of the earlier HBN.100, and thus followed the optimized layout established with that precursor study of having a circular-section fuselage, low-mounted wing, twin engines in underwing pods and what might be termed a conventional landing gear and tail. After several ups and downs the overall size was fixed in 1969, and in particular the fuselage diameter settled at 18 ft 6 in (222 in, 5.64 m), a value since confirmed on countless occasions as the correct one.

Lacking much firm input from potential customers, AI naturally kept the design as flexible as possible. It was always obvious that there would be room inside the main wing box for fuel for much greater ranges. At first it was thought that, by simply making more of the wing into an integral tank, the range could ultimately be extended to about 2,100 nm (2,418 miles, 3,892 km), but the A300B design proved in practice to have more potential for range-stretch than any previous airliner, and today the Dash-600 version carries 267 passengers and baggage, with full airline reserves, over sectors as long as 4,400 nm (5,065 miles, 8,154 km)! By older standards this makes it very much a long-hauler. Indeed the derived A310-300 carries a full payload 5,000 nm (5,757 miles, 9,266 km), in what is probably the most efficient trucking job in the entire history of air transport.

It was also arranged that the fuselage could be lengthened to increase passenger capacity by 25 per cent without the need to modify the geometry of the landing gear or rear fuselage shape. It is typically ironic to note that, whereas in 1968 the airlines were shouting 'make it smaller', as soon as the design was frozen they began calling for extra capacity. It was too late to lengthen the first two prototypes, but every A300B built subsequently has been about 10 ft (3 m) longer, and in the latest Dash-600 the rear fuselage (basically that previously designed for the A310) enables two extra rows of seats to be accommodated within a longer cabin housed inside the same overall length. Today AI has gone way beyond the original 'too big' A300, and has recently responded to market forces by offering the A330 seating up to 350 mixed-class passengers in a lengthened fuselage.

At all times great attention has been paid to flight performance and safety. It would be foolish to claim any unique level of safety in consequence, but the fact remains that the A300B and A310 are the only large subsonic passenger jets in history to have established a perfect safety record. Not one has ever been grounded. Luck clearly plays some role in such matters, but with over 4 million hours flown by over 350 aircraft it is certainly fair to claim that the original Airbus is the safest vehicle ever offered to passengers. Almost the only time Airbus passengers ever experienced the slightest discomfort was on the occasion of the famous hijack to Entebbe! This contrasts with the slick conclusions of the media at the start of the project, when, to quote a British national daily, it was thought to be 'blatant folly' to carry so many people with so few engines.

Throughout the entire design and development of the A300B there was an almost total absence of trouble, to a degree never before attained with any large transport. The media would have have loved to have been able to 'knock' the Airbus, but to them good news is no news. Very little was ever said to explain that this kind of success is never attained by chance, but by the most meticulous attention to detail everywhere. Except for the engine installation, which was almost straight DC-10-30 (but with slightly revised accessories, and with no need for the American transport's drag-inducing fences on either side near the top of the cowl), almost every part of the A300B was absolutely optimized for the job, and subjected to prolonged and intensive refinement. Occasionally facilities outside the original three main partner-nations were used, including a tunnel at NLR Amsterdam and many supplier-company research departments in the USA, such as Westinghouse on the basic electric power system. Thanks to a combination of skilled and experienced manpower, skilled and experienced management and a deliberate policy of multinational critical design analysis, the author has no doubt that, with this aircraft, far more than ever before of the 'unpredictable' problems were identified and avoided before they could happen.

Few aircraft have looked more unexcitingly 'normal' than the first A300B. In fact its normality belied the design's unequalled aerodynamic refinement, and though this was true of every potential problem area it was especially true of the wings. As already described, research at Hatfield in 1959–65 had progressively allowed the refinement of wings of improved profile, known as rooftop or rear-loaded aerofoils, which go most of the way towards the true supercritical wing. In fact, the latter has never been fully achieved except on very special NASA research aircraft. A practical commercial transport would find it difficult to achieve the necessary curved underside at the trailing edge and still incorporate effective high-lift flaps. Moreover, even if the aircraft were to be built with such a wing, after half an hour its surface would no longer achieve the necessary laminar airflow. Perhaps the truest test of the A300B wing is that almost a decade later Boeing, no slouch in wing design, gave the 767 a wing with much more area, 3.5 degrees more sweep, thinner profile and another ten years of technology, and achieved a slower cruise Mach number and higher approach speeds. A detail point to be made is that comparisons really are odious, and arguments over relative aspect ratio often overlook the fact that European and US wings are measured in completely different ways.

Superficially the wing of an A300B does not look very different from that of a 707. They are similar in size, and the only obvious difference is that the 707 wing has more sweep. In fact, the way they generate lift could hardly be more different. The older wing accelerates the air violently as it rushes up and over the leading edge, leading to the most intense suction along a quite narrow strip of the upper surface between the leading edge and about 10 per cent chord (one-tenth of the way back across the wing). This narrow strip virtually lifts the aircraft; the rest of the wing does not achieve much. It works, but the tremendous acceleration of flow over this upper forward portion of the wing means that the speed of sound is reached when the true airspeed of the aircraft is only about 460 kt or Mach 0.8. As soon as this happens a shockwave forms, immediately aft of the crest of the aerofoil, causing sudden rise in aerodynamic drag.

In the past the only way to make an aircraft cruise faster on the same power was to make the wing thinner or sweep it back more acutely. Both are undesirable on several counts. More sweep means poorer low-speed performance and longer takeoff and landing runs, and also possible control deficiencies. A thinner wing has to have much thicker skins in order to achieve the required strength and resistance to bending, and this makes it much heavier, as well as reducing the volume available for fuel. The sharp leading edge is also totally unsuited to lift at high angles, and needs complex systems to modify its profile.

What Hatfield pioneered, and which has since been adopted by virtually all builders of subsonic jets, was to reshape the wing profile with a blunter leading edge, flatter top, greater depth (with bulged underside) and downturned rear portion. Such a wing behaves in a way dramatically different from the traditional type. As the air encounters the wing it is still speeded up as it rushes up over the leading edge, but the acceleration is barely half as great as before. Instead of having a violent peak in speed, the air speeds up only modestly; but it then retains this increased speed right back across the top of the wing, and even maintains a much higher speed than before as it traverses the aft section. As a result, instead of generating intense lift across a narrow strip near the leading edge, the new wing generates powerful lift over virtually the entire area. The centre of pressure, the point at each aerofoil section through which the resultant lift force acts, is shifted from near the leading edge to a point roughly at mid-chord or even aft of this. A diagram appears on page 89.

The advantages of the rear-loaded or rooftop section are very great. The bluff rounded leading edge is much better at low speeds and high angles, while still being efficient at cruising speed. Delaying the onset of shockwaves enables the cruising

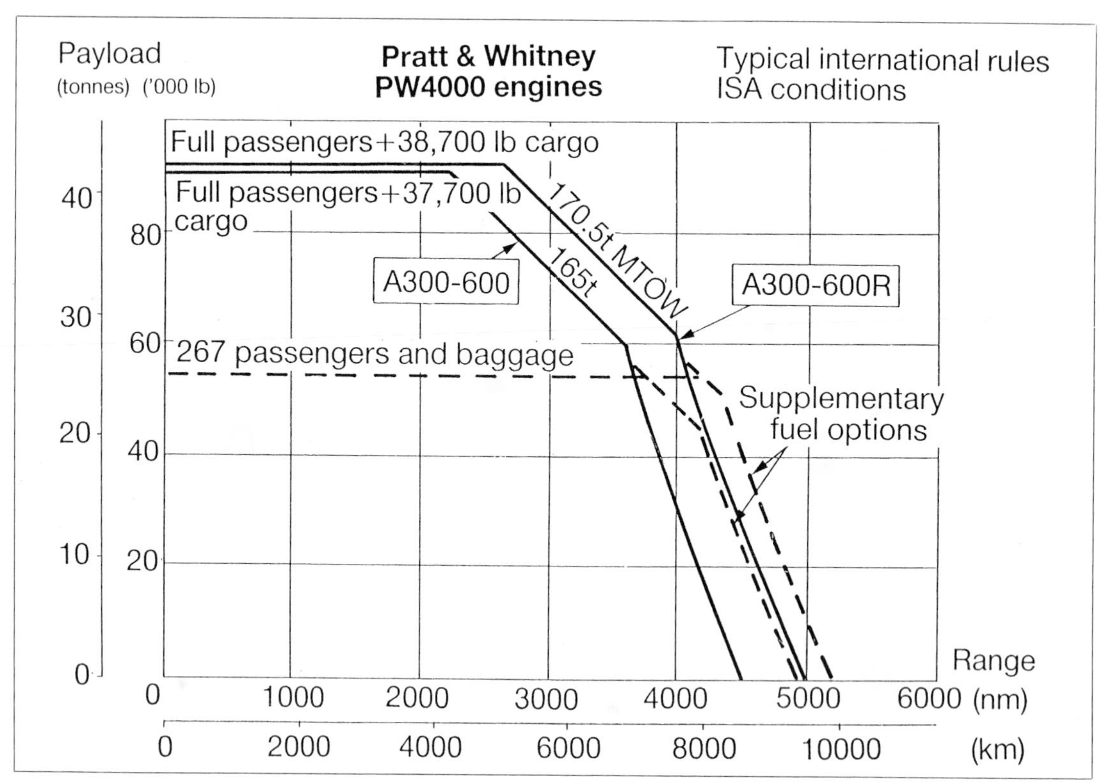

Payload/range curves for today's aircraft (with PW4000 engines). It seems hard to believe that the A300B was designed to carry 239 passengers just 1,187 nm (2200 km)!

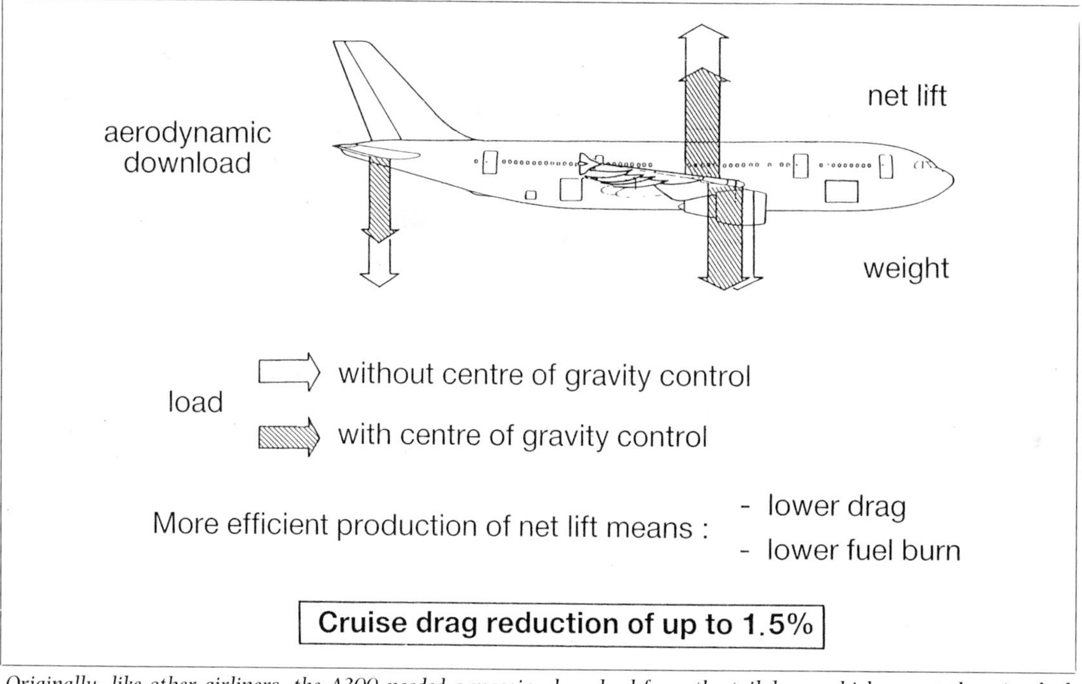

Originally, like other airliners, the A300 needed a massive download from the tailplane, which meant the wing had to generate far more lift than that needed to support the weight. Today the fuel-filled tail of the -600R gets the download internally, taking the strain off the wing and reducing drag

Mach number to be raised, say, from Mach 0.82 to Mach 0.85 or more for a given propulsive thrust. Alternatively, and this is usually the preferred choice, the wing can be made noticeably deeper, so thinner skins can be used, saving 1 to 1.5 tons in weight on a single wing of A300B size and further improving low-speed characteristics. The increased internal volume was not needed for fuel in the early Airbuses, which have a capacity of 9,460 Imp gal (43,000 lit), but it enables later versions to have tremendous stretch in range, so that today's A300-600 carries 13,836 Imp gal (62,900 lit) without any change in the external size of the wing.

Of course, everything possible was then done to increase lift coefficient in the high-lift regime for takeoff and landing. Prolonged testing gradually refined the profiles and locations of the leading-edge slats, which initially comprised five sections outboard of the pod pylon, a big gap at the pylon and a sixth slat section inboard, terminating well out from the fuselage. The final arrangement comprises just three long slat sections forming an unbroken strip from the tip to near the root, with no gap at the pylon. This gapless slat was not achieved on the DC-10 and TriStar. South African Airways has severe high-altitude airport problems, and to increase payload and performance in WAT-limited (weight/altitude/temperature) conditions the A300B2K was developed with reduced slat angles (16 degrees instead of 20) linked to a Krüger flap extended from the leading-edge root, and with the final inboard gap sealed by a small Krüger section hinged out from the fuselage. This seemingly perfect leading-edge arrangement soon became standard.

On the trailing edge are wide-chord tabbed Fowler flaps, two sections outboard of the trailing-edge kink and a single section inboard. The latter is separated from the other sections by a small all-speed aileron in line with the jet. The flaps cover 84 per cent of each semi-span, and when fully extended increase chord by 25 per cent. In this high-lift regime the slotted tabs on the flap trailing edges increase lift coefficient to a remarkable 2.85. Even at takeoff setting of 15 degrees the L/D is appreciably higher than the best achieved with more complicated double- or triple-slotted flaps, the lift coefficient being nearly 2.7, assisted by downward rotation of the neutral position of the all-speed aileron. Effectiveness of this high-lift system was startlingly better than prediction. As a result two flap takeoff settings were deleted, as well as the final landing setting together with its planned load-relief system, resulting in major simplification. All-speed aileron droop was reduced to only 9 degrees.

Along the top of the wing are hydraulically driven hinged surfaces used as spoilers for roll control, as airbrakes and as lift dumpers. The original scheme was to use conventional outboard ailerons, then (coming inboard) two sections of spoiler, then three sections of airbrake, then the all-speed aileron driven to ±30 degrees, and finally two sections of lift dumper preselected to open on touchdown. The extreme efficiency of the roll system enabled roll rates to be increased, and the system simplified to have other benefits. The modified configuration used on the B2 and B4 aircraft comprises: a low-speed outboard aileron, with gearing slaved to slat extension; three sections of spoiler; two sections of airbrake; the all-speed aileron, restricted to ± 23 degrees; and two inboard sections of airbrake. After the rear fuselage had been reinforced at Frame 91 to bear the greater fuselage torque, the cockpit handwheel could be slammed to 60 degrees at maximum speed or Mach, giving full roll at 25 degrees per second with no limitation.

The roll-control system was further simplified in the A300-600 and A310 by eliminating the low-speed ailerons. Most Airbuses in current production have simple fixed outer wings. In addition, the wingtips of the A300-600 (GE engines, and probably later with the PW4000) and A310-200 and -300 all have carefully sculpted wingtip fences which reduce fuel burn, as described later.

The conventional tail unit comprises a fixed fin, powered one-piece rudder, powered elevators and irreversible trimming tailplane. Whenever the aircraft is trimmed, in any flight regime, the elevator remains at zero deflection except when dive/climb is commanded.

Powered flight controls, deicing and similar topics are dealt with later, in a section on systems.

Background to the fuselage cross-section has already emphasized how carefully this vital parameter was studied before deciding on an 18 ft 6 in (5.64-m) circle. The floor is a little below the mid-position, giving a centreline cabin interior height of 8 ft 4 in (2.54 m) and an underfloor hold height of 5 ft 9 in (1.76 m). Though high-strength steels and titanium are used at the points of highest stress, virtually the entire structure is conventional aluminium alloy, with machined panels along the passenger windows and other areas with stressed cutouts. The entire fuselage is pressurized, as explained later, except for the nose radome, the extreme tail section, the area under the main wing box and the compartments for the nose and main landing gears. The underfloor area includes not only two large holds for containerized loads, plus a rear hold for loose (bulk) cargo, but also beautifully arranged compartments at a convenient height for maintenance personnel where are grouped avionics, electrics, air-conditioning, fuel, hydraulics and other systems. Leaving any lever or switch in an incorrect position inhibits closure of the compartment door and is indicated in the cockpit.

Typical of the items that would, at least in part, have been British, had not the British government withdrawn from the programme, all three units of the landing gear were originally of Dowty design. When Britain withdrew, they were handed to the French company Messier-Hispano-Bugatti for manufacture. Later US (Bendix or Goodyear) wheels and brakes became available as customer options. All units could hardly be more straightforward. The twin-wheel nose unit is steerable to 65 degrees left/right (95 degrees on tow), and retracts forwards. The bogie main units are pivoted to forgings carried off the rear of the wing box in such a way that, in an abnormally heavy landing, the gear breaks off without any fracture of main structure and without causing any fuel leak. Each unit retracts inwards, the bogie lying in the fuselage in a bay closed by doors hinged each side of the centreline. All units can free-fall and lock down in the absence of hydraulic power. Originally tyre pressure was to be 150 lb/sq in (10.54 kg/cm^2), but with increasing weight it rose on the main tyres to 180 lb/sq in, or 161 with optional wide tyres.

The underwing engine location has already enabled AI to offer almost the entire current range of CF6, JT9D and PW4000-series engines; indeed the CF6-80C2 and PW4056, both engines of record power and of the very first importance, in each case made their first flights aboard the A300-600. In each case the pylon picks up at the same points on the main wing box but serves as interface to quite different attachments on the engine. Aerodynamically all pylons are precisely optimized for ideal airflow and minimum pod/wing interference, and the pods themselves are also essentially ideally configured despite their having distinctly different shapes. In all cases the engine axis is tilted 3 degrees down from the major aircraft axis, and 1 degree inwards. All pods incorporate fan reversers for ground operation, and acoustic panels to minimize external noise.

Before turning to the systems a little should be said about the structure of the wing, because each wing is an impressive piece of hardware even without its secondary structure and movable surfaces. The left and right wing boxes are joined at the sides of the fuselage to a massive centre section integral with the fuselage. Structurally each wing box comprises front and rear spars, a centre spar extending as far as the engine pylon rib, inter-spar ribs and three large machined skins above and three more below. Almost every one of these parts is machined from solid, and after being hand-finished and shot-blasted with small glass beads the skins are pressed to the correct curvature and the complete wing box then assembled using Drivmatic riveting and interference-fit bolts. A few crucial joints are made with TaperLok titanium bolts. Completed wing boxes, with leading and trailing ribs and the main-gear attachment forgings, are then flown by Super Guppy to Bremen for completion, as described in Chapter 4. The appreciably different wing of the A310 is described in Chapter 3.

Not only the main wing box but every part of the primary structure is finished to a standard of corrosion protection which, when the A300B first flew, was unique in the industry. There is no bare metal anywhere! Some joints are protected by eight different layers or coatings, and no operator has ever experienced much corrosion. As for fatigue, the complete second airframe was put into a massive water tank and fatigue-tested for 120,000 hours, and numerous other parts have been individually fatigue-tested for similar or greater periods. The unrivalled resistance to ageing of Airbus airframes has a major influence on their resale value; indeed some Airbuses have been bought secondhand for more than the original price.

This aircraft, seen on takeoff at Toulouse, was the very first A300B2 production aircraft. It first flew in June 1973 as F-ODCX in Lufthansa colours (see colour picture). It was repainted in the new AI house livery as F-WUAD, as seen here. Now see below

Today the same aircraft, reregistered F-BUAD, has completed almost 15 years of often crucial work as the main Airbus Industrie 'house' flying testbed. Millions have gasped at its recent displays showing what the pilot can do, in complete safety, with the flight-control system of the A320

Two of Eastern Air Lines' A300s pause at Miami alongside a DC-9 and a 727. The Eastern order was a massive coup for AI and sent shockwaves throughout the US airline industry. It was also the key which unlocked the closed minds of the world's airlines

A slow fly-by by aircraft 34 (F-WLGB, later VT-EDV), the first B2 for Indian Airlines. On page 47 an account begins of ferrying the second Indian B2 (No 36, F-WUAT/VT-EDW) from Toulouse to Hamburg for interior furnishing. At that time IA had signed for three A300s; today the airline has ten

The static-test airframe quickly showed how, with generally very minor strengthening, the aircraft gross weight could be increased from the original B2 figure of 137 *tonnes* to today's Dash-600R weight of 170.5 *tonnes* (375,900 lb). In contrast a typical OWE (operating weight empty) has grown only from 85 *tonnes* (187,390 lb) to 88.2 *tonnes* (195,500 lb). This has enabled the product potential, the payload multiplied by the range it can be carried, to be increased from 225,900 passenger nautical miles in the B2 to 1,174,800 pnm in the 600R! This truly staggering difference puts today's same-size aircraft in a totally different category.

A little should be said here about accomodation and furnishing. It is a fundamental feature of all widebody passenger jets that each row of seats is broken at two places to give two parallel aisles running the length of the cabin. Indeed, the description TA (twin-aisle) is used by Airbus Industrie in preference to widebody, in particular to distinguish between the big A300/310 family and the SA (single-aisle) A320 described in Chapter 6. All TA cabins have a feeling of spaciousness absent from smaller aircraft, but it must be remembered that, at least in the original conception, the A300B was a short-haul aircraft. This is inevitably equated by the airlines with less room per passenger. Indirectly it leads to other problems. On short sectors there is little time to serve perhaps 300 meals, and the author has seen Airbuses with six meal trolleys at work, three in each aisle, which hardly facilitates nipping along to the toilet.

On the original B2 and B4 aircraft the almost universal basic furnishing included a galley and two toilets behind the cockpit and two galleys and four toilets at the rear. Operators were given the option of a big underfloor galley, but on short sectors the extra serving time is a major problem and all initial customers adopted the above-floor arrangement, each adjacent to a 42-in (1.07-m) service door. In addition to the service doors there are four outward-opening parallel-arm Type A plug-type passenger doors, two at the front and two at the rear, and a Type III emergency exit on each side aft of the wing.

The datum passenger layout in the B2 and B4 is 261 seats eight-abreast (2-2 + 2-2) at a seat pitch of 34 in (864 mm), with 19-in (483-mm) aisles. Airbus Industrie deliberately rejected the 19 ft 6 in fuselage because they were convinced short-haul operators would use the extra width not to install wider seats but nine-abreast seating, resulting in poorer standards. The standard (baseline) seat has a width of 40.4 in (1.03 m), and for almost all passengers this is excellent, even on long hauls. In the author's view little purpose is served by changing to seven-abreast seating with wider (long-range type) seats, though with the 767 Boeing has always claimed that seven-abreast, in that aircraft's narrower cabin, is in some way superior. Of course, the greater the number of passengers, the less will be the aisle room and overhead storage volume per passenger. When the original A300B2 was introduced by Air France the overhead lockers were considered so spacious that the airline actually

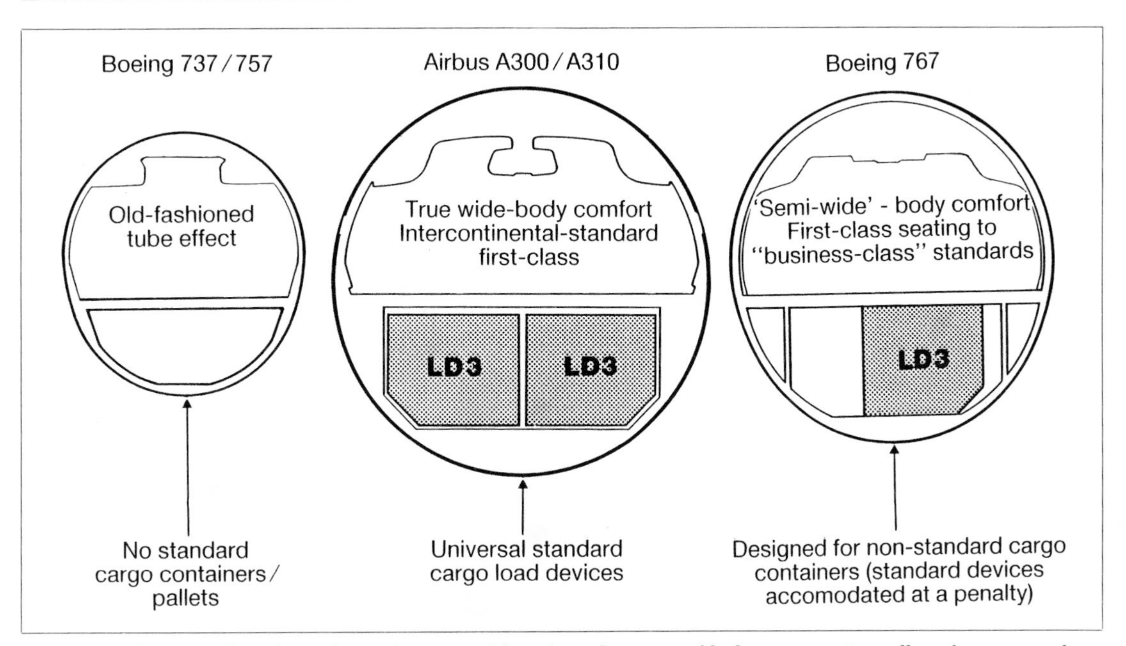

They say there are 'lies, damn lies and statistics' but these diagrams of body cross-section, all to the same scale, speak for themselves. Time will show whether British Airways will continue to attract passengers and cargo with an all-Boeing fleet. It was Béteille who lifted the cabin floor to match LD3s.

encouraged passengers to carry their baggage with them. Operators have always had the option of adding a double row of overhead lockers down the centre of the cabin.

Turning to the cockpit, this was originally designed as a very good example of conventional ideas. In the B2 and B4 the two pilots face ahead, with the console between them. CM3 (crew-member 3, nominally an engineer) sits behind on the right, and because his big panels are on the right wall this later became known as the SFCC, for side-facing crew cockpit. A fourth seat on the left is for an observer. All seats are electrically adjustable vertically and in the horizontal plane, and the CM3 and observer seats can traverse across the deck. To give a flavour of flying an early B2, the following was written by John Belson, *Flight International* staff man, for the issue of 11 December 1976.

We begin to push back from 'the cattle trough' (*l'abreuvoir*), as Airbus Industrie's Toulouse flight-test centre is known locally, at 1530 hr. Our mount, the second A300B2 for Indian Airlines, made its three-hour maiden flight only two days previously. After an evaluation sortie from Toulouse we will go on to the Finkenwerder base of Airbus Industrie partner MBB. There, seven miles from Hamburg, internal furnishings and seats are fitted to all production A300s.

Although sales of the big twin have been disappointing this year, 36 A300s have already been sold and options are held on a further 21. So far 26 of the type have entered service, and Air Inter, Indian Airlines and South African Airways are each due to take their next aircraft before the end of the year.

A300B2 is the designation given to the basic aircraft certificated at a take-off weight of 142 *tonnes*. Changes to the fuel system, increased fuel capacity and the addition of small Krüger flaps at the wing root allow the B4 to take off at 157.5 *tonnes* and fly 2,100 nm with a 53,000 lb payload. Fitting the same Krüger flaps to the basic aircraft, while leaving out the associated increase in fuel capacity and take-off weight, provides the stable with its hot-and-high performer—the A300B2K, which lifts seven tonnes more than the basic aircraft.

Recently announced is the B4-FC freighter conversion, which also offers a maximum take-off weight of 157.5 *tonnes* with a freight payload of 40 *tonnes* over 1,900 nm, or 28 *tonnes* over 2,700 nm.

Air France, the first customer, is full of praise for the A300. This year Lufthansa introduced the type and has found it extraordinarily trouble-free: of the German flag carrier's first 1,000 A300 flights, only one was cancelled for technical reasons.

Indian Airlines selected the B2 for its domestic routes last year. Three A300s are firmly ordered and a further three are on option; the first IAL machine, No 34 off the line, was delivered last month.

On entering the A300's 'office' I am immediately impressed by the attention to detail betokened by such items as tailored flight-bag locations outboard of the pilots' seats (you can actually take some forgotten item from your bag easily and safely), an illuminated board for letdown charts, ample storage for pens and pencils, and an emergency-checklist holder at the rear of the pedestal. The pilots' seats are electrically operated and can act as very effective toe-crushers if the flight deck is full of unwanted guests. But at least one is left with no excuse for not carefully adjusting seat height. Close to the centre windscreen pillar are three horizontal 'eyeballs' with which each pilot aligns himself to ensure that his eyes are always at the same position, both fore-and-aft and vertically.

Flight-deck layout is clear and uncluttered. Because Indian Airlines has not specified inertial navigation as part of its avionics fit, the forward centre console area offers plenty of additional space in which to display letdown charts or take-off performance parameters.

The conventional control column features comfortable hand grips. The outboard grip incorporates a rocker switch for pitch-trim autopilot disconnect, intercom and a manual autopilot control.

The captain's and first officer's instrument panels are duplicated. Each accommodates a basic 'T' of ASI (airspeed indicator), ADI (attitude director indicator), vertical-strip radio altimeter and servo altimeter, and HSI (horizontal situation indicator), with a vertical-speed indicator mounted to the right of the HSI. Dual radio-magnetic indicators for VOR and ADF flank the HSI, and a quartz-crystal clock with light-emitting diode readout occupies the bottom left of each pilot's panel.

Engine instruments on the centre panel are few, comprising twin N_1 (fan speed), exhaust-gas temperature, N_2 (core-engine speed) and fuel-flow analog/digital indicators. Dominating the centre panel is the master warning system. Its upper section presents mixed red and amber warnings which demand pilot action, while the lower duplicates system warnings to alert crew members. The take-off inhibit facility is cancelled by raising the undercarriage or pressing the neighbouring recall button. The squat pedestal groups the pitch-trim wheel, speed-brake control, throttles and combined slat/flap lever ahead of the radio and radar controls.

TRANSAVIA HOLLAND

SUID - AFRIKAANSE LUGDIENS
ZS-SDB

Page 49 *The eighth A300, a B2, was leased in 1974 to Air Siam. It is pictured in May 1976 as F-ODHC in the livery of TEA, to whom it was leased as PH-TVL* Apollo 76, *before finding a permanent career with Air Inter as F-BUAF*

Left *ZS-SDB, the second of SAA's Kruger-flapped B2Ks, on flight test in November 1976. The observatory of the Pic du Midi (9,466 ft) is every bit as good a backcloth as Mount Rainier, favoured by Boeing. A month later this aircraft,* Gemsbok, *arrived in Jo'burg; Capt John Lamprecht said 'We love it already'*

Above *Kenya's first A310-300 was delivered on 16 May 1986. After the ceremony it was flown to London, took on a full passenger load and then went on non-stop to Nairobi. This first day was typical of all that have followed. Kenya would not argue with the author's belief that the Dash-300 is, on a strict ton-miles per pound of fuel basis, the most efficient airliner yet built*

Above *Though it looks very much like the first A300B2 delivered to Lufthansa in 1976 this aircraft, the first A300-600 for the same carrier, does about three times as big a job. The only obvious external differences are the small tip fences and the absence of a dorsal ADF fairing. In the distance is Toulouse-Blagnac's airport terminal*

Top right *This A300B front end, having been flown from Germany and fastened to a nose made at Toulouse St Martin, then travelled by night through the centre of Toulouse on its way to CEAT for structural testing*

Right *After the first flight of an A310 on 3 April 1982; from left, flight-test engineers Jean-Pierre Flamant and Günter Scherer; Bernard Ziegler; Bernard Lathière; Pierre Baud; FT engineer Gérard Guyot; and Jean Pierson, at that time boss of the Toulouse plant*

aerospatiale

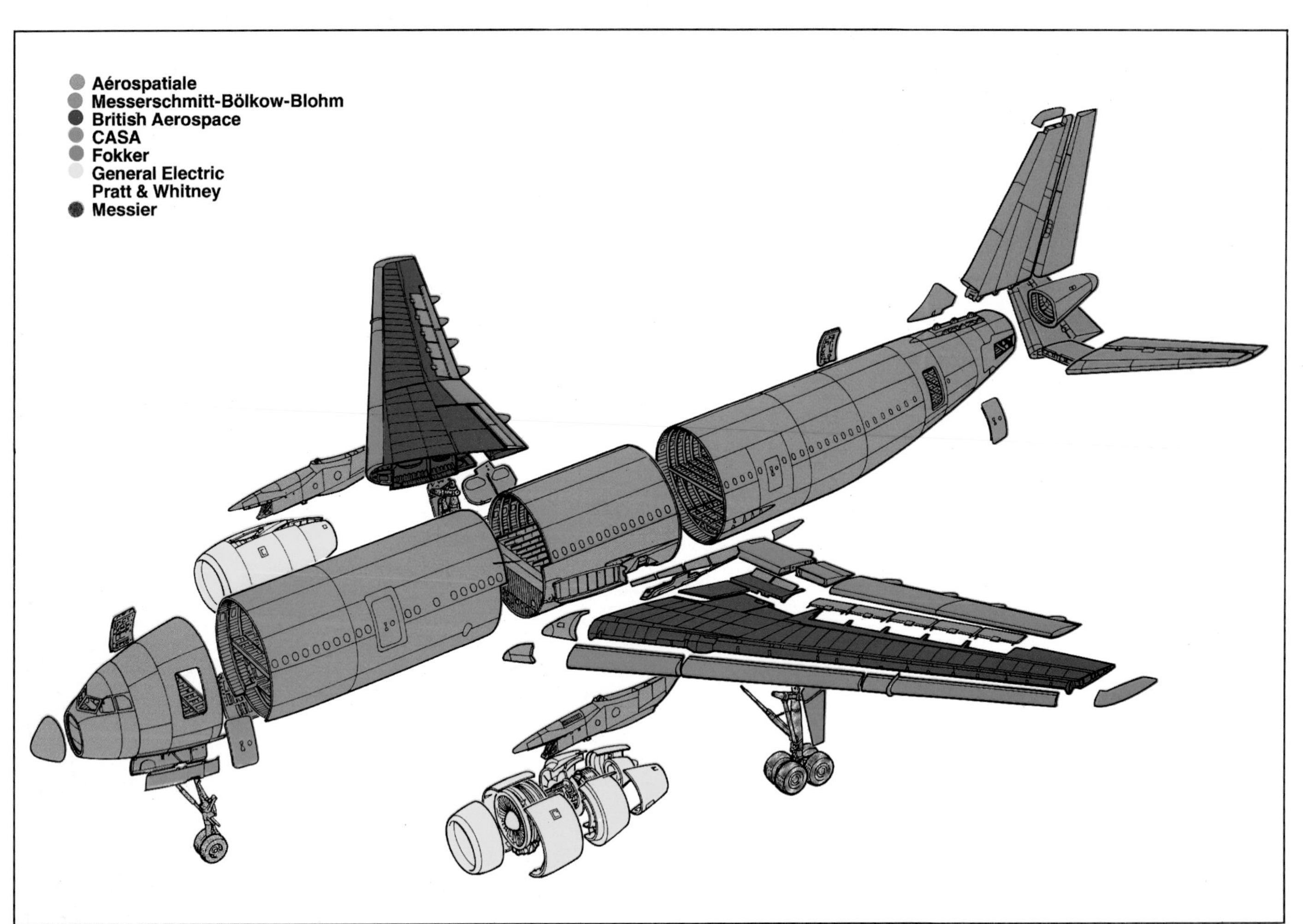
Aérospatiale
Messerschmitt-Bölkow-Blohm
British Aerospace
CASA
Fokker
General Electric
Pratt & Whitney
Messier

swissair

Top left *How production of the A300-600 is shared out among the Airbus Industrie partners and (in yellow and grey) their major suppliers. The distribution of work has been almost the same throughout the 15 years of A300B manufacture*

Above *Pierre Baud, Vice-President of the AI Flight Division, is seen here about to start up an A300-600. This particular aircraft (with temporary French registration WWAB) has the traditional handwheel or yoke, and the ADI (altitude/director indicator) or PFD (primary flight display) is above the HSI (horizontal situation indicator) or nav display, instead of the other way round*

Left *In 17 days in February/March 1983 the No 5 A310, in Swissair configuration, completed a faultless demonstration tour through the Middle and Far East. It is seen here at San'a (Sanaa), capital of the Yemen*

Overleaf *A rare opportunity to compare the A300B4 and A310 occurred in late 1984 when two leased aircraft for PanAm were on flight test together. The B4 is one of 12 'white tail' aircraft for services in the Caribbean. The 310-200 shows off its new standardized pylon strut and cowl, in this case for JT9D-7R4D engines. Today PanAm has brand-new A310-300s with PW4152 engines*

PAN AM
PAN AM
PAN AM
PAN AM
F-WZMI

I'm settled comfortably into the left-hand seat, and Airbus Industrie test pilot Udo Günzel is sitting at my right. It's an odd-numbered day of the month, so we elect to use the No 1 systems wherever there is a choice—the transponder, pressurization, airborne radar and ignition are all duplicated, for instance. (This rough-and-ready convention is used worldwide to ensure that duplicated systems are used equally.)

Having moved the start switch to the 'arm' position and checked that the auxiliary power unit is providing enough air pressure, I start the No 1 engine. At ten per cent N_2 I open the high-pressure cock and monitor exhaust-gas temperature (EGT) while Udo starts the stopwatch. A temperature rise must show up within 25 sec; thereafter EGT is limited to 900°C during the starting sequence. On this occasion it rises to 615°C, and a digital readout confirms the pointer indication. Starting tail-to-wind is possible in winds up to 50 kt, but N_1 build-up is slow and EGT is usually higher. Selecting ground idle for the General Electric CF6-50 fitted to the A300 gives a core speed of 65 per cent of nominal maximum revolutions, N_1 (fan speed) of 25 per cent, 390°C EGT, and 570 kg/hr fuel flow.

CF6-50 reliability has been exceptional, with only two engine-originating in-flight shutdowns recorded by the A300 fleet up to the beginning of last month. The A300's -50 is fully interchangeable with the DC-10-30 powerplant.

From start-up onwards the pilot is primarily interested in N_1—the fan provides 85 per cent of thrust—and EGT. Throttle movement is remarkably small, with a mere 35 degrees displacement of the two throttles unleashing 102,000 lb of thrust. There are no intermediate stops on the quadrant, so care must be taken not to exceed engine limitations.

After-starting checks are quickly completed by flight engineer Erwin Mayhofer, and a final word with the groundcrew confirms that all is clear for taxiing—a laconic 'Au revoir' sends us on our way. About 50 per cent N_1 is required to move the aircraft, but once under way idle power is usually sufficient to keep it rolling.

A nosewheel/rudder interconnect provides 6 degrees of steering directly from the rudder pedals, so on straight runs there is no need to use the nosewheel tiller. The aircraft is positioned while taxiing by keeping the taxiway centreline just to the right of the autoland warning light on the glareshield. Perched 18 ft above the ground it is difficult to estimate taxiing speed—the more so without INS groundspeed information—and it is important to check by looking out through the side windows.

The view from the flight deck is good, taking in a total 135 degrees either side of the nose, but the ground is invisible up to 50 ft in front of the aircraft. At a decision height of 100 ft and runway visual range of 1,200 ft, eight approach lights are visible, a big improvement on older types with more obtrusive nose profiles. The nose gear is several feet behind the flight deck, something which needs to be borne in mind while turning on the ground, and the aircraft tends to stop in a tight turn unless about 35 per cent N_1 is used.

The pre-take-off data card shows our weight to be low, 105.7 *tonnes*, and at 26.2 per cent the centre of gravity dictates a pitch-trim setting of +1.2 degrees. With flaps at 8 degrees the relevant speeds work out at V_1 123 kt, V_R 125 kt, V_2 127 kt, flap retraction (V_3) 136 kt, slat retraction (V_4) 177 kt, and final take-off speed (V_{FTO}) 203 kt. Safe pitch attitude in the event of an engine failure is calculated at 14 degrees. Our weight is unrepresentative of airline operation for two reasons: no internal furnishings, seats, galleys or toilets are fitted, and we are carrying just enough fuel for the sortie because after arrival at Finkenwerder the aircraft will be defuelled to allow furnishings to be fitted.

Airbus Industrie has spent two years refining its presentation of the performance data used by commercial operators to optimize take-off weights. The company is well aware that 'the simpler you make it, the more you lose.' Accordingly, A300 flight-deck literature includes a single sheet on which is presented all of the customary information, plus a number of correction factors. These the pilot applies to data derived from the main table to arrive at a maximum take-off weight figure much closer to the true capability of the aircraft. This simple expedient helps to keep to a minimum operations at unrealistically, and uneconomically, low take-off weights.

At this point one must choose between using a fixed V_2/V_S (the ratio of free-air safety speed to stalling speed) and the full range of flap settings, or selecting from only one or two flap positions and varying V_2/V_S. Airbus Industrie favours the latter approach for the A300. By regulation V_2 should never be less than 1.2 V_S, and an upper limit of $V_2 = 1.35\ V_S$ is imposed by tyre speed, brake energy and aircraft weight constraints. This V_2 range makes it possible to optimize take-off weight in every case, and is particularly useful when the take-off is weight/altitude/temperature limited.

The twin-engined A300 is required to maintain a 2.4 per cent gross second-segment climb gradient on one engine. The increased take-off speeds permitted by the variable V_2 technique make it possible to trade off excess runway length for a steeper climb. But surprisingly, neither Air France nor Lufthansa yet fully uses variable V_2, preferring instead to retain simple payload tables where runway length permits, and adapting V_2 only on short, high-elevation runways.

In normal operations the A300's autothrottle system (ATS) is continuously armed and can be used either in N_1 or speed mode. If power is not applied when the aircraft levels after a descent, ATS is programmed to ensure a safe flying speed by moving the throttles to the value displayed by the N_1 limit computer. When conditions allow, reductions in take-off thrust greatly prolong engine life. But current regulations allow only a ten per cent reduction, roughly equal to a four per cent drop in N_1. Maximum N_1 for the prevailing flight conditions is calculated and displayed by the N_1 limit computer, and automatically repeated by moving indicator bugs inside the two N_1 indicators for six flight phases: take-off, flexible take-off, climb, cruise, maximum continuous and go-around.

The computer takes account of aircraft speed, atmospheric conditions and engine-air bleed for anti-icing and air-conditioning. The maximum temperature ('flex temperature') at which the aircraft is able to perform a balanced take-off is selected manually, and the required N_1 for the prevailing conditions is displayed at a touch of the 'Flex TO' button. Even if the true take-off power required is less than 90 per cent, the computer will indicate a reduction no greater than the mandatory ten per cent. Flexible take-off power calculations assume an engine failure at V_1, and no power increase is required should an engine actually be lost.

For take-off one of the two autothrottle triggers automatically advances the throttles to the figure displayed by the N_1 limit computer. Above 60 kt the N_1 limit computer is 'frozen' until another mode is selected, and the amber section of the master warning system is inhibited until the undercarriage has been retracted. Any red warning, an EGT above 950°C, an engine failure or jammed flight controls all call for a mandatory abort below V_1. But a failure of the air-data computer or attitude director, nosewheel vibration or hot brakes are not regarded as reasons for discontinuing a takeoff.

With the briefing completed, I confirm the take-off configuration with the check button, and then depress the port ATS trigger. Both throttles open automatically, and I concentrate on the take-off run while the flight engineer monitors engine response. The calm conditions make directional control straightforward, with the nosewheel-steering/rudder interconnect helping a lot in this respect. The flight engineer reports 'power set' at 70 kt, and as speed increases past V_1 I move my right hand from the throttles to the control wheel. When V_R is called I ease back on the yoke, aiming for an initial pitch attitude of 18 degrees. Ground effect slows the rotation rate as 10 degrees pitch attitude is passed, an effect emphasized by the expanded scale of the ADI, which gives an initial impression of an over-steep attitude. The low weight makes the aircraft very sprightly, and we easily better the target speed of V_2 plus 10 kt.

A standard noise-abatement take-off calls for the maintenance of V_2+10 kt to 3,000 ft before climb power is set and pitch attitude reduced to 10 degrees. Flaps are retracted at V_3 and slats come in above V_4, allowing pitch attitude to decrease to about $7\frac{1}{2}$ degrees. Today we elect to fly a Toulouse 'Blue' circuit at 1,500 ft. In the take-off configuration, 75 per cent N_1 gives a comfortable 160 kt and I command No 1 autopilot to follow my flight direct in preparation for an automatic approach.

Having agreed earlier that an automatic approach was the best way to introduce me to the landing phase, we brief for a touch-and-go landing to be followed by a practice engine failure after V_2. The mode indicator confirms with green captions that we are steering compass headings and that we have acquired the pre-selected height. Selection of land mode as we fly downwind illuminates the amber V/L (VOR/LOC), G/S (glidescope) and LAND ARM and the white LAND 2 capacity captions. Turning base leg, I progressively reduce speed towards the target V_3+10 kt (146 kt) as the aircraft establishes itself on the localizer. Two dots below the glidepath I select gear down, followed by 25 degrees of flaps at one dot to go. The mode indicator confirms that all is well by showing green V/L and G/S.

Passing the outer marker I reduce speed to the V_{APP} of 120 kt and engage the second autopilot and flight director. V_{REF} is defined for aircraft weight and configuration, and a speed correction is applied to take account of wind and abnormal configurations. A 20 kt headwind dictates a wind correction of 10 kt, while a single-engined approach calls for a 5 kt addition. The higher of the two figures is added to V_{REF} to arrive at the target speed, V_{APP}. Comparison of two command and two monitoring channels in parallel provides fail-operational safety.

The mode indicator displays green LAND ARM and white LAND 3 capacity captions and we slide down the 3 degree ILS glidepath as if on rails. The flight engineer continues his regular call-out of radio-altitude as flare height approaches, the throttles close as '20 ft reduction' is heard, and the engineer has just enough time to call '10 ft' before a gentle touchdown prompts us to disconnect the autopilot, raise flaps to 8 degrees, select go-around N_1 and continue the touch-and-go. Feeling more at home this time, I smartly rotate to 18 degrees when V_R is called and am ready for the expected practice engine failure. This proves to be almost a non-event. About 85 per cent of the CF6's thrust comes from the fan, which has very high inertia. Though airspeed is lost at once, the fan winds down slowly and the asymmetry makes itself felt only by degrees. The rudder load is modest but lateral control may be difficult if corrective rudder is not fed in progressively. Oscillations in aileron control can result from the lag associated with rudder-induced roll, and spoiler-induced drag can complicate lateral control if the ailerons are not neutral.

The answer to a CF6-50C failure on take-off is definitely *not* to rush into corrective action with too much rudder. Pitch attitude should however be reduced to the safe value displayed by the flight-director pitch bar—14 degrees on this occasion. I have the undercarriage raised and adjust the rudder trim to neutralize the ailerons while climbing to 2,000 ft at V_2. Not wishing to make my first manual approach asymmetric, I restore symmetric power and fly a normal visual circuit.

With speed down to 150 kt, I lower the gear and, 45 sec later, set flaps to 25 degrees and turn towards the runway. The A300 is a slippery ship and even 25 degrees of flap produces little extra drag on the approach. The classic relationship of stick for speed and power for descent rate must be respected, and the approach should be set up in good time, especially at our low all-up weight. At 800 ft/min using 65 per cent N_1 the approach looks good, and I allow the speed to decay to 120 kt at 100 ft. The landing and final approach attitudes are very similar, and the flare consists essentially of 'breaking' the glidepath without re-trimming. Passing 30 ft I break the glide to check the rate of descent and, guided by the flight engineer's chant of '30 ft, 20 ft reduction, 10 ft,' I set the aircraft firmly down on 15R. The regular height calls are particularly useful, especially if a steady descent is arrested for any reason.

During the touch-and-go Udo Günzel simulates another engine failure, this time just above V_1, and on this occasion I keep the asymmetric configuration for the subsequent circuit and landing. V_{APP} goes up 5 kt to 125 kt, and 78 per cent N_1 proves about right for the approach. Airbus Industrie recommends an N_1 increase of about 15 per cent on the live engine when asymmetric, but our light weight calls for a rather lower figure. I brief for a touch-and-go and ask the flight engineer to centralize the rudder trim during the ground roll instead of removing it before touchdown. Some pilots prefer to land with rudder trim neutral, but I prefer to be prepared for a late overshoot by landing with some trim applied. For an asymmetric overshoot the go-around lever would be depressed and 12 degrees pitch attitude selected, and the aircraft climbed away at a speed in excess of V_{REF}.

I have no difficulty in handling the asymmetric A300, which offers a power-to-weight ratio unsurpassed by other twin-engined airliners, but at higher weights care must be taken to maintain correct speeds. For this Airbus Industrie recommends use of the autopilot, although not of autothrottle. I use the normal two-engined technique for flare and touchdown—making a better landing than when symmetric—and select normal power on both engines for the roll and a climb to FL100. Cleaned up, we climb at 300 kt and head south for the Pyrenees and a short photographic session with the company's Paris 3. General manoeuvring at higher airspeeds is satisfying, and the aircraft responds so well that its size and inertia are never apparent.

AI's Flight Test Department is housed in a building called l'abreuvoir (the cattle trough), with direct access to each day's flight decks (on this day in May 1986, two 300s, two 310-200s and two 310-300s). The building was being enlarged ready for 320 testing

THY TURK HAVA YOLLARI - TURKISH AIRLINES
JA8237
TOA

N_1 is set at 72 per cent for the 220 kt cruise at FL100, and when posing for the Paris 3 we select altitude hold on the autopilot while retaining manual roll control.

The A300 owes its good cruise performance to a super-critical wing section unique among commercial transport aircraft. Producing more lift over its aft portion, the section has made possible a lighter, more efficient wing. Excellent airfield performance is achieved by the addition of powerful high-lift devices, but once cleaned up the wing is equally efficient in a high-speed medium-range cruise.

Full-span leading-edge slats are extended on the approach to 25 degrees for maximum lift coefficient, with optimum take-off lift/drag being found at 16 degrees. The large double-slotted flaps occupy 84 per cent of the wing span, increasing the chord by 24 per cent. The flap-track fairings are prominent beneath the wing, but Airbus Industrie says that they contribute only four per cent of total cruise drag.

With flaps and slats extended, the stall develops from the root trailing edge, spreading forward and outwards to the engine pylon. Blocking the slot behind part of the inboard slat produces a good pitch-down at the stall for only a small loss in maximum lift coefficient.

With the Paris 3 well clear I briefly sample the A300's low-speed manners. The flight manual predicts that clean and at a weight of 95.4 *tonnes* the stick-shaker should activate at 150 kt. Pitch attitude is 8 degrees when the shaker finally fires, and I recover by gently lowering the nose to about 5 degrees, extending the slats and increasing power. With slats extended to 16 degrees, undercarriage down and 8 degrees flap, the stick-shaker fires at 104 kt with the pitch attitude at 16 degrees. Recovery is effected by lowering the nose and increasing power.

I do not subscribe to the wholesale stalling of large transport aircraft, preferring instead to rely on the airworthiness authorities to determine that such aircraft have acceptable stalling characteristics. In fact, I would regard proficiency in the handling of emergency descents as being an equally important flight-deck skill. Airbus Industrie recommends that rapid descents should be initiated by reducing power to flight idle, extending airbrakes, and banking to 30 degrees while lowering the nose to −15 degrees pitch attitude. Rolling level after turning through 45 degrees leaves the A300 stabilized and descending at more than 6,000 ft/min.

One hour after takeoff and we are climbing at 320 kt to FL180 as we head for the Toulouse VOR. Communications and radar surveillance during the photographic session were handled by a flight-test radar unit. For the next phase of the flight we change to civil air traffic control, which clears us to climb to FL280 for a Toulouse Uniform Five departure towards Mende.

This part of the sortie allows me to sample the A300 within its intended route-flying environment. The No 1 flight-director and autopilot sets are in use, and after arriving overhead Mende at our final FL310 cruise height I couple to the outbound radial to remain on the Upper Green Five airway. We settle at Mach 0.83 and 310 kt IAS, 12 kt less than the indicated maximum. Cruise N_1 is 98 per cent, somewhat less than the maximum N_1 of 106.2, EGT 675°C and outside air temperature −40°C, and I read a true airspeed of 491 kt directly from the panel. Fuel flow is 2,820 kg/hr for each engine, and a six-minute check of fuel consumed confirms this rate. Cabin differential pressure is 6.7 lb/sq in, equal to a comfortable

The twin-aisle widebodies are all assembled on this one short line at Toulouse-St Martin. Here in 1983 can be seen the tail of an A310-200 for Swissair followed by aircraft No 261, one of the last A300s for Eastern. The only items actually made here are noses (background)

Korean Air was one of the first customers for the A300B, boldly ordering six B4s at a time when other world airlines hung back. Today it has 13, including two of these A300F4 cargo versions with a payload of over 105,000 lb

5,000 ft cabin altitude, and the Sun is setting behind the left wing.

With 664 nm to run we estimate flying time to go at 1 hr 37 min. But Hamburg is offering a cloudbase of 500 ft and less than 2 nm visibility—fine for an alternate but below the 600 ft/2 nm minimum for an approach to Finkenwerder. But there is over $1\frac{1}{2}$ hr to go and the front may have cleared by the time we arrive, so we press on for Hamburg International. Fuel remaining totals 19,000 kg, almost 2,000 kg up on the flight-plan minimum.

I select CONTOUR on the Bendix digital weather radar, hoping to pinpoint the nastiness associated with the lightning flashing away to the north. An occasional contour shows ahead, but a slight turn to the east as we pass St Prex will take us well clear.

We keep both VOR and DME receivers tuned to the same beacon most of the time, leaving control on the left-hand side. If Udo wants to take control, the No 1 autopilot can remain in use, but VOR control will have to be transferred to the right-hand side. Each VHF control box incorporates a frequency-preset facility and a transfer switch, a boon to anyone who has ever suffered the forgotten-frequency syndrome. Panel lighting is first-class, incorporating automatic dimming of warning lights and captions.

The slight turbulence which we are encountering causes the A300 no distress at all—I am told that passengers find little to complain of during the cruise, and operations without a yaw damper have little effect on handling.

In airline service, the A300B2's optimum cruise height after a 142-*tonne* maximum-weight takeoff in standard conditions is FL310. Ceiling under the same conditions is FL340, but this falls to about FL150 in the single-engine case. Optimum drift-down level at 140 *tonnes* is just under FL200 at 235 kt. With 20 *tonnes* of fuel remaining, a 140-*tonne* A300 can fly 1,200 nm on one engine at FL200 and 250 kt. An allowance of 3,100 kg of fuel is made for holding and landing, and sector time is 3 hr 34 min in nil-wind conditions.

The need for low direct operating costs in the short/medium-haul market dictates the use of a twin, which sometimes results in operational inflexibility. The US requirement that twins should always be within 1 hr of an alternate airfield when flying at the single-engine cruise speed effectively limits the trans-ocean abilities of such aircraft. But minimum takeoff requirements provide few difficulties in service, although a twin with one engine out has to operate to a minimum decision height of 100 ft. Air Inter has specified a Category IIIB fit for its three A300s, including a ground-roll monitor which will also be used for takeoff.

We're twenty minutes out of Hamburg, and Finkenwerder is now reporting two octas of cloud at 1,800 ft and 20 km visibility, with a turbulent 250 degrees/18 gusting 28 kt surface wind. It's dark, the runway is relatively short (5,985 ft), narrow and wet, and I'm happy to leave the approach and landing to Udo. The initial descent is flown at 300 kt, slowing to the 275 kt turbulence speed as we enter cloud; descent rate is around 3,000 ft/min. The weight is now down to an improbably light 86.1 tons, and the significant speeds are V_{APP} 115 kt (allowing a 5 kt margin above the 110 kt $_{MCA}$), V_3 153 kt, V_4 171 kt, and final takeoff speed, should an overshoot be necessary, 198 kt. Even at the maximum landing weight of 133 *tonnes* only 4,300 ft of destination runway is required.

As we descend through 10,000 ft the air temperature is near 0°C, prompting the selection of nacelle anti-icing, but the powerful wing-inspection lights reveal no ice formation. Hamburg radar clears us in steps down to 2,200 ft and finally to 800 ft on a heading of 050 degrees downwind for a visual approach to Finkenwerder. The final turn is flown around a 600 ft high lighted chimney which looks more than just close (the Hamburg traffic pattern rules out even a 1,000 ft circuit height), and turbulence adds to the difficulties of flying a steeper-than-usual glidepath with a very light aircraft. Finkenwerder's single runway is only 98 ft wide and makes the approach seem high, but with only the sea for an undershoot and no approach lights any tendency to go low should be firmly resisted.

Udo brakes heavily after touchdown, selecting reverse thrust while the spoilers deploy automatically. We slow to walking pace with 2,000 ft of runway remaining. The taxi/takeoff lights in the nose clearly illuminate the runway, and though we are provided with marshalling help as we turn in the pan at the end of the runway, the A300's side taxi floodlights provide a clear sight of the area. With the auxiliary power unit providing all the ground power requirements, I close the high-pressure cocks of both CF6-50s at the conclusion of a sortie which has offered a taste of most aspects of A300 operations.

Over the years the electromechanical dial instruments began to be replaced by multifunction colour electronic displays, and AI have from the start been a world leader in this important development. In addition, AI recognized ahead of most of its rivals that the SFCC inevitably posed problems. A basic design criterion was that the aircraft should be safely flyable by any two crew-members without either having to leave his seat, and also that any crew-member should be able readily to monitor the actions of the others. It was gradually found that this is almost impossible. Suppose a cabin discharge valve were to jam wide open. Loss of pressure would show as 'abnormal cabin rate' (of climb) on CM3's side panel. CM3 would be very busy trying to sort out the problem, and, facing the panel, would be poorly placed for talking with the captain. Good communication would be difficult, especially if, as would almost certainly happen in this case, the crew donned their masks. CM1 (captain) would feel pain in his ears, but this might equally be caused by sudden overpressure. The relevant instruments, cabin VSI and cabin altimeter, are too far away to read and out of arm's reach. CM2 cannot read them either, because he sees the panel edge-on. Nobody could effectively monitor CM3's actions, and under stress he and CM1 might take dangerously incorrect decisions.

This was one of the very few cases in which AI's new and severe cockpit design criteria proved not fully attainable. Moreover, despite political pressures, there has for many years been a steady trend towards reducing flight crew numbers and eliminating members who are not rated pilots. AI studied the problem carefully and in 1979 boldly announced the FFCC (forward-facing crew cockpit). Here there are just two pilots, with two observer seats behind them which need not be occupied. At first glance this may seem a retrograde step; surely three heads are better than two? In practice there can be an engineer seated behind the pilots, so nobody need lose his job, but it would be naïve not to recognize the strong pressure from airlines for a crew comprising just two pilots. In December 1979 Europilote, with Ifalpa backing and representing a considered trade-union viewpoint, totally rejected the FFCC. Its main argument was that the limited main and overhead panel space facing the pilots was inadequate for the amount of information. This is untrue. Closer study has shown that, in fact, modern electronic displays facing the pilots can present more than 12 times as much systems information as can a traditional side panel, and present it in an infinitely more immediate and assimilable form, with no need for interpretation.

In particular, the FFCC presents everything in clear view to the pilots. Their ability to see everything, monitor everything and reach everything is perfect. A third man sitting behind would be needed only if the two pilots were suddenly to become incapacitated—a rare occurrence indeed! Thus, the FFCC at last extends to the vital area of the human crew the philosophy of redundancy and fail-safe operation long built into the inanimate systems. It was an original design feature of the A310, described in the next chapter, and is now standard on the A300-600.

In the matter of avionics a great deal is left to customer choice, but certain basic systems are standard. One obvious one is the AFCS (automatic flight control system), a joint product of SFENA, SI and Bodenseewerk in the B2 and B4, with every conceivable kind of special automatic facility. In today's Dash-600 aircraft a more advanced fully digital system is used, with distributed computers serving special functions. A single or twin FCC (flight-control computer) serves flight director and autopilot functions, a single or dual TCC (thrust-control computer) manages all speed and thrust control from before brake-release until the aircraft is parked, twin SI FMCs (flight-management computers) and two CDUs (control display units) provide a total flight-augmentation management system in both the horizontal and vertical planes, twin FACs (flight-augmentation computers) provide safety functions such as yaw damping, electric pitch trim and flight-envelope monitoring and protection, a DFA (delayed flap approach) can be added to the TCC for decelerated final approach, and an optical windshield guidance display can be added to the glare-shield for use in zero visibility.

The basic twin-ILS installation can be augmented with a radar altimeter and dual FCCs for blind landing down to Cat.IIIB. The weather radar has usually been the Bendix RDR-IF, but late aircraft and A310s have the Collins WXR-700 or Bendix RDR-4A. There is always provision for a second radar, and for an INS (inertial navigation system), GPWS (ground-proximity warning system), and in the A310 an Omega global navigation system. All recent aircraft have a comprehensive DFDS (digital flight-data system) with acquisition units and recorders, and they also have an increasingly popular option in an SRS (speed reference system) with built-in windshear protection. Of course, there are the usual (normally duplicated) VHF and HF radio, with Selcal and provision for DABS (discrete-address beacon system), VOR, DME, marker-beacon receivers, ADF and ATC transponders, as well as interphone and passenger address systems, and various forms of taped or filmed inflight entertainment.

Although the flight-control surfaces have been listed, nothing has been said of the operative system. All surfaces are fully powered from the three hydraulic systems, without manual reversion. The designers had probably unrivalled experience dating back to the early 1950s with the Comet and Caravelle and, more recently, the Trident.

On early B1, B2 and B4 aircraft roll control is provided by low-speed outboard ailerons at the tips and all-speed inboard ailerons, backed up by two (originally three) spoiler sections ahead of the outer flaps. All four ailerons are each driven by three power units, one in each of the three hydraulic systems to give triplex redundancy. The outboard ailerons have variable gearing slaved to slat extension angle, and as speed increases through the 190-kt level a lock-out mechanism centralizes and locks these surfaces. In current A300/310 aircraft there are no low-speed ailerons. The all-speed ailerons are linked through a non-linear gearing unit to the spoilers, and differential linkage allows all spoilers to open symmetrically as lift dumpers after landing, along with the five sections of airbrake on each wing.

The one-piece rudder, which in the A300-600 and A310 is made of CFRP (carbon-fibre reinforced plastics), is driven by three power units, one in each system as before. A yaw damper is fitted, but stability even near the ceiling is so good it is hardly needed. Auto-compensation for asymmetric thrust was studied but found unnecessary. Pitch control is provided by the simple left and right elevators, each driven by triplex hydraulic power units. They are hinged to the variable-incidence trimming tailplane, which is driven by a fail-safe ball screwjack driven by two independent hydraulic motors which are electrically controlled with an additional mechanical input. Trim is effected by switches on the control wheels or (in recent aircraft) sidestick controllers, or alternatively by trimwheels on the console. The aircraft can be safely flown on the elevators with the tailplane jammed in any flight position, and safely flown on the tailplane with the elevators jammed in any flight position.

Likewise, in the roll-control worst case, with two ailerons on one wing both locked, the opposite wing can fly the aircraft safely. All axes have spring-loaded artificial-feel systems, that for pitch being modified by q-feel (sensitive to dynamic air pressure, to avoid overstressing the aircraft) and compensated for tailplane position. In short, the very newest of the traditional pre-FBW (fly by wire) solutions.

The extremely powerful leading-edge slat and trailing-edge flap systems are all similar. In the fuselage are duplex hydraulic motors driving low-friction torque shafts running along the wing and carrying angle boxes at frequent intervals. The latter drive ball screwjacks attached to the moving surfaces. Slat drive tracks are housed in sealed cans inside the front of the integral wing tanks; in recent aircraft these cans are deep-drawn in SPF/DB (superplastic formed/diffusion bonded) titanium. The flap tracks are enclosed in fairings under the rear of the wing; though these look enormous, they contribute less than 4 per cent of total aircraft drag. Hydraulic system failure to one slat or flap motor leaves its partner driving at half-speed. Drive power is instantly cut off should the slats or flaps reach a specified very low level of asymmetry.

Originally there were three airbrakes on each wing, plus two lift dumpers inboard, the function of the latter being to kill lift from the inboard wing and, by throwing weight on the main wheels, increase braking power. Recent aircraft have no fewer than 14 surfaces (four spoilers and ten airbrakes) which can all be used as lift dumpers. The latest aerodynamic feature on the A300 family is introduction of wingtip fences, or winglets, on the A300-600 series.

To operate a triplex-type flight-control system demands three completely independent hydraulic systems. Following the terminology pioneered with the Comet almost 40 years ago, these are called the Blue, Green and Yellow systems, each filled with fire-resistant phosphate-ester fluid at a working pressure of 3,000 lb/sq in (207 *bars*, 210 kg/cm^2) generated by two self-regulating pumps. The Blue circuit has one pump on No 1 (left) engine and one driven by the emergency drop-out RAT (ram-air turbine). The RAT is a Dowty Rotol product normally retracted inside the lower right wing root. In the B2 and B4 aircraft the Blue system drives all the flight-control surfaces and the No 1 flap motor. Green has one pump on each engine and supplies all flight-control surfaces, slats, airbrakes, landing gear, steering and wheel brakes. Yellow has a pump on No 2 (right) engine and one on the RAT, and drives all flight-control surfaces, No 2 slat motor, No 2 flap motor, airbrakes, wheel brakes, steering and landing-gear emergency release. In the A300-600 the circuits all drive every flight-control surface as before, but are modified in other respects. Blue serves airbrake 1, spoiler/airbrake 4, spoiler 7, yaw damper and slats. Green serves spoiler 6, flaps, slats, Krügers, landing gear, steering, tailplane trim, artificial feel and all three autopilot axes. Yellow serves airbrake 2, spoiler/airbrake 3, spoiler 5, flaps, wheel brakes, tailplane trim, artificial feel, all three autopilot axes, yaw damper and cargo doors.

Motor/pump units can transfer power from any circuit to any other, without transfer of fluid. An electrically driven pump charges the brake accumulator for towing, and the APU drives a larger pump to provide ground maintenance power.

The APU (auxiliary power unit) has always been a Garrett (originally AiResearch) gas-turbine unit installed in the tailcone. Early in A300B development a great improvement in operating and relight envelope was gained by providing a two-position inlet door, switching from the Flight to the Ground configuration as soon as the main landing gear is compressed. The APU was originally a TSCP-700-5, as used on the DC-10, but current Dash-600 and 310 aircraft have the much improved Model

331-250. In both types the jetpipe is angled diagonally up at the tail, and noise on the ground is muted. The best comment on the installation is that in all cases the operating and relight envelopes are higher than Garrett's own specification. The APU provides bleed air for starting the main engines and for air-conditioning the passenger and flight compartments from sea level to 15,000 ft (4,572 m), and remains operable to near the maximum aircraft operating height of 40,000 ft (12,192 m). The APU also drives at constant rpm to a 90-kVA oil-spray-cooled generator similar to those driven by the main engines, and further drives a hydraulic pump for ground maintenance power.

Primary electric power is supplied at 400 Hz, 115/200-V, by two Westinghouse IDGs (integrated-drive generators), one on each main engine. The IDG comprises an alternator and constant-speed drive with an output at a steady 8,000 rpm. Rating of each machine is 90 kVA, with overload of 112.5 kVA for 5 min and 150 kVA for 5 sec. Three TRUs (transformer/rectifier units) supply 28-V DC, and three nickel-cadmium batteries supply power for APU starting and all emergency supplies including 115-V 400-Hz power for essential instruments, navigation and lighting, via completely separate circuits.

Bleed air for air-conditioning is tapped from both engines and/or from the APU. On the ground the latter can provide full interior conditioning, and conditioned air can be supplied direct to the cabin via external connections. When the two air-conditioning packs under the floor are not in use, a plain ram inlet can provide fresh air. Maximum cabin dP (differential pressure) is 8.25 lb/sq in (570 mb) in the B2, B4 and 310, and 8.32 lb/sq in (574 mb) in the Dash-600. Total environmental control is provided by two identical systems, each of which automatically switches over from active to standby, or vice versa, after each flight. Auto pre-pressurization after closing the doors gives a gradual build-up, and eliminates pressure excursions during takeoff. On letdown, pressure is automatically brought to that at the landing airport.

There has never been any need for major airframe anti-icing. Instead hot-air anti-icing is restricted to the engine fan inlet and pod inlet, and the slat sections outboard of the engine. Raw AC electricity is used to anti-ice the flight-deck front windows and demist the side windows, and on demand to heat all air-data sensors, pitot probes, static ports and waste-water drain masts.

The fuel system is elegant and simple. In all early aircraft there were just two integral tanks in each wing, formed by sealing the wing structure. Like every other part of the airframe, the metal structure is painted and all joints sealed. In the wing box Thiokol flexible sealing compound is used to ensure a fuel-tight joint at every mating surface. This compound and others are used in layers to ensure perfect protection against any form of corrosion. Along the centres of the three under-surface skins are oval manholes; in current aircraft the cover plates are among the major SPF/DB titanium parts, with significant gains in simplicity, light weight and

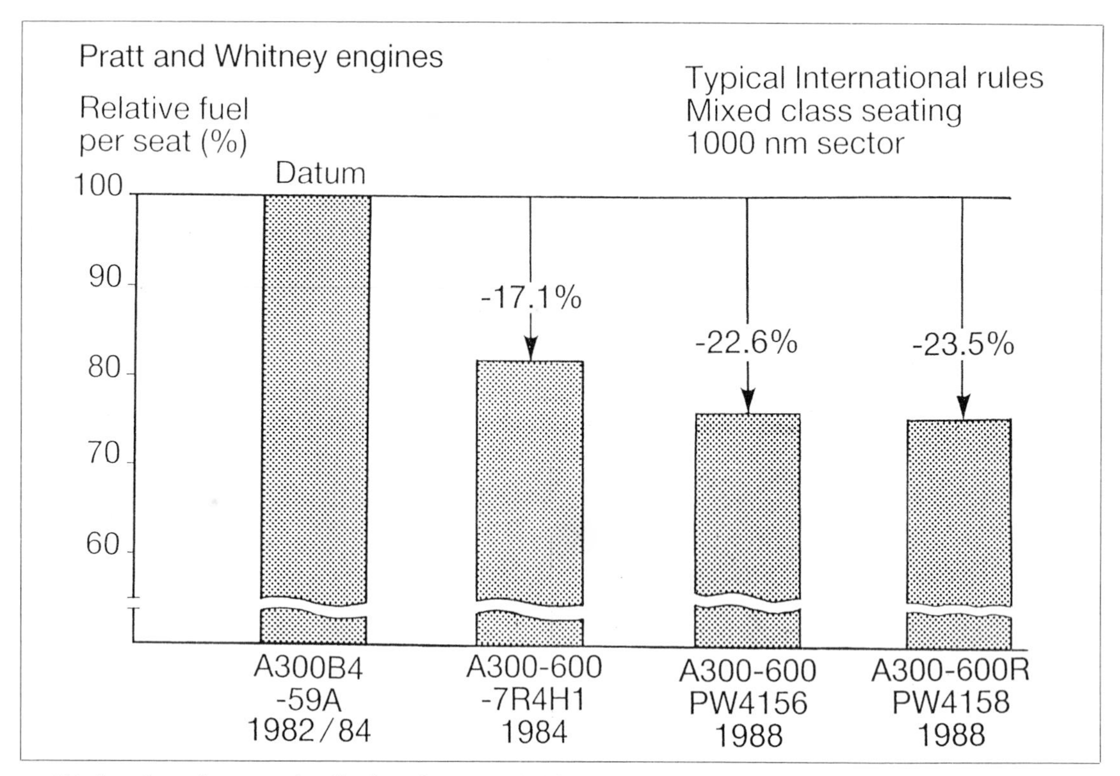

This bar chart shows graphically the reduction in fuel burn per seat achieved by today's Dash-600 and 600R. Similar figures would be shown with GE engines, and had the datum been the first A300B1 the overall reduction would have exceeded 35 per cent

low cost, each cover being in effect a single exceedingly complex piece of metal formed in a manner resembling glassblowing. The four tanks incorporate baffles to prevent sloshing of the fuel during wing flexure in turbulence or flight manoeuvres, whilst permitting fuel and any water present to drain along the lower skin, and air to pass from one tank to another at the top. At the wingtips are vent surge tanks.

The system is filled via two standard 2.5-in (63.5-mm) couplings side-by-side in the underside of the right wing, just ahead of the flaps and outboard of the kink. Two similar couplings can be fitted in the left wing, but these are seldom specified because at 50 lb/sq in (3.45 *bar*) the standard pair take fuel at 500 gal/min (1,125 lit or 600.5 US gal/min). Fuel is supplied to the engines by twin submerged pumps in each tank. Each pump has a different electricity supply from its neighbour, and all can be withdrawn in their canisters without draining the tank. A special pump and supply line feeds the APU in the tail. There are numerous special extra features to ensure total flexibility in operation and safety, following every conceivable eventuality. For example a fuel-proof rib is inserted in the leading edge so that, should a burst turbine pierce the front spar, no fuel can reach the pylon. The LP (low-pressure) shut-off valve is located between the pylon attachments, the safest place possible, and an electrically actuated shut-off valve is added behind the rear spar to control supply following severance of the cables to the manual LP shut-off valve. A typical further example of fail-safe design is seen in the manual tank transfer valve in the ground control panel; the handle is so shaped that, if it is left in the 'open' position, the cover over the refuel/defuel panel cannot be closed.

Usable capacity in the B1 and B2 was 9,460 gal (43,000 litres). The B4 was planned as a four-tank aircraft with 12,450 gal (56,600 litres), but was actually put into production with a fifth integral tank in the centre section increasing capacity to 13,133 gal (59,700 litres). The B4-200 has a further optional tank which replaces two LD3 containers in the rear cargo hold, adding a further 1,320 gal (6,000 litres). In the A300-600 the standard five-tank system has been refined to increase capacity to 13,836 gal (62,900 litres) without any encroachment on cargo space. The A310 fuel system is described in the next chapter.

Of course, main engines, APU and cargo holds are fully provided with smoke and fire detection systems, automatic and manually controlled fire extinguishing systems, and with firewalls to shield main structure from the effects of any fire. Gaseous oxygen bottles are used to provide emergency oxygen to the flight crew, with a modular box gaseous system serving all areas of the passenger cabin, with emergency sets for cabin staff.

The remainder of this, the longest chapter in the book, traces the story of the A300B and A300-600 from the first flight onwards. The first flight, on 28 October 1972, was pretty well a textbook example of how an ideal first flight should go. Director of flight test Bernard Ziegler, who in those days wore his headset over a baseball cap, said that most of the modifications that were going to be needed were in order to remove things and make the aircraft simpler, because it was performing so far beyond prediction. Admittedly, some of the modificiations had a tremendous positive effect, notably on rate of roll. Almost the only snags encountered, apart from the odd bit of local noise or vibration, were inability of the autopilot to hold course after simulated engine failure at low altitude, and a tendency of the flaps to jam on retraction, caused by differences between static and sliding friction. By the end of February 1973 the overall flight-test programme was described as 'two months ahead of schedule'. The only visible modifications at that date were the addition of extremely small slat fences near the junction between the two outer slats, and small vortex generators ahead of the low-speed ailerons on the outer wings, which were later eliminated as were the ailerons themselves. The tiny slat fences, added at Flight 28, produce a more positive nose-down pitch in a clean stall at aft CG. They remain on all aircraft prior to the A300-600.

During early flight development the prototype was often flown at an IAS as low as 88–89 kt (163 km/h). Stalls were immaculate, and aerodynamic warning abundant, though from the start a stick shaker was fitted to comply with British certification requirements. The onset of buffet in manoeuvres did not appear anywhere near the

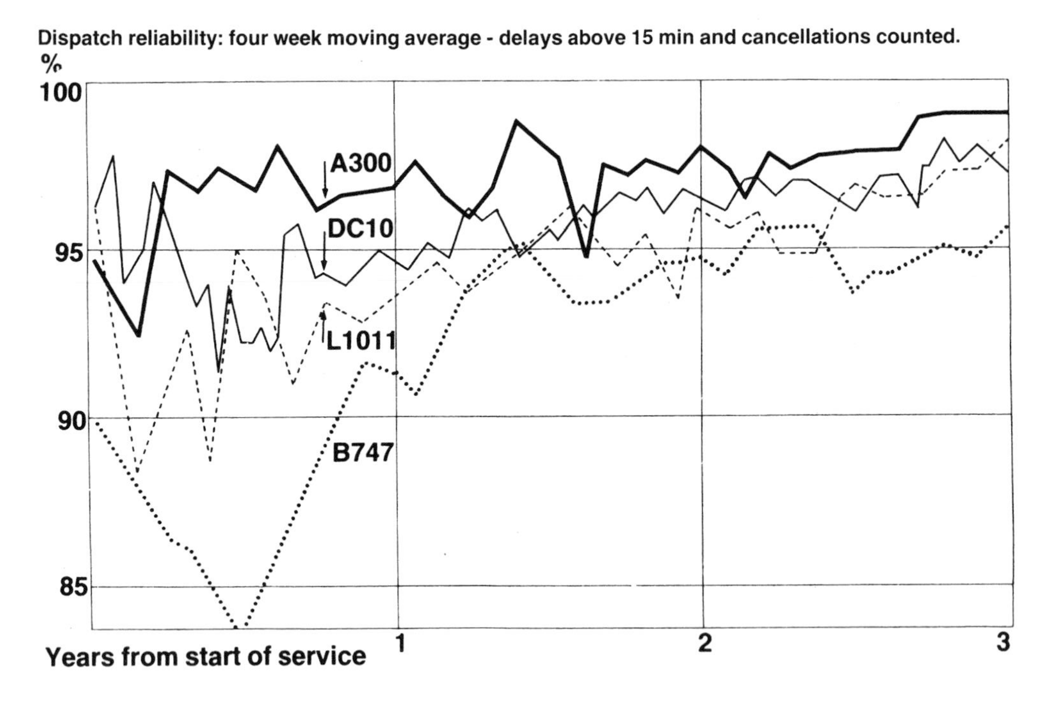

No problem! Each of these plots begins on the date the type entered scheduled service and records all delays exceeding 15 minutes attributable to the aircraft during the first three years of service

predicted values; for example, at Mach 0.8 at 30,000 ft (9,144 m) the predicted point was in a turn pulling 1.2G, but no buffet was ever felt prior to 1.75G. Despite the small wing (compared with the later 767) it proved possible to take off at MTOW and climb straight to almost 40,000 ft (12.2 km), though in practice few sectors are planned at heights above 31,000 ft (9,450 m). In general there was every kind of evidence that the A300B would not only be a fantastic success but would in due course be certificated at weights much higher than the original 132 *tonnes* (291,000 lb). In the early days there was also some interest in RTOL (restricted takeoff and landing) versions, matched to runways of about 5,000 ft (1,524 m), but this interest progressively evaporated, except among AI's own pilots who fly into Hamburg Finkenwerder! Indeed the field length of the early B4-200 was almost double this value, without affecting sales in the slightest. Today's Dash-600 has takeoff field lengths from about 7,700 ft (2,347 m) at sea level.

From the early project-study period much attention was paid to both the cargo and the military markets. Both would need a wide above-floor cargo door, and this was finally settled at a width of 3.58 m (11 ft 9 in), a little wider than that of cargo DC-10s and KC-10s. A firm offer of a multirole tanker/transport was made to the Federal German Luftwaffe as early as February 1973, but—very remarkably, in the author's opinion—this fell on deaf ears. Had military A300Bs been launched early in the programme, the RAF would not be in such a sorry state of disarray in 1987 with regard to its long-overdue AWACS type aircraft, nor would it have had to rebuild second-hand TriStars.

The first prototype, re-registered F-OCAZ, made an important sales tour of the Americas in the month beginning 18 September 1973. An engine-change at Chicago was caused by minor damage at Mexico City due to a failed fuel nozzle; though there was no measurable fall in engine performance, there was an oil-pressure warning, and Ziegler chose to shut down that engine and make a single-engine landing at 7,300-ft high Mexico City. Apart from this there was no trouble of the slightest significance. The punishing trip of 21,000 nm (39,000 km) involved 22 inter-city sectors and 38 demonstration flights for well over 2,200 guests, 55 pilots from the 19 airlines visited sampling the controls, and everyone being deeply impressed by such factors as rate of climb, amazing quietness (at New York not one sound monitor detected the aircraft's takeoff) and impeccable handling.

After only a few days at Toulouse F-OCAZ then made a nine-day tour through the Middle East to India, starting on 31 October 1973. For most of this trip the captain was AI's Jacques Grangette, assisted by Capt Philipp Davies of Air France, and with a single temporary INS fitted and monitored by Pierre Caneill, AI Deputy Director of Flight Test. The whole trip went like clockwork—apart from a Pakistani request for an unplanned landing to be made at Karachi which cost $405 including $125 for the use of steps! Béteille commented on the difficulty of pricing the aircraft in the face of revaluations of European currencies against the US dollar, and rapidly rising inflation in most partner countries. While at Delhi Indian Airlines were offered three B2s at $15 million each, clearly an unrepeatable price. The table below lists sectors and fuel burn on this trip. Today's A300-600s would do even better.

Date	Stage	Distance		Flight time		Fuel used	
		nm	(km)	hr	min	lb	(*tonne*)
October 31	Toulouse–Athens	1,276	(2,365)	3	00	40,500	(18.4)
November 2	Athens–Tehran	1,392	(2,580)	3	05	44,000	(20.01)
	Tehran–Karachi	1,216	(2,253)	2	45	36,400	(16.5)
	Karachi–Delhi	628	(1,164)	1	45	22,100	(10.01)
November 4	Delhi–Bombay	608	(1,127)	1	45	24,700	(11.21)
	Bombay–Delhi	608	(1,127)	1	50	26,800	(12.19)
November 5	Delhi–Tehran	1,470	(2,724)	3	40	53,000	(24.02)
	Tehran–Athens	1,390	(2,576)	3	35	48,500	(22.1)
	Athens–Toulouse	1,207	(2,237)	3	05	41,900	(19.03)

As 1974 dawned, AI progressively moved from Paris, where it was bursting at the seams, near the assembly plant at Toulouse. On 15 January the first staff occupied the virgin-site HQ building a mile or so to the south, towards the city at first called Route de Lectoure and later named for Lucien Servanty. Sales director Robert Blanchet henceforth headed a major marketing and PR organization, with four main sales regions: North America headed by an American, Europe headed by a German, the Middle and Far East headed by a Briton and Africa and South America headed by a Frenchman.

In April 1974 the Hanover show static park was dominated by the big European, while a small trickle of orders was announced—those of Transbrasil, SATA and Sterling never being taken up. In the same month Robert Blanchet gave first details of the proposed four-CFM56 version for ultra-long routes. Later called the B11, it eventually became the A340 (Chapter 11) a full 12 years later!

A key date in the A300B programme was 15 March 1974, when the B2-100 was type certificated by DGAC of France and LBA of West Germany. At this time four aircraft, two B1s and two B2s, had flown 1,500 hours in just over 16 months, which by any standard was a most encouraging start.

Another key date, perhaps even more publicly significant, was the entry into service of the A300B2 on Air France's Paris–London route on Thursday 23 May 1974. While B1 No 1 was on tour to the Far East and Australia, F-BVGA, officially designated as a B2-A1, at last began not only earning money but also winning masses of friends. As noted in the first chapter, the cabin staff were universally of the opinion that the big twin was 100 per cent French, and the author soon learned that there was little point in trying to argue.

Around the world, the entry into service of what ought to have been regarded as the first of the new generation of mass people-movers passed off with scarcely any news-coverage at all, and quietness seemed to be the A300B's hallmark. Australia carried out detailed noise testing during the type's first visit, and the Minister of Transport, C K Jones, then described the Airbus as 'the quietest commercial aircraft there is'. A little later the British Department of Trade announced that not one of the first 100 scheduled services to London Heathrow ever appeared on any of its noise monitors, which generally meant a level distinctly below 90 EPNdB. On 30 May 1974 American FAA certification was granted. No US airline appeared to evince the slightest interest; they preferred noisy, fuel-guzzling narrow-bodies.

By October the B2-1A was flying on Air France routes to London, Nice, Marseilles and Algiers, with increasingly frequent appearances at Beirut, Damascus, Cairo and Tunis. On the original Orly–Heathrow route over 113,000 passengers had been carried, with load factor averaging 65.7 per cent. Technical dispatch reliability was 97.8 per cent, but there were prolonged delays due to inability of the airport gates to get the large group of passengers on board quickly enough.

In service the aircraft itself caused hardly any bother at all, and the appalling overall dispatch reliability (to 15 min) of 62 per cent was caused almost exclusively by delays in handling the boarding passengers. The total of 431 delays due to 'police procedures and loading' was simply unacceptable, and the problem was especially acute at major airports where a single telescopic loading jetty was used, aligned with the left forward door and pouring everyone through the forward First Class section. It took many months for the airports to learn how to cope with the first short-haul wide-body, and many observers commented that part of the trouble was lack of fanfare. When the 747 entered service with PanAm the whole world knew about it, but with the capacious A300B the airports hardly took any notice and failed to match up to it. This was tough on a splendid vehicle which, said Air France V-P Commercial Claude Lalanne, was 'an extraordinarily trouble-free aircraft, much better than either the 727 or 747 . . .'

By this time AI had published details of its proposed next three versions, the stretched (six extra seat rows, 322 European mixed-class seats) B9, the cut-back (seven rows shorter, 218 European seats) B10, and the long-haul four-CFM56 B11 with an increased wingspan. But the basic task of getting customers continued to prove elusive. One of the very first and most important customers, Iberia, cancelled in October 1974 when its four B4s were well advanced in construction. The airline invoked a clause permitting it to cancel if a certain number (50) of sales had not been achieved by a given date, which underscores the uphill struggle AI had to get anywhere. Much later, and at higher prices, the Spanish airline came back.

In the winter 1974–75 the second B1 prototype, sold to TEA of Belgium as OO-TEF, was leased to Air Algerie in order to carry pilgrims on their annual journey to Mecca. Despite being smaller than all subsequent A300Bs, this B1 was fitted out with 323 passenger seats and then, with no back-up aircraft, undertook a gruelling schedule involving ten hours' flying on each of 50 consecutive days, with inexperienced maintenance personnel at airports totally unfamiliar with the type. Its regularity was 100 per cent.

The first B4, the ninth aircraft built, first flew on 26 December 1974. With fuel capacity raised from 43,000 to 59,700 litres, it began a new standard heavier and longer-ranged family with various detail improvements.

In February 1975 Henri Ziegler retired after most ably serving as AI's first chairman, through what was in many respects an extremely difficult period. His successor was Bernard Lathière, likewise an Aérospatiale nominee, who immediately held a Press conference. In an impressive public debut he announced a commitment to build 54 aircraft, though firm orders stood at only 20 (and time was to prove some of these not to be firm at all). He stated that dispatch reliability was 'better than that of the DC-10 and TriStar at the same stage of their careers' (in fact it was better than the reliability of the big trijets even in February 1975), and Claude Lalanne of Air France took the microphone and described the A300B as 'extremely easy to introduce, easier than the 727, 747 and even the Caravelle'. Lathière called the Airbus 'the bread and butter of the European aerospace worker . . . We cannot call the TriStar a European aircraft, and I regret that A300B sales teams find themselves up against not only American diplomatic resistance but also that of British embassies too . . .' Yet again, he expressed the hope for an RB.211-engined version.

In late March 1975 the FAA issued a Notice of Proposed Rulemaking demanding major and exceedingly expensive structural modifications to the DC-10, 747 and TriStar, following two DC-10 accidents involving main-floor collapse caused by explosive failure of underfloor cargo doors. The A300B was not mentioned, and an earlier FAA committee had noted that 'The Airbus . . . can experience at least a 16 sq ft hole in either of the two cargo compartments at 38,000 ft altitude without floor damage'. In any case, in the basic design of the A300B all systems and subsystems were segregated to an extent never before seen, as depicted in two diagrams. No possible survivable damage to the pressurized fuselage could cause more than mild inconvenience, and certainly could not present a threat to continued safe flight. The one door which might be shut in a hurry, and improperly locked, that to bulk baggage/cargo, is of the plug type, opening inwards.

Also in March 1975 the first B4 made the longest flights by any Airbus at that date. The sectors were: Geneva-Kuwait (2,530 nm, 4,688 km) and Kuwait–Toulouse (2,600 nm, 4,818 km). What is more interesting is, first, that the original design range of the A300 was to be 810 nm, 1,500 km, and, much more important, today's A300-600R can carry a capacity payload with full airline reserves and diversion fuel over a sector distance of 4,400 nm (8,154 km)!

While Air France services rapidly gained momentum, especially in improved aircraft utilization, the other chief AI national flag carrier, Lufthansa, joined with the third, Iberia, in considering cancellation. Lufthansa had timidly ordered three B2s with four on option, and throughout April 1975 discussed invoking a clause in its contract permitting cancellation if fewer than 50 aircraft—including 20 from outside the Atlas group comprising Air France, Alitalia, Lufthansa and Sabena—had been ordered by 1 April 1975. The airline's Technical Director, Reinhardt Abraham, at last announced that it had decided not to cancel, but that this remained a possibility and was being studied by Lufthansa's lawyers. This was perhaps the most amazing example of a major world airline, whose country was a 45 per cent AI shareholder, utterly failing to consider the aircraft on its merits. (Today the number of Lufthansa Airbus aircraft, including options, totals 99.)

In August 1975 McDonnell Douglas published details of its proposed DC-X-200, not quite as bad as the DC-10 Twin but still a singularly unattractive big twin with a body of DC-10 cross-section (diameter, 19 ft 9 in, 6.02 m) and CF6-60 engines hung on a new wing more like that of an A300B but smaller. There was no way McDonnell

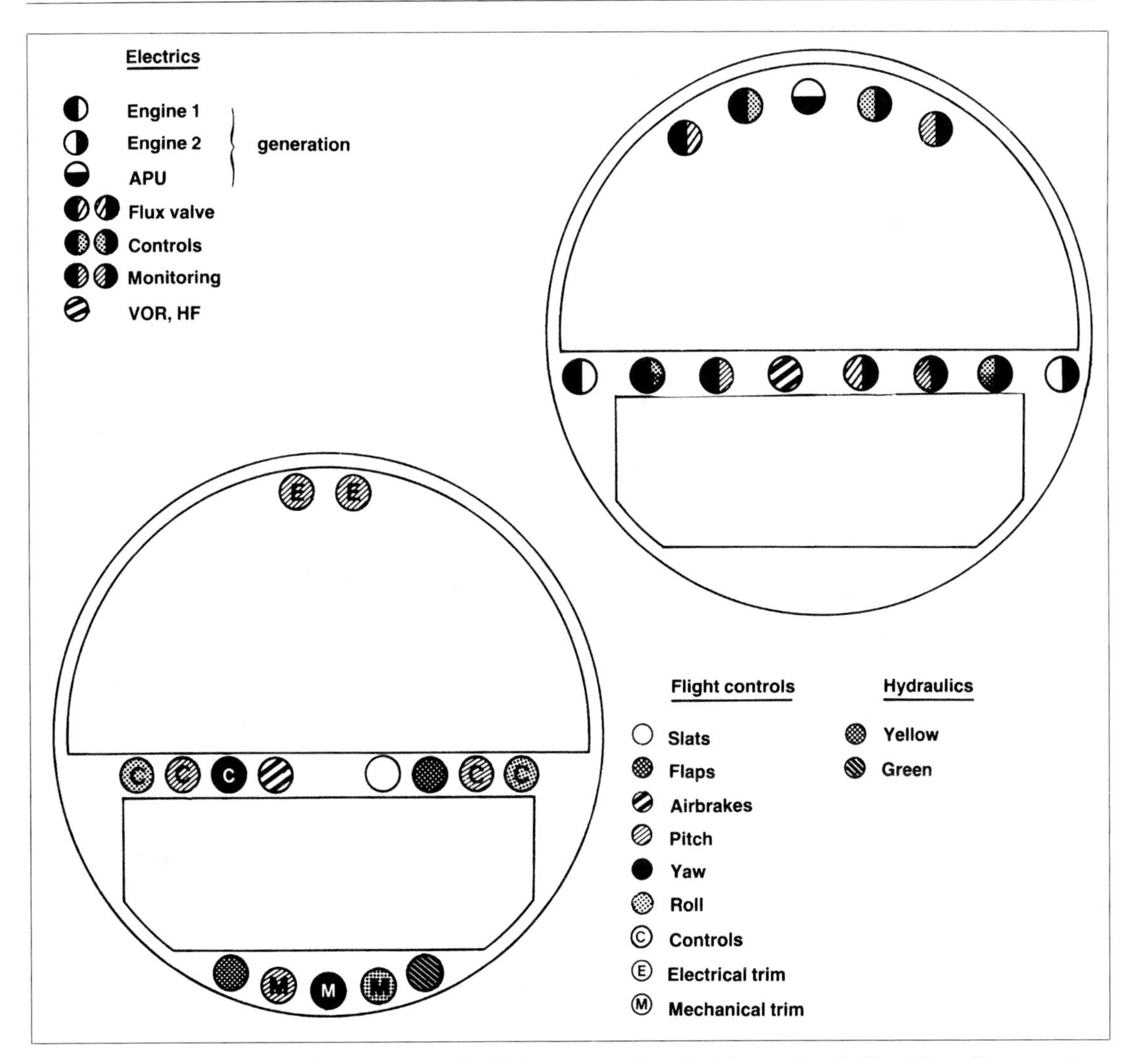

The matchless safety record of the A300B and A310 was not achieved without a lot of effort. These diagrams show the wide segregation of power and control runs in the fuselage roof, belly and floor

Douglas could have met their claim to have aircraft-kilometre costs '20 per cent better than the Airbus' and this ill-conceived project was never built. This was despite almost clinching a deal with the British Aircraft Corporation in which BAC would have collaborated on both the X-200 and also on a proposed RB.211-engined DC-10-30R. Warren Kraemer, McDD V-P Europe, devoted great energy in the second half of 1975 to proving to all and sundry that, while Airbus Industrie could be ignored, the true future of Britain lay with Rolls-engined DC-10s and the projected X-200. Meanwhile Boeing's chief proposal to fill the gap between the 727 and 747 was the 7X7, a trijet with 201 seats in a 16 ft 6 in (5.03-m) fuselage, looking rather like a smaller DC-10.

By September 1975 Air France reported it could make a profit on a typical A300B sector with either 100 passengers and no cargo or 16 *tonnes* of cargo and no passengers, the latter weight being little more than half the available cargo capacity under the floor. TEA, still using the original B1 prototype, reported that on package holidays between Brussels and Palma its Boeing 720s used *130 per cent* more fuel per seat. One of the few 1975 sales successes, South African Airways, specified a new variant designated B2K (later restyled B2-200). This featured the improved high-lift system at the leading-edge root first fitted to the B4, in which Krüger flaps swung out from the wing and a small additional portion swung out from the fuselage to fill the root gap in a perfect and unique manner. The SAA aircraft was the first 'hot and high' A300B variant, though it did not fly until 30 July 1976, as aircraft No 32. Also in September 1975, Béteille confirmed that the basic A300B had 'enough fin and rudder' for engines of over 54,000-lb thrust, leading to the virtual certainty of B4-200 certification at 165 *tonnes*. 'With this weight', he told the author, 'we have a transatlantic aeroplane.' But he was realist enough to recognize that for political reasons the European big twin would never get certificated for such trans-oceanic routes 'until the USA itself has a rival to us'.

The year 1976 was Airbus Industrie's worst year. Unbelievably, despite the dramatically superior performance, reliability, passenger-appeal, quietness and economy of the product, airlines stayed away in droves and total sales for the calendar year amounted to just one aircraft. So poor did prospects seem that in April Aérospatiale PDG Gen Jacques Mitterand announced that, following continuing negative responses from Britain, the French giant would have to look to the USA for collaboration on future commercial aircraft, and that Boeing was Aérospatiale's first choice. Indeed, a simultaneous statement from Bonn that Germany would not support 'any but the A300 programme' was actually regarded as a 'serious setback'.

In January 1977, following months of encouraging negotiation with Western Airlines, AI was somewhat shattered when the US carrier announced that it was instead buying DC-10-10s and 727s. As neither of the US types could come anywhere near the efficiency, economy and environmental acceptability of the A300B, one could not but agree with French Transport Minister Marcel Cavaillé who expressed 'astonishment'—the more so as Western themselves had earlier described the European aircraft as 'clearly a superior buy'. Disappointment in Bonn and at MBB was acute, especially as, following the sales famine of 1976, production rate was cut to 1.5 per month. In this time of bleak near-despair there was a tendency to blame one's partners, and the Germans certainly felt the French were to blame for the loss of Western.

What AI did not know was that this was to be the end of the beginning. In April 1977 PanAm Chairman William T Seawell publicly stated that the A300B was being considered for internal German services—a study that did bear fruit, but not until much later. In the same month came the first order for 15 months: four for Thai International. But of much greater consequence was a leasing agreement with

Eastern Airlines of Miami. Following some weeks of rumours, the US giant made the portentious announcement on Monday 4 May 1977, stating that four A300B4s would be leased—on 'liberal' terms—for six months in the busy winter traffic season of 1977–78, backing up TriStars and 727s. The deal was clinched by George Warde (pronounced Wardy), newly appointed President of AI North America. Eastern President, and ex-Astronaut, Frank Borman managed to persuade his board to 'throw the A300 into the fire'. The four aircraft would be put on a brutal 10-hours-per-day schedule to demonstrate: that AI as a team could really perform; that AI (or rather Aeroformation) could train crews; that AI could support its aircraft in service; and that the A300 would really prove as good as the evidence indicated. Eastern was serious, said Borman, and wanted to negotiate the eventual purchase not just of the four aircraft but of many more.

In fact, Eastern was in a unique position to apply the 'fly before buy' philosophy, for the first time in modern commercial aviation. The airline's financial and equipment position was poor in the extreme, and it could not afford the massive re-equipment needed to beat Delta and other rivals. AI in Europe understood, and its hunger for orders and group of white-tail A300s at Toulouse (aircraft built, but with no airline markings to paint on) led to a sale of four of the latter to the Bank of America, which via its subsidiary Bamerlease leased them back to Airbus Industrie Leasing Corporation, which freely sub-leased them to Eastern. Eastern did pay many incidental costs, however.

Eastern's V-P Planning, Dr Mort Erlich, said that, making every possible negative assumption and adverse allowance, the A300B4 still burned 6 per cent less fuel per seat-mile than the airline's TriStars, and 26 per cent less than its 727s. Soon after handover of the first Eastern aircraft on 30 August 1977 Paul Johnstone, Eastern V-P Operations Service, said 'The A300 is, right now, as good as or perhaps even a little better than anything US manufacturers are suggesting—the 7X7, 7N7 or DC-X-200'. This was the kind of thing the author had been expecting to hear from many airlines and for many years, and it was a long time coming.

Summer 1977 saw AI penetrate the Middle East with Egyptair, which began by leasing aircraft from TEA and Germanair. The 165-*tonne* gross weight was funded to certification, and sanction was given for an A300 with the Pratt & Whitney JT9D-59A engine in a Rohr nacelle similar to that of the DC-10-40. And the B10 studies were refined into the B10X-13, with a new and smaller wing; lacking a British commitment, the preliminary design and tunnel-testing of the proposed B10 wing was started at VFW-Fokker and the Dutch NLR research centre.

Though Eastern's initial investment in the A300 was primarily not financial, it was very soon clear that from top to bottom the airline was banking on this being the right aircraft, and planning went ahead to buy 28. The four free white-tail leases, N201EA to N204EA (Nos 41–44 off the Toulouse line) were intensively used for training, route and station proving and publicity, though revenue flying was gradually slotted in from mid-November 1977. The word Airbus was comprehensively eliminated from all Eastern thinking—oddly, Delta responded with a no-frills 'all-American Aerobus' service, using old DC-8-61s—and everywhere the aircraft was referred to merely as the 'A-300 Whisperliner', with a hyphen. GE alone received publicity as the supplier of the engines. The 100th revenue service came on 5 December, with a 100 per cent dispatch reliability, and full service at over 10 hours per day began on 13 December. Around Christmas Bill Sweetman of *Flight International* visited Miami, to be told by an Eastern V-P 'Any airline chief executive who doesn't get off his fanny and go to Toulouse to find out what the economics of this aircraft are all about will have to answer to his board'.

At the start of 1978 Boeing's Tex Boullioun—who has probably sold more jetliners than any other ten men—gave first details of what were to become the 757 and 767, though both were still to change radically. The twin-aisle aircraft was a 180-seater, 7-abreast, with engines in the 35,000–40,000-lb class. Unlike previous Boeings, with small wings fitted with sophisticated high-lift devices, it was to have a big wing with simple high-lift devices. In contrast, Airbus continued to plan the B10 around a very clever new and smaller wing, as outlined in the next chapter.

On 6 April 1978 Eastern signed for 23 A300B4s, with options for nine more as well as 25 of the planned B10 version. Immediately US manufacturers called for 'protection from European imports', and three subcommittees of the US Congress began studying the fine print, immediately latching on to an 'operating cost support' clause which paid Eastern a small subsidy to cover the supposed difference in operating cost between the B4 and the smaller B10, which Eastern said it really wanted. This seemed hardly necessary, as according to Frank Borman the actual measured fuel per seat-mile on Eastern's routes was 20 per cent lower than for the TriStars and 34.6 per cent lower than for the 727 fleet. The President added 'No new aircraft ever placed in service by Eastern has functioned from the outset with as few mechanical problems and other flight-delay snags as the A300 . . .' The whole deal was worth $778 million. AI lent the airline $96 million and GE lent $45 million, at interest rates which were to reflect the airline's future profitability. European banks lent $250 million at 8.25 per cent, on terms 'consistent with the Ex-Im Bank's financing of US aircraft exports'.

Eventually Eastern planned to standardize on the CF6-50C2 engine, and this new 52,500-lb engine, in a refined and very efficient pod, made its first flight on the No 3 A300 prototype at Blagnac on 10 May 1978. This was the first of several occasions on which a new US engine was to make its first flight aboard an Airbus.

AI entered 1979 with a firm order-book of 123 aircraft, of which 70 were gained in 1978! As noted in the next chapter, it also had commitments for over 60 of the new A310 (previously the A300B10), which was launched in July 1978. A total of 60 aircraft had flown 230,000 hours in 160,000 flights, with a worldwide dispatch reliability exceeding 98 per cent. Production was at two per month, rising to three in late 1979 and to four in late 1980. And AI had become dominant twin-aisle builder for Europe, the Middle East and Far East.

In 1978 AI had adopted a striking house livery comprising stripes of dark blue, red, orange and yellow in that order. This was used as cheat line on company demonstrator aircraft; later demonstrators, such as the Dash-600 and A310-300, have a white fuselage with the stripes used only on the vertical tail. As 1979 dawned AI gained its 21st customer in TDA, Japan's busy Toa Domestic Airlines, which requested and received permission to adopt the AI livery on its own aircraft.

In March 1979 AI reached agreement with Air France and Lufthansa for the inservice test of CFRP (carbon-fibre reinforced plastics) components replacing metal items on aircraft already delivered. The selected parts comprised outboard spoilers, main landing-gear fairings, fin leading edge, cabin floor vertical support rods and, on the first Lufthansa aircraft, D-AIAA, a complete rudder. AI was convinced CFRP parts would offer advantages in weight and manufacturing cost, but wanted at least two years' service experience to confirm resistance to impact damage, that maintenance would not be more expensive, and to prove its methods for conducting away lightning strikes. In the same month Hatfield announced details of its own wing design for the A310, as related in the next chapter.

On 5 March 1979 Bruce N Torell, President of Pratt & Whitney, showed how important he considered AI to be by visiting Toulouse for the roll-out of the first aircraft for SAS, the first with his company's engines. The twin JT9D-59As, each rated at 53,000 lb, and the most powerful turbofan engines on any civil airliner at that time, behaved impeccably on the first flight on 28 April, when the entire flight envelope was covered, as well as an automatic approach and automatic go-around.

A little later, on 17 May, the first of several aircraft was flown from Toulouse to VFW's Lemwerder factory for conversion into the first A300C4-200 convertible. The customer was Hapag-Lloyd of West Germany. The 83rd aircraft off the line, the first freighter had a 6-m section removed from the forward fuselage (itself previously made in Germany) and a new section, made by VFW at Einswarden, spliced in. The new section contained a passenger door plus the new upward-opening cargo door, 3.58 m wide and 2.56 m high, a little larger than the door on cargo DC-10s. Other differences included a reinforced main floor throughout, smoke detection systems in the main cabin, and special passenger/cargo interior trim. Ball mats, roller tracks and electric drives could be fitted to the normal seat rails. Though seemingly crazy, the conversion of completed aircraft was shown by AI to be cheaper as well as quicker than incorporating everything into the Toulouse line. This first C4 was rolled out and flown on 9 November 1979.

In 1979 AI took orders and options for 221 aircraft, several times more than its total order-book a year previously. Rather suddenly, and without doubt very largely because of Eastern, the European group had at last become recognized on the world scene. Production rate was increased by all means practical, and prices and lead-times went up. At the start of 1980 AI was selling aircraft priced at $35 million for delivery in 1984. And not least of the about-facers was Britain's Rolls-Royce which, after having taken a conscious decision to walk way from the Airbus at the start of the programme, now tried desperately hard to get back. At the 1979 Paris airshow the engine company announced an agreement with AI, under the terms of which it would pay all the development and certification costs of an A300B powered by the RB.211-524. British Airways, who could have been the launch customer, kept on buying Boeings, and foams at the mouth if the word Airbus is mentioned.

Though Eastern's main fleet comprises B4 aircraft, at the start of 1980 it took delivery of two short-haul B2s, previously used by Iran Air before the overthrow of the Shah. Many airlines tried to get these low-time aircraft, but Eastern needed them to operate the NY–Boston shuttle in a one-class configuration with 280 seats. It later received permission to operate into Washington National, the barrier there having been purely political, and vast numbers of passengers have now shuttled in the B2s from DC and Boston Logan to New York. At the latter city the airport used was La Guardia, whose pile-supported runway extensions caused a limitation on gross weight. Like many such restrictions, this was eventually forgotten.

The January 1981 issue of *British Aerospace Quarterly* contained a eulogy of the A300B based on comments by Dieter Kramer, Lufthansa Manager of Maintenance Engineering. His message was that the A300B is a very advanced piece of machinery, packed with electronics, yet at least as reliable as older and simpler aircraft. His closing sentence was 'I think they spent a lot of time thinking about this aircraft. Its performance is quite superior to any other shorthaul aircraft we operate. The airplane is different. If you try to operate it from instincts you'll have it on the ground for days, but if you follow the book it's unsurpassed'. But to the author there was unconscious humour in Editor Rosalind K Ellingsworth's introduction: 'When Airbus Industrie was designing the A300, Lufthansa was right there assuring they got the airplane they wanted; and they did'. As readers of this book may by now be aware, nothing could be further from the truth; the German flag-carrier's attitude was cool to the point of open hostility until a year after first flight.

As explained earlier, one of the most significant single advances in the A300 story has been the FFCC (forward-facing crew cockpit). This made its first flight on Tuesday 6 October 1981. The aircraft was the first B4-200 for Garuda Indonesian, and the two pilots were Chief Test Pilot Jimmy Phillips and Flight Division V-P Pierre Baud. The first flight by any widebody aircraft with a two-man flight crew, this historic mission lasted 3 hr 40 min, the last 2 hr being after dark. Baud commented, 'Whatever the care taken and the amount of experience put into the development of a flight deck, only actual flight can confirm, and quite ruthlessly, the rightness of the decisions taken. In this respect, today's flight gave us full satisfaction, and we are now fully optimistic about the progress of the extremely complex flight-test campaign, which will be finalized by the end of the year'.

On 3 April 1982 the first A310 (there was no prototype) made its first flight. In many respects a later aircraft than the A300, it incorporated numerous features which AI saw could be transferred with advantage to the A300. Much of 1981–82 was thus spent planning the resulting A300-600, 'the world's largest twinjet', which was soon ordered by Saudi Arabia, Thailand and Kuwait, followed by others. Planned for the principal high-density routes, the Dash-600 soon demonstrated outstanding potential and today the 600R offers payload/range capability that far surpasses that of early DC-10 trijets.

Although the Dash-600 looks like the very first A300B ever built, it is in fact a considerably different aircraft, crammed with technical innovations. Among the latter are a fuselage incorporating the rear fuselage of the A310, with the rear pressure bulkhead moved aft to give a longer cabin and shorter unpressurized section. This enables two extra seat rows to be accomodated, and the Dash-600 can be certificated for up to 375 passengers. To restore tail moment arm the fuselage aft of the wing is lengthened by a single frame, 21 in (520 mm). Also borrowed from the A310 is the smaller tailplane. The wing is basically that of the A300 but with important detail changes, notably the use of simpler flaps without tabs but with the

Repeatedly the AI engineering story has been 'better than prediction, make it simpler'. Here the A300-600's one-piece flap can be seen, with extra camber from a downward-curved rear portion instead of a hinged tab

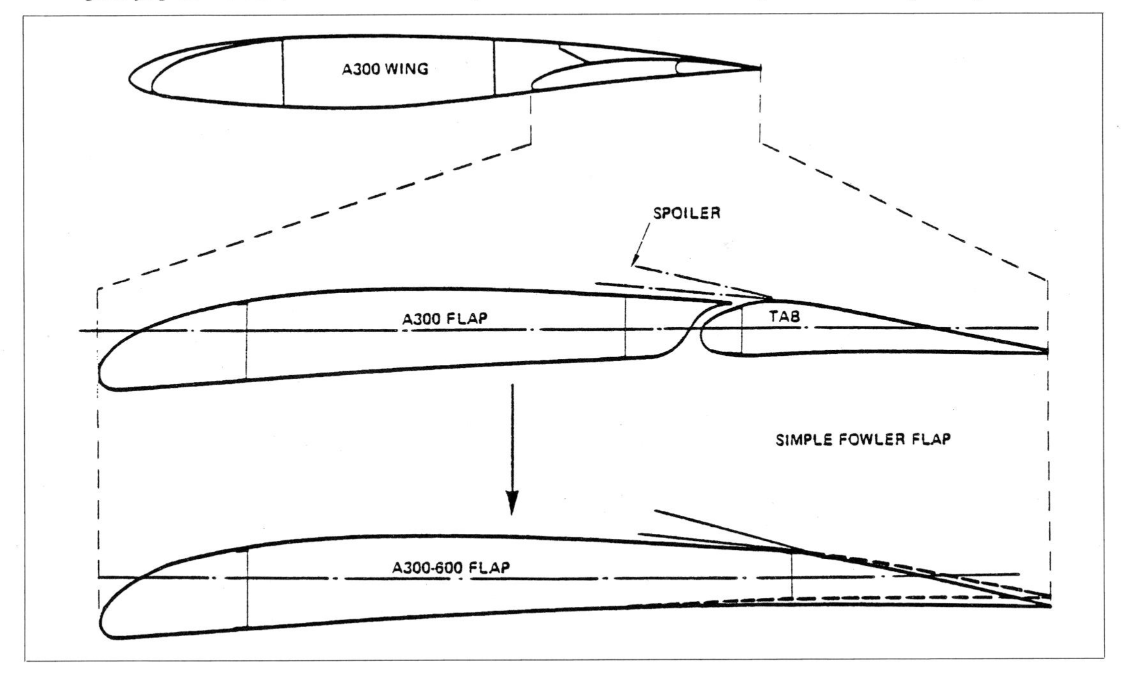

trailing edge curved slightly downwards. Despite the simplification, landing lift coefficient is increased by 8 per cent. Also eliminated are the slat fences and outboard low-speed ailerons. Altogether, drag is reduced by 4 per cent in cruise and 4.5 per cent in second-segment climb.

The entire airframe is lightened wherever possible by use of composites and modern high-strength alloys, designed to reduce crack propagation rates and improve resistance to corrosion. The engines are new, those in the first (Saudia) series being the Pratt & Whitney JT9D-7R4H1 of 56,000 lb thrust. Later the even more powerful General Electric CF6-80C2 was fitted, followed in 1986 by the Pratt & Whitney PW4056 and 4058. All these engines are extremely advanced and efficient in design, and are installed in nacelles whose drag has been reduced and whose weight has been dramatically lowered through widespread use of composites.

Not least, the entire Dash-600 is an electronically digital aircraft. The FFCC cockpit is more advanced even than that of Garuda and virtually identical to that of the A310. Pilots qualified on the one type need no significant training to qualify on the other. Flight controls, including spoilers and airbrakes, are of the FBW (fly by wire) type, and the entire aircraft incorporates much of the very newest thinking in data highways and the use of distributed self-checking processors and recorders. A further big plus is that this biggest of all Airbuses was designed to meet the very latest standard of FAR Pt 25, the continually changing 'bible' to which virtually all major commercial transports are certificated. The first A300-600 made its first flight on 8 July 1983, and, despite the colossal magnitude of the programme, involving many tons of documentation, the aircraft was certificated on 29 February 1984, with 7R4H1 engines. In March certificates were awarded to Saudia's -620, and to the Kuwaiti C620 convertible passenger/freighter aircraft, with a cargo payload of 110,782 lb (50,250 kg).

On 20 March 1985 the first aircraft flew with CF6-80C2 engines. This variant has an appreciably greater range, part of which is due to its use of wingtip fences (winglets), though smaller than those of the A310-200 and -300. It also has carbon brakes and an even newer two-man cockpit. Lufthansa is one of its customers. Newest model of all, first flown in 1987, the A300-600R incorporates the integral trimming fuel tank in the tailplane first seen in the A310-300. Other features include greater use of composites in the airframe, wingtip fences and carbon brakes, and with PW4058 engines and 19,300 US gal of fuel this aircraft carries 267 passengers (20 First and 247 Economy) with full baggage, and up to 23 LD3 containers, over a range of 4,400 nm (8,154 km)! Yet it looks like the first A300B of 1972.

3

THE A310

IRONY IS NOT UNCOMMON in big aerospace programmes. Long before the first Airbus flew, the project staff had identified nine possible variations on the basic A300B design, known as the B1 to B9. Apart from the original production models, the B2 and B4, not one of these variations was built. The irony is that the only derived aircraft so far to have become reality is a tenth variation, studied in 1973, as the A300B10 and later called the A310.

In passing, it will be recalled that the designation A300 meant 'Airbus, 300 seats'. When this was cut back in size, instead of being called the A250 or A270—these being typical ballpark passenger capacities—it became the A300B. The subsequent adoption of the designation A310 for a smaller aircraft confirmed for all time AI's disinterest in making the designation give a clue to size, and this is even more clearly seen in today's A320, which seats only half this number!

Certainly, AI suffered from an almost total lack of helpful feedback from the world's airlines when it was setting up shop in 1967–70. It was for this reason that the A300 was scaled down in body length and diameter into the A300B. Then, when the A300B1 prototypes were in build, several airlines began to ask for greater capacity, so—except for the first two aircraft, which are B1s—every A300 has been longer and more capable. But, in parallel with the sustained demand for the A300 family, which in today's Dash-600 series has grown internally into what is by a wide margin the most capacious and capable twin-engined transport ever built, there has from the beginning been a strong market sector that has regarded these aircraft as too big. Some operators simply do not have the traffic to fill an A300, others want greater service frequency, while others were concerned for their own reasons to try to reduce aircraft-mile costs, even at the cost of fractionally higher seat-mile costs. Swissair and Lufthansa specifically asked AI to consider this.

On the face of it, it is simple—especially having already slightly stretched a basic design—to make a jetliner appreciably smaller. In practice the problems are very large indeed. If the objective is to offer superior economy, everything possible must be done to minimize direct operating cost. This is strongly influenced by the amortized capital cost of the aircraft, which in turn depends crucially on the costs of R&D

(research and development). To keep down the R&D costs the simplest thing is just to build a shorter-fuselage version of the existing aircraft, and several early B10 projects were called B10MC, from Minimum Change; but this is in various ways inefficient. In the case of the A300, cutting it back to around 220 seats, which was always the kind of capacity many airlines said they wanted, would have left the small body riding on a big oversized wing, landing on an undercarriage matched to much higher weights, and pulling so much extra hardware through the sky that it would have burned more fuel than necessary.

A further major complicating factor was monetary inflation. Throughout the 1970s this often overlooked factor became ever-worse in most countries, including the Airbus partners. In Britain it galloped into the 20–35 per cent per year level in 1978–80, making nonsense of years of detailed pricing which tried to look ahead to the late 1980s and beyond. The total R&D bill for the A300 had been exemplary, but how could AI produce a smaller aircraft offering lower costs if, because of inflation, its development were to cost even more than that of its big ancestor?

The author talked at length with AI executives at this time. Many, including Béteille and Commercial Director Dan Krook, were of the opinion that the best solution was simply to put fewer seats into an A300B2 or B4. Such an aircraft would incur no R&D bill whatsoever, but with a few other trivial changes could achieve slightly reduced aircraft-mile costs whilst offering a marvellous and uniform standard of passenger comfort. Even the Production Director, famed engineer Felix Kracht (whose daughter Barbara has almost from the very beginning headed AI's public-relations staff), had grave misgivings about trying to design a totally new wing to support a cut-down fuselage.

The battle ebbed to and fro, and throughout the mid-1970s AI's management was to a considerable degree riven in twain, with a strong faction who were known as the 'antis' (anti-B10). Further spanners were cast into the works by the totally uncertain objectives of the top management in France and Britain. At Aérospatiale almost all the board from Gen Mitterrand down were by late 1975 ready to hop into bed with Boeing, which was regarded as by far the best US partner with which to stride forward into the future. Boeing said 'as you have the best cross-section, you can build the fuselage'. The scheme was called the BB10, B for Boeing but someone suggested Brigitte Bardot ought to be the grandmother. This was looked at by the two, basically rival firms in the first quarter of 1976. But, to muddy the waters still further, in the UK British Aerospace wished to rejoin AI, but could make no political progress in the face of the stonewall opposition of British Airways and Rolls-Royce. It must be remembered that at this time it was still possible to say, of the A300B, that it was 'the wrong design' or that it would 'never sell'. These were Rolls-Royce's arguments, whilst British Airways simply fell over backwards to justify its wish to buy everything American in sight, from 737s, through 7N7s and 7X7s, up through various additional TriStars to more 747s. Indeed, by July 1976 the airline's European Division was so vehemently opposed to any consideration of an A300 or a B10 that the magazine *Flight International* ran a feature headed '220-seater: ED mans the barricades'.

British Aerospace, already building wings for AI as a subcontractor and aware that Britain is not actually part of the USA but part of Europe, could only wring its corporate hands. Just to help things along, the French Government started off reopened talks with a British team in late May 1976 by announcing a precondition for any attempt by British Aerospace to rejoin AI as a full partner: an order from British Airways. This may have had a bearing on the British airline's antipathy.

Whilst all this turmoil was going on, AI began discussions with Western Airlines in the hope that this might at last be its hoped-for breakthrough into the US market. The A300B was still the only big twin on the market, and despite the absence of the smaller B10, which was close to the American operator's ideal, the advantages of the bigger A300B over any rival were so great that, as reported earlier, the airline went on public record as saying it was 'clearly a superior buy'. At the eleventh hour Western announced its scarcely believable choice of the DC-10-10 and more 727s. These could easily be assimilated into the existing fleet, but on almost every other count the choice was a very poor second to buying a fleet of A300Bs. What clinched the deal was that Boeing and Douglas made Western offers it thought it simply could not refuse, but such deals are seldom good in the long term. What brought the deal into this chapter is that the AI negotiating team was led by Dan Krook, the avowed leader of the anti-B10 faction at Toulouse. Loss of the order led to a few recriminations, and some people in AI pointed fingers at Krook. In the author's view there was some merit in the arguments of the 'anti' brigade, but it should have been clear that in the longer term AI did need to offer a smaller aircraft, with everything possible done to make it modern, uncompromised and efficient. Later in 1979 Krook returned to Amsterdam as Fokker's head of marketing, his replacement being Warde.

As the talking in 1977 droned on, BAe continued to wheel and deal with Boeing on the 7N7 and possible stretched 737s, and with McDonnell Douglas on the DC-10-30R and proposed DC-X-200. Chairman Lord Beswick publicly stated that the objective really remained collaboration with Europe, if possible on a new jetliner entirely. In his view, the market would not 'stand more than one European type'. As most of the chief West European companies had just formed a loose consortium called JET (from Joint European Transport), based at Weybridge to look at narrow-body aircraft in the 150-seat class (see Chapter 6), this seemed pretty conclusively to rule out any notion of a B10, at least with British participation. This was tough, because at Hatfield—without any commercial cover or contract—work had begun on a completely new and idealized wing for the B10, which by late 1977 had begun to look very promising.

Though this all-new wing would be costly, it was significantly better than the best part-new alternative, which was to keep the existing wing box and build on to it smaller and simpler leading and trailing edges. Not many people were enamoured of this obviously compromised solution except BAe, and the British favoured it—despite Hatfield's new wing study—because it virtually guaranteed that BAe would keep on making the giant wing boxes for all Airbuses. By October 1977 the two baseline B10s were the B10X with a brand-new wing and the B10Y with a botched-up wing. (The author entirely failed to reach a personal conclusion.) It was said that, apart from the British, everyone favoured the uncompromised B10X, but this is a gross oversimplification; the decision was far from simple.

It was taken, however, and AI decided to back the ideal B10X, which fairly soon became restyled A300-10. Immediately plans were put in hand for a completely new wing to be designed on the Continent, the obvious partner being VFW-Fokker. Stepping down as that company's Chairman in May 1978 Gerritt Klapwijk said that, though he hoped to see BAe come in as full partners and take on the wing, AI could not rely on this ever happening, especially in the face of steadfast disinterest by British Airways. Accordingly, plans were going ahead at Bremen for design of the best possible new wing, and very soon Aérospatiale began offering assistance to what became known as the IWDT (Integrated Wing Design Team). For a while in early 1978 the other German AI partner, MBB, did its own detailed wing study under Engineering Director Dr Heribert Flosdorf—today AI's Executive V-P—but at no time seriously wished to tackle the manufacturing programme.

The A310 was first exhibited in the form of a model at the Hanover airshow in April 1978. Whereas studies had generally been on the basis of a wing area of 2,250 sq ft (209 m^2) the model had a wing equivalent to 2,360 sq ft (219.25 m^2). The fuselage was 12 frames shorter than that of the A300, passenger capacity being 195/245. But the design continued to be refined, and almost every part was to change in the course of the next 12 months. During this period, on 9 June 1978, Swissair and Lufthansa defined their joint specification for the A310, and a month later these airlines announced their intention to place launch orders. AI announced that the 310 was going ahead at full speed. On 15 March 1979 Swissair signed for 10, while Lufthansa said it wanted 10, costing with spares $240 million, showing that the large R&D cost (estimated at the time at $850 million) was not being amortized on aircraft for early customers. Lufthansa also placed options on a further 15 aircraft (later this airline's orders and options were to rise to 50). A little later Air France signified its wish to begin with an order for four, plus more for Iberia. The expected engine was the CF6-45, essentially a standard CF6-50A derated to the lower thrust of 46,500 lb to reduce costs. Lufthansa said it calculated aircraft-mile DOC to be 15 per cent lower than that of its B2 fleet, though a typical passenger load would be reduced by 20 per cent.

At the 1978 Farnborough show the British Secretary of State for Industry, Eric

Varley, announced that BAe wished to become a full partner in AI from 1 January 1979, taking a 20 per cent shareholding and playing 'a full part in the development and manufacture of the A310'. (The sweet pill was simultaneously soured by his announcement of British Airways' and Rolls-Royce's total commitment to the Boeing 757, previously the 7N7). This government-backed wish to return to the AI fold after ten years at last opened the way to BAe participation in the A310 wing on a formal basis. Indeed, if we read the bible, *Jane's*, we learn that the A310 wing was 'designed by the British Aerospace Aircraft Group'. On the other hand, writing in the monthly company magazine *Aérospatiale* for October 1978 Jacques Morriset unequivocally reported 'The A310's wings will therefore be Franco-German'. What actually happened was very much in between these simplistic statements.

As already reported, Aérospatiale, Hawker Siddeley, MBB and VFW-Fokker all did prolonged studies of B10 wings. These were rationalized by autumn 1978 into two supposedly rival designs, one by British Aerospace at Hatfield and the other by the IWDT at Bremen. Both groups started out with the premise that the objective was to reduce area and weight whilst holding span as close as possible to the original value.

Every Airbus has had the enormous advantage of a so-called supercritical wing with a flattish top and bulged underside as shown. But the wings have got better. The best so far is that of the A310, but the A300-600 has come some way towards equalling it

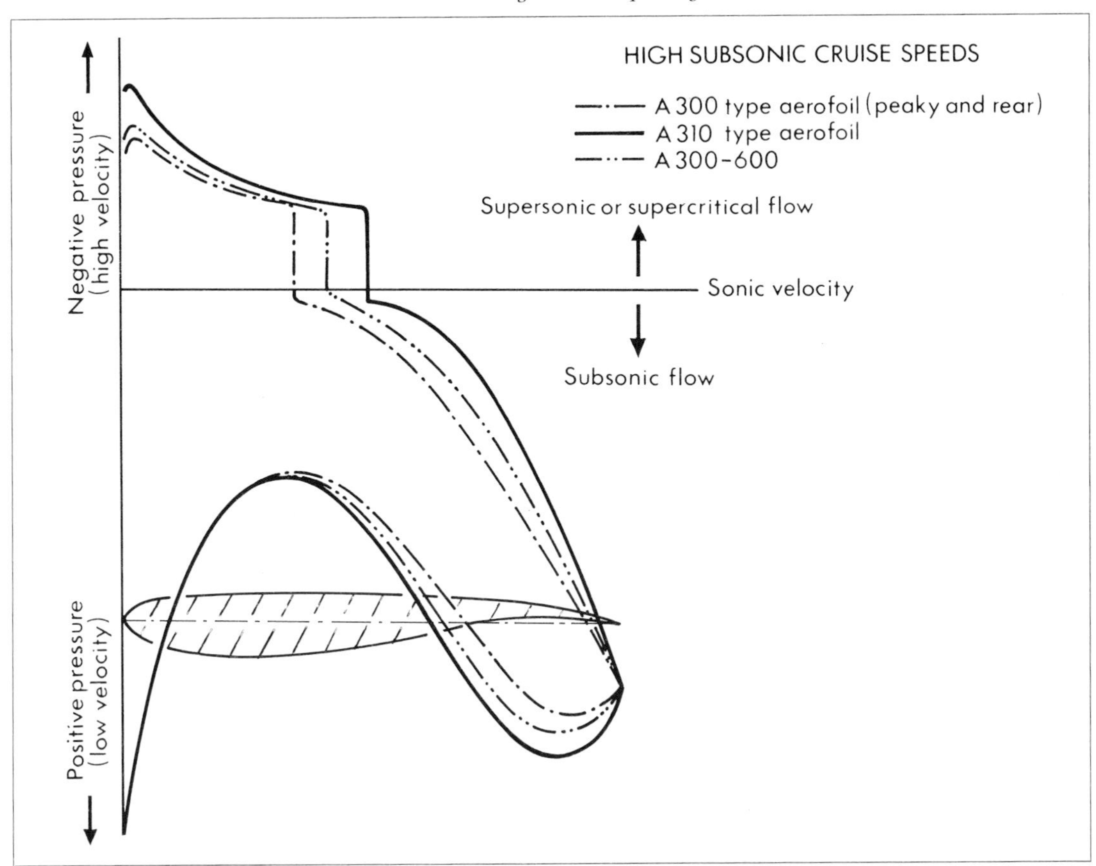

This would obviously result in higher aspect ratio (slenderness in plan view), which gives better range-efficiency. But the two groups came up with wings differing in many respects, and the interesting thing is that each group saw good in the rival offering. Very broadly, the Bremen wing was more conventional, with a deep supercritical section from root to tip, and fitted with linkages carrying Fowler flaps. The Hatfield wing had fractionally greater (15.2 per cent) thickness/chord ratio at the root, but the inboard wing tapered sharply in thickness from below, giving considerable dihedral inboard, to reach a t/c ratio at the kink of only 11.8 per cent, falling further to 10.8 per cent at the tip. On the other hand, Hatfield used double-slotted flaps. Bremen frankly found the Hatfield wing weight estimate, slightly below their own, hard to believe in view of the thinner outer panel. There was no doubt Hatfield offered lower drag, however, as well as ample fuel capacity as a result of the deep root, and they stuck to their weight.

The good news was that, as must always be the case with all partners in any collaborative project, nobody wanted to score off anyone else, and attitudes were invariably positive and generous. This paved the way for the return of BAe to AI in January 1979, and the assignment of responsibility of the entire wing to the British partner. Even though AI recognized that it was to some degree engaged in a race with Boeing on the 767, and that handing it all to BAe would cause some delay (the estimated magnitude of which varied wildly, depending whose opinion was sought), there was soon almost unanimous agreement that BAe was the right partner to look after this vital new wing. The proper course was simple: in effect, lock everyone in a room and let them out only when they had merged the work of all partners into the best possible wing. Thus, 33 French and German engineers came to Hatfield and got to grips with their British colleagues, generally adopting the British wing, but with Fowler flaps outboard and with what the Bremen men called a 'vaned Fowler' inboard; to save face, Hatfield described the inboard flap as 'double slotted'.

Béteille said, 'BAe is doing a fantastic job pulling the whole thing together, and the whole wing is now, in January 1979, back on schedule. We know exact weights and drags, and are close to signing contracts with the launch customers . . . We have had the benefit of three very good wing teams, though the British team has had the most experience. The compromise that we have had the responsibility to choose is certainly better, and could not have been done by any one team alone'. Production Director Kracht added, 'The discussions between the different wing schools have been very fruitful, and the final wing will be significantly better than the best originally achieved. . . . This superb wing will be built in the same shops and by the same people as the A300 wing, so that we can benefit from the experience . . .'

On 1 April 1979 Lufthansa signed not for 10 of the new jetliners but for 25, with another 25 on option! Two days later KLM Royal Dutch Airlines placed its biggest-ever order, and its first for any non-American jet, signing for ten plus ten on option, at

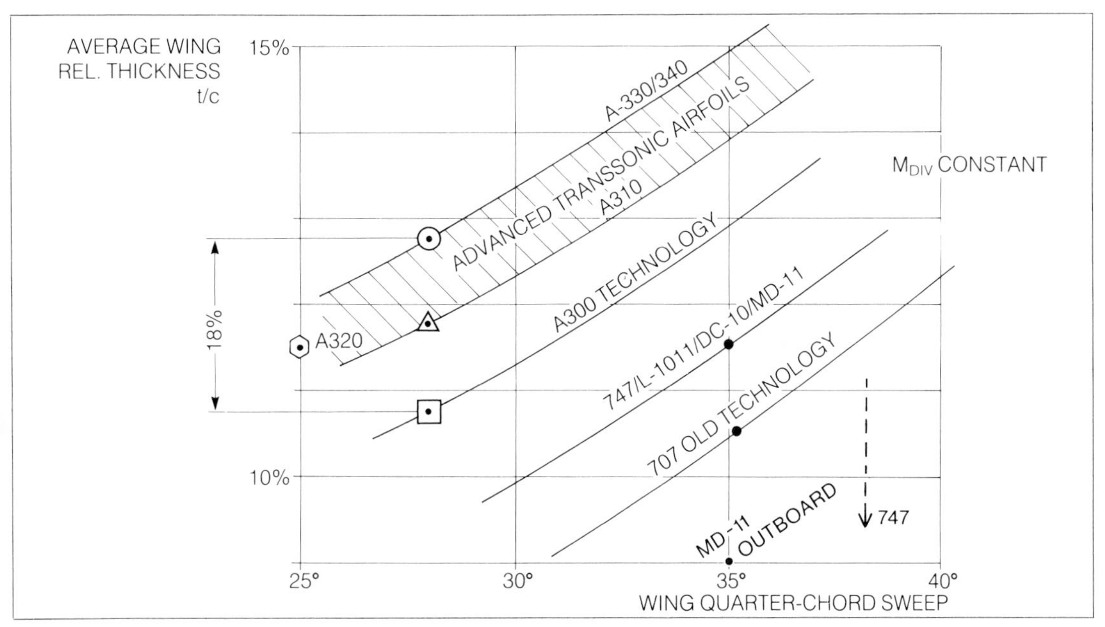

Wings in a nutshell: whereas the objective used to be less thickness and more sweep (and the 747 is off the map with a mean t/c of 7.8 per cent) today the objective is just the opposite. The square, triangle and circle respectively represent the A300, 310 and 330/340

Guilders 10^9 (£238 million). By this time the A310 had begun a firm process of growth, with ever-greater fuel capacity and range. Weights naturally grew, so that instead of the CF6-45 Swissair selected the Pratt & Whitney 7R4C of 48,000 lb thrust, while Lufthansa and KLM picked the new and lightened CF6-80A2 of 50,000 lb. GE's bold development of the new Dash-80 family, which has today led to the almost totally new 80C2, reduced commonality with the mass of A300 engines but brought so many benefits that it has influenced some A300 customers to buy GE.

At the end of April 1979 AI disclosed its plan to offer a developed A310 able to carry a full payload 3,500 nm (6,486 km). This was the beginning of a process of development which had already also begun to transform the big A300, but not even AI had any notion how far beyond prediction the A310 would prove to be. Back in 1979 there were three models on offer: the 310-100 short-hauler, for 2,000-nm sectors, which nobody had bought and which (it seems likely) nobody ever will; the Dash-200, the initial production model bought by the launch customers and able to fly 3,000-nm sectors; and the new developed variant, at that time undesignated but which quite naturally later became the 310-300, planned for 3,500 nm. The long-hauler retained the original fuel capacity (technical figures appear later in the 310 description) but was structurally strengthened to operate at an MTOW increased from 291,010 lb (132 *tonnes*) to 310,000 lb (140.6 *tonnes*), which would permit it to uplift a capacity fuel load simultaneously with a full passenger load, the latter then being a nominal 194 economy plus 20 First Class. Market reaction was positive, and from early 1979 AI concentrated its 310 marketing on the longer-ranged versions.

What was not then apparent was the truly dramatic way in which the 310 would deliver performance not even dreamed of, to the point where it would emerge not only as a viable replacement for the 707 and DC-8 but as a true long-hauler.

As explained elsewhere, the 310 was one of the key factors in the return of Britain as a full partner in AI, effective from 1 January 1979. Just four months later another partner joined, but only on the A310. This was the Belgian consortium Belairbus, formed with capital of 50 million Belgian francs by the Belgian government (one-third), which also injected 200 million francs to fund the first year and tooling costs, the Walloon (Flemish) development authority (one-third) and an industrial group comprising SONACA (formerly Avions Fairey), FN (*Fabrique Nationale Herstal*) and Asco, an engineering company (one-third). Belairbus did not accept design responsibility but took on the production of all A310 slats, slat tracks and Krüger flaps, as well as participation in future developments of these items. By the time production started Belairbus also took on the production of the large wing/body fairing, made of composite CFRP and Kevlar materials.

In October 1979 British Caledonian concluded a long and intense evaluation of the A310-200 against the Boeing 767. In true British style BCal seemed to be reluctant to accept that the European aircraft might actually be superior, despite such obvious advantages as lower sector costs, greater passenger seat and aisle widths (for any given seat configuration) and the use of standard underfloor containers. Only slightly later another British operator, which has the patriotic name Britannia, picked the 767 and got massive (and seemingly patriotic!) media publicity by doing so. It later wrote in its house magazine that the American aircraft was superior because 'The wide-bodied, twin-aisle design facilitates eight-across seating, and the two-four-two layout means that no passenger is more than one seat away from the aisle', which is just like an A310 except that the total width available inside the cabin is 15 ft 6 in in the 767 compared with 17 ft 4 in in the European airliner. Britannia also eulogized the 'specially designed' (ie, non-standard) baggage containers and the promise of 'the smoothest ride qualities of any airliner in commercial service'. Now the author has boundless respect for Boeing, and the 767 is a fine aircraft, but he always finds it amusing when people make choices of this magnitude without being able to give any reason that appears to have the slightest germ of truth or commonsense behind it.

At the end of 1979 there came the political showdown on the FFCC (forward-facing crew cockpit). In the author's view the opposition was 99.9 per cent due to quite natural fears in a highly unionized profession that fewer people on the flight deck was going to be bad news for the pilots. Already the surging growth of the airlines had been replaced by real or imagined fears of retrenchment, and the 1973 'fuel crisis' and many other factors had conspired to increase competition and drive one operator after another out of business—Court Line and Laker in Britain, for example, and in the USA a whole shoal of operators from Braniff downwards. But such factors are

Condor Flugdienst received the first of three A310-200s on 10 January 1985, since when they have been joined by three more, all used on intensive charters

Left *A November 1986 view of the assembly line. Aircraft 442 in the foreground was the first of 12 A310-300s for PanAm. It was delivered in June 1987, the first aircraft in service anywhere with PW4000 type engines*

Below *Kenya got its first A310-300 in May 1986. This carrier picked the General Electric CF6-80C2*

difficult to put across. Not so safety, and so safety was the plank on which ALPA, Ifalpa and Europilote argued vehemently throughout 1979 for the retention of the traditional cockpit with two pilots up front and an engineer at the rear facing the right-hand wall. Europilote said it 'must act now, while the FFCC is still a concept. Once it is a fact it will be too late'. Strike action was never far from the surface at countless pilot-union meetings.

At this difficult period AI stood out as leader of the bad guys who were actively promoting the FFCC. Indeed, a year earlier Boeing had spinelessly said that, provided its competitors did the same, it would build nothing but three-man widebody cockpits. The author was reminded forcibly of the situation on the railways, where the steam-era footplate crew of driver (US = engineer) and fireman had been replaced on diesels and electrics by a driver and a 'second man' who had no valid role to perform. On London's underground it was soon shown that no up-front driver at all was needed, and the battle to win computerized trains manned only by a guard amidships may be imagined. All that was really needed in the case of the FFCC was a little missionary zeal, combined with massive amounts of education. Once pilots had actually flown the FFCC, either for real or in a simulator, they rather suddenly began to appreciate that it is an entirely new ball game. Instead of trying to crowd all the old flight-engineer instruments and controls into overcrowded overhead panels, the FFCC presents the two pilots with big multifunction displays which tell them nothing except whatever they need to know, in whatever detail they wish.

The A310 cockpit is described later. Today it is accepted as an industry leader, loved by its pilots and the source of no trouble at all. But, like so many examples of visible change in the human world, at the outset it caused prolonged and acrimonious argument. To a small degree it paralleled the Airbus itself: in the early days there was a widespread opinion that 300 passengers on two engines was unsafe. The author pointed out to Lathière that 80 years earlier transatlantic passengers judged the safety of a liner by how many funnels it had, and that in this century numerous giant ships had been built with false funnels to avoid losing customers. We never had Airbuses with false pods, but we were faced with a rather similar situation regarding 'safety in numbers', plus the massive overlying problem of trade-union protection of jobs. Not that the FFCC was a new idea: smaller jets, such as the One-Eleven and 737, had used two-pilot cockpits for years, but with traditional instruments filling every nook and cranny. Where the A310 FFCC was totally new was that, thanks to the replacement of traditional instruments by big multicolour, multifunction CRT (cathode-ray tube) displays, each area of panel could be made to display from dozens to hundreds of different items. If nothing was going wrong in a system, nothing need be displayed. If something were to go wrong, that fact would be instantly and stridently communicated to the crew, who could then call up more and more detail in a way utterly impossible with the traditional three-man cockpit.

From 1979 AI opened its doors to visiting pilots who wished to try the FFCC simulator. Though not representative of a definitive A310 flight deck, and in fact used almost entirely as a vital development tool for the ergonomics and software, this simulator did at least enable pilots to 'suck it and see' even in a primitive way. Most of the visitors were the captains with fairly open minds; the hardest 'antis' did not wish to go near it. Thus, having no rigid preconceived notions, pilot after pilot came away not only impressed but deeply excited. One from Air France said 'I don't want to go back to my own cockpit; it now seems to me prehistoric'. In any case, there was a natural conflict between the airlines, which wanted the modern two-man FFCC, and the pilot unions. The latter often took refuge in the suggestion that, the more pairs of eyes there are, the better; but two recent mid-air collisions, and a landing a kilometre short of the threshold, all occurred when there were *five* flight crew in the cockpit.

AI was very much the meat in the sandwich. When absolutely pinned to the wall and screwed down firmly, AI could be made to admit that, in its considered view, the new-technology FFCC was not only much more efficient but safer; problems in crew communication with the old cockpit were discussed in the previous chapter. AI pilots, men of vast experience and integrity, shared this view to a man. Their personal contacts, and the growing number of customer pilots who visited Toulouse, very gradually helped educate the vast body of line pilots in existing and potential customers, but it took a long time. In January 1979 Lufthansa published a technical paper which attempted to demonstrate the enhanced safety of the FFCC. If anything, it inflamed the more militant Lufthansa flight crews worse than before. Europilote activity stepped up sharply, and by November Air France capitulated and agreed to equip its A310s with a traditional SFCC (side-facing crew cockpit) similar to that of its B2s (AI Tech Director J Roeder hit his brow and said 'I just don't believe it!'). Within two weeks the Belgian pilot union, ABPNL, announced its total refusal to fly Sabena 310s with any but the traditional arrangement, and the next day Lufthansa pilots threatened a series of strikes if its 25 new A310s did not also have the old SFCC.

Far from the European aggro, Garuda in Indonesia completed a training course at Aeroformation on the FFCC and put it into service with its first A300B4-220 in December 1981. This was despite the fact that their aircraft did not have the new 'glass cockpit' of the A310, being equipped with a traditional front panel plus a new pushbutton overhead panel similar to that of the new FFCC. AI pilots worked closely with the Indonesians to evaluate and refine all the new concepts, so that a truly refined FFCC could be built into the No 3 A300B, the AI test and demo aircraft, in late 1981. Initially all this work was aimed solely at the A310, though AI never doubted that in due course it would read across to the A300 family.

Throughout the late 1970s Rolls-Royce continued to discuss with the British government, British Aerospace, AI and a host of existing or (more often) potential customer airlines how it could get back aboard the Airbus. Ralph Robins, who today is RR's MD, told the author 'I regret our misjudgement of the importance of Airbus Industrie. Of course ours was a different company, with different leadership, but we had the whole Airbus programme in our pocket and we did nothing with it—not that we were in a position to do so, as it transpired'. He went on to comment on his company's willingness to go ahead even on as small a market-base as 30 ship-sets (engine pods for 30 aircraft), but, he said, 'HM Government will have to help a bit with the certification costs'. Over in Connecticut and Ohio they were more fortunate, and the Ohio company had the advantage of being virtually standard supplier of engines on the A300B, unless a customer had special reasons to the contrary. On the new 310, however, everything was up for grabs, and this time the Connecticut group, part of United Technologies, was rather more lean and hungry.

During 1979 Pratt & Whitney's board decided they simply had to try harder: AI was going to survive and prosper, and GE really had to be given the hardest possible run for their money. The A300 family was solidly based on GE, but even at this early date talks were held to see how far the planned next-generation PW4000 series engine might carve out a niche in future A300s as big as that gained by GE's new CF6-80 series. But much more immediate markets were showing in the A310 programme, and here Pratt & Whitney decided the key to gaining a much bigger fraction of A310 power—perhaps more than half—lay in the big order for Air France. The famed builder of what it called 'dependable engines' sent the whole first team over to Paris to make the French airline an offer it simply could not refuse. Though it offered the JT9D-7R4D1 engine at a typical market price, it added into the contract: offset work for French industry, mainly for SNECMA, worth 30 per cent of all current and future orders for JT9D engines for Airbus aircraft; and completely free overhaul and upgrading to later standards of all the JT9D engines in the older 747s in the Air France fleet!

In normal circumstances this could hardly have failed, especially as P&W and SNECMA had a long history of collaboration; indeed, at one time the US firm had held 10 per cent of SNECMA's stock and had seats on the board. It will be recalled that, had it not been for the abrupt purchase of Bristol Siddeley by Rolls in 1966, the Airbus would have been launched with JT9Ds made partly in Europe by SNECMA and Bristol Siddeley. Air France considered Pratt & Whitney's offer carefully, and well they might; but by this time GE too could pull political strings. Not only did it have almost the whole of the A300B programme, but it also had much more than P&W going with SNECMA, including manufacture of CF6 parts for Airbuses and also DC-10s. Even more important, GE and SNECMA had lately launched a new engine, the CFM56, on a 50/50 basis; much later this was to be the launch engine for the next, and totally new, Airbus, the A320. GE simply refused to be licked, and matched P&W blow for blow. Moreover, its engines were lighter; and widebodies are limited in payload on weight, not on volume. At the end of the day, the only place where GE could not equal

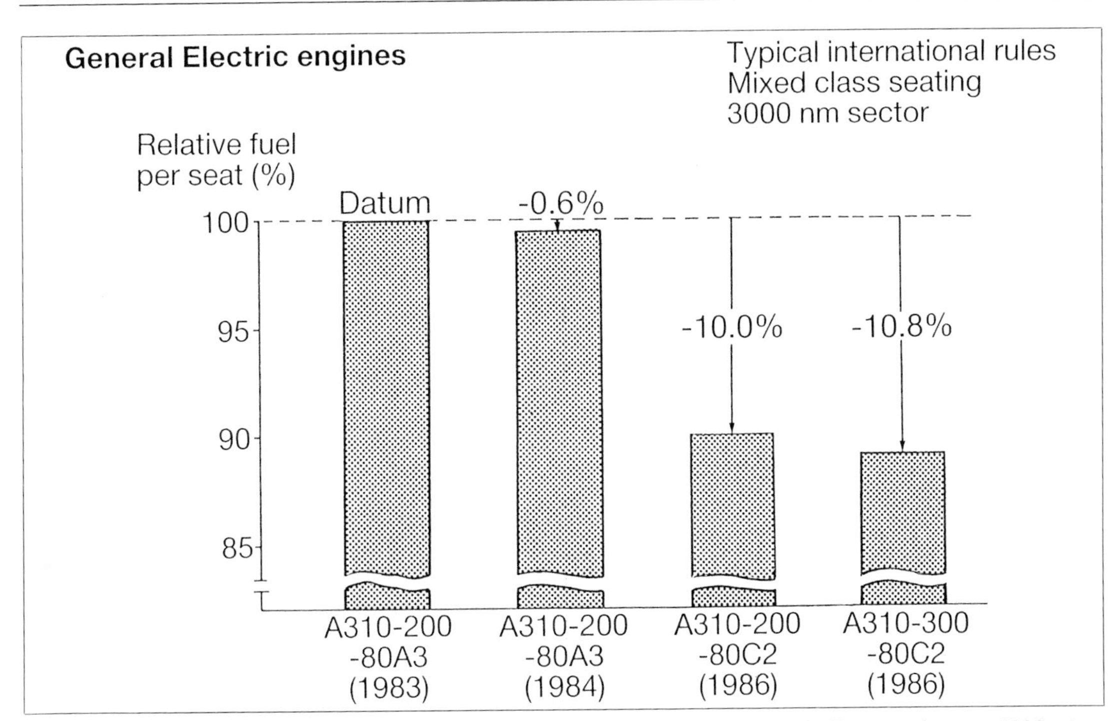

As a comparison with the diagram of page 70, this shows the improvement in fuel efficiency of recent A310s, in this case over a 3,000-nm sector and with GE engines. Payload/range productivity has climbed over 75 per cent

its rival was that P&W needed only 15 months to upgrade the Air France 747 engines, whereas—not having worked on JT9Ds before—GE had to offer a schedule of 30 months. But evaluating the proposals took over six months, and it was not until the end of 1979 that the French airline announced it was buying CF6-80A1 engines worth $30 million for its first five A310s, and would later need many more. Pratt's President, Richard Carlson, told the author 'The French government wasn't on our side'.

In 1979 Asad Nasr, successor to Sheikh Alimuddin as Chairman of MEA (popular Middle East Airlines of the Lebanon), announced his intention of carrying out a searching evaluation of the 767 and 310. At the end of 1980 he announced an order for five of the AI product, plus no fewer than 14 options. At once he was besieged by GE, P&W and also by Rolls-Royce, which saw in a combination of MEA, Kuwait and, especially, Saudia, almost its only hope of launching its RB.211 into the Airbus programme. Adam Butler, junior Minister for Industry, said that he was talking with the Derby company about 'the funding of the non-recurring costs' involved in the development of a Rolls-engined Airbus, while BAe said it was completing the design of the special pylon strut required to hang the shorter but heavier RB.211-524 on the A310 wing. Sadly for Rolls, it never was able to sew up any deal involving RB.211-engined Airbuses, for the Middle East or anywhere else, and sadly for AI the disastrous religious war in the Lebanon killed MEA's A310 order also.

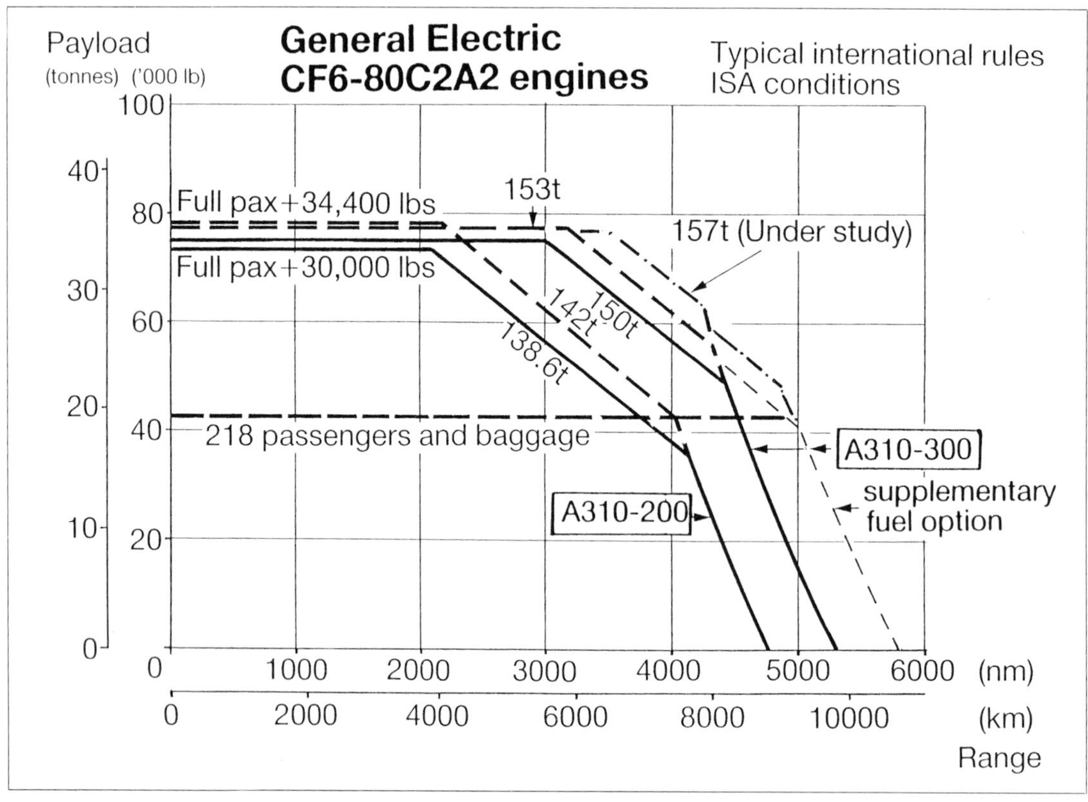

As noted in the text, Airbus Industrie began by aiming their big twins at the short-haul maket! This payload/range plot for today's A310s (with GE engines) shows how far AI has come

Around Christmas 1980 BAe began gathering the bits of its first A310 wing box into its first new jig at Chester. The wing itself is described later, and the factories and production process in the next chapter. This first wing box was taken out of its jig on 7 April 1981, and later flown to Bremen. It was said at the time that in 1981 currency each A310 wingset was worth £1.4 million to BAe, but as A300 wingsets had been priced around £2 million two years earlier (when inflation was almost 30 per cent) this was an underestimate. This was unquestionably the worst period in the whole history of AI for trying to reconcile prices in all the currencies involved, which never stayed in the same relationship to each other for two days together. Mike Goldsmith, MD of BAe's Hatfield/Chester Division, said he had read that the total BAe share of A310 launch cost was £250 million, over the period 1978–85. First, he said he did not believe the figure was so high; second, he said it was ludicrous in a time of such galloping inflation to predict 1985 prices. Fortunately for Britain, and for the AI programmes, Britain got its financial act together with the Thatcher government, and prediction of costs and prices over what might be termed 'big-league aviation' timescales once again became a practical proposition. Some of the predicted costs, in fact, were actually revised downwards, as British inflation was forced down to around 4 per cent!

In the winter of 1981–82 major sections of the first A310s began coming together at Toulouse. There was no prototype, though for many reasons Nos 01 to 04 differed, even if only temporarily, from the regular customer aircraft. They were given special attention, over a longer than normal period, in the Toulouse final assembly hall. The chief reason for this, especially with Nos 01 and 02, was the need to pack almost every part of the aircraft with instrumentation. The biggest non-standard structural features were an emergency escape route through the nose-gear bay for the test crew, and provision for in-flight explosive jettisoning of a cargo hold door to demonstrate compliance with the severe FAA ruling on floor strength following explosive decompression beneath it.

AI did not start a new C/n (construction number) sequence, but numbered the 310s in with the 300s. Thus, the first two were Nos 162 and 172. Both were 310-220s, with Pratt & Whitney engines and destined for Swissair. Despite this, however, the first aircraft, initially with French experimental registration F-WZLH, looked like a Swissair aircraft on the right side only. Seen from the left it was pure Lufthansa, apart from having the wrong logo on the engine pod (the German airline having selected GE). To the author's knowledge this was the first time a new airliner had been rolled out painted in this way in the livery of two totally different customers. Moreover, seeing the 310 for the first time, the author found it hard to explain why, from some angles, it should be instantly identifiable for what it was, whereas from others it should be difficult to distinguish from an A300. In any case, having the hardware at last on the ramp, this is a good point at which to break off and describe the A310, concentrating on its new features.

Though the body is significantly different, the really new feature is the wing. There is not the slightest doubt that developing the wing of the 310 was one of the biggest challenges and biggest successes in the history of commercial transport aircraft. To recap: at the start of the B10 studies the general consensus was that, to minimize development cost, all that need be done was to cut down on the length of the body and make as few other changes as possible. At an early stage, prior to 1976, there were hopes that an acceptable compromise would be to bolt new leading and trailing sections on the existing A300B wing box, but the author soon formed the view that even those who proposed this did not fully believe in it. As already related, the final answer was a totally new wing. To the casual observer there may not seem much difference. Closer inspection shows that the A310 wing is smaller, especially in chord. Looking a little closer still shows that it differs startlingly in head-on view. The A300 wing is conventional, having normal taper in depth from root to tip, the root merely being faired into the body with small fillets. In contrast, the A310 wing starts off with depth actually greater than that of the older wing, the undersurface at the root extending at its deepest point well down the lower curve of the body. The undersurface then sweeps sharply upwards until at the pylon the total wing thickness is appreciably less than it is for the A300 wing at this point. This is despite the fact that the thickness/chord ratio is actually greater (11.8 per cent against the older wing's 10.5 per cent), because the actual chord is so much less.

To some degree the A310 can be said to have a 'blended' wing/body shape reminiscent of the latest fighters, such as the F-16 Fighting Falcon; but, unlike the fighters, the A310 blending is entirely on the undersurface. The advantages include reduced wing/body interference at high Mach numbers, greater internal volume for fuel, and, above all, to gain enough root depth to carry the severe structural loads with the lowest possible wing weight. The engines are hung further inboard than on the A300B, and further ahead of the wing. Great care was needed to achieve a common design of pylon strut which can be used with any GE, P&W or RR engine; in practice engines by the first two suppliers are in use, each having its own type of pylon built around the common structural beam and wing pick-ups. Once when the author was in Toulouse the discussion chanced on the practicability of flying an A310 with one GE engine and one P&W, and no insoluble problem could be unearthed (though it is a complex matter).

Structurally the new wing is simpler than the original A300 wing, except for the skins. The simplification is mainly the elimination of the inboard third spar; the result is an almost perfect two-spar wing box, the front spar being straight and the rear spar changing direction at the kink. Aft of the inboard section is an added portion with a false rear spar, as on the A300, whose inboard end carries the main landing gear. Rib design and spacing is little altered, though of course chord is reduced and the profile therefore relatively deeper, especially towards the root.

The skins, however, are completely new. As in the A300 family there are on the first A310s a forward and aft top skin and an outboard top skin, and a forward and aft bottom skin and an outboard bottom skin. There the similarity ends. On the A300 the forward and aft inboard skins are of short span, extending only to the kink; the outboard skins are the giants. On the A310 the forward and aft skins cover almost the entire wing; the outboard skins are tiddlers, covering just the dry portion of wing box between the tank end rib and the tip. Advantages include a lighter skin joint and reinforcing straps, because the loads outboard are about one-tenth as high as at the kink, and elimination of a chordwise skin joint in the tankage. By 1986 the outboard joint had been eliminated; now there are just two skins above and two below. Further weight saving comes from eliminating the third spar, another advantage being that only one row of manholes is needed in the inboard underskin.

The complicating factor where the skins are concerned is that double curvature is needed. In making the A300 wing the skins are merely stretch-wrapped in the traditional way, but in the A310 wing the underskins have to be curved not only in

Right *Making a fin out of carbon fibre may not sound much until you see the fin of the A310! It saves 254 lb in weight and has only one-twentieth as many parts. It is the largest carbon primary structure in production in the world*

MBB

side elevation, around the profile of the aerofoil, but also in the head-on view. In the author's opinion the machine-tool industry has yet to come up with an elegant way of making thick double-curvature skins of such dimensions. In the case of the A310 the method is saturation shot-peening. Almost the entire surface of the machined skin is subjected to bombardment by small but very hard steel balls moving at extremely high speed, each impact causing a microscopic outward stretch in all directions of the surface at that point. Thus, shot-peening just one side of the sheet would progressively make it look like an inverted trough or saucer. In the case of the A310 both sides have to be blasted, to curve it around the aerofoil profile and also to curve it around in front view. No suitable equipment existed in Britain for work on this scale, so the skins for the first 40 A310s were begun as slabs from Alcoa (Aluminum Company of America), machined by Rockwell and shot-peened by MIC (Metal Improvement Co) in New Jersey. Eventually MIC set up shop at Osmaston Road, Derby, in the heart of the Rolls-Royce landscape, and from the 41st wing-set this has curved the wing skins machined at Chester.

In true Airbus tradition the high-lift system of the new wing delivered more performance than was needed, and it was progressively simplified. Among the over-20,000 hours of tunnel testing have been a multitude of slat and flap arrangements, but from near the start of the programme the emphasis has been on reducing cruise drag rather than on increasing low-speed lift. Only brief examinations were made of flaps of the double-slotted type, and even less of the use of plain hinges carried far below the wing in fairings as is the case on the DC-10, but for a long time it was thought that a double-slotted flap might be used on the inboard section. The final answer is simple and elegant. All flaps remain Fowlers, running aft and down on tracks. The tabs on the flap trailing edges are omitted, but the inboard flap sections are vaned; in other words, they can be regarded as tracked double-slotted. A further improvement in drag and simplicity resulted from making the outboard flaps in a single section, reducing the number of faired tracks on each wing from four to three. The latter are of new low-drag design and of CFRP construction, made by Fokker.

Though the first two A310s were fitted with outboard low-speed ailerons, these were already known to be redundant. Roll control is exercised by the small all-speed trailing-edge ailerons augmented by electrically signalled spoilers. The three outermost sections above each wing are the roll-control spoilers. These open only on the downgoing wing in the turn, controlled by the new digital flight-control system via two computers, each with its own software to give complete system redundancy. Inboard are four sections serving as airbrakes, two outboard of the wing kink and two ahead of the inboard flap. All 14 surfaces flick open after landing to serve as lift dumpers. All are primarily of CFRP construction, made by MBB.

Left *The main landing gear of an A310 is a delight to the structural engineer, quite apart from such colossal advantages as carbon brakes and radial tyres, which save weight and last much longer*

On the leading edge are three large sections of slat, made by Belairbus, with a single Krüger flap filling the gap between the inboard slat and the root. No other jetliner has ever had such a neat and efficient wing. The gap at the leading-edge root is filled beautifully, but without the need for the A300's extra small 'Krüger' swinging out from the wall of the fuselage. Even the small fence above the outer slat has vanished, leaving the 310 with an absolutely clean wing, with not one vortex generator or fence and with no gap in the slats even at the root or at the engine pylon struts.

Structurally, everything possible was done at the outset to incorporate every new material considered to have reached a proper level of maturity. In terms of weight-saving the biggest item was the use of new high-purity aluminium alloys in the upper wing skins and stringers, saving a little over 300 kg (660 lb). As noted, on the current 310 a further 90 kg (200 lb) is saved by eliminating the main wing skin joints and using unbroken skins from root to tip. Lesser amounts have been saved by the use of SPF/DB (superplastic formed and diffusion-bonded) titanium to make the complex but one-piece inspection covers along the undersides of the tanks and several of the cans inside the front of each tank which accomodate the slat tracks. In the light secondary structure extensive use is made of non-metallic materials, including CFRP, GRP and Kevlar, Nomex-filled GRP being particularly prevalent.

Turning to the fuselage, this is again an example of something which, like a Beethoven symphony, was repeatedly altered and yet eventually came out pretty well perfect. AI played tunes on the number of frames, and on the (not necessarily related) number of seat rows. At the end of the day the fuselage was made shorter than that of the A300 by 13 frames, but, by completely redesigning the rear fuselage, the rear pressure bulkhead was moved closer to the tail and the cabin is shorter by only 11 frames. Apart from this shortening, and elimination of the left/right forward passenger doors, the 310 body differs from the 300 only in small areas of refinement, and the manufacturing breakdown between MBB and (nose and lower centre section) Aérospatiale is unchanged.

In planning the vertical tail it was at first thought that the reduced moment arm would be roughly in the same ratio as the reduction in engine thrust, compared with the A300, and so the fin and rudder were left unchanged. In contrast, despite the shorter rear fuselage, the horizontal tail as finally designed is smaller than that of the A300B2 and B4, span being reduced from 16.94 m (55 ft 7 in) to 16.26 m (53 ft 4 in) and total area from 69.5 to 64.0 m^2 (748.1 to 688.89 sq ft). This further reduces weight and drag, and it is especially significant that the smaller horizontal tail has also become standard on the biggest Airbus of all, the A300-600. No customer has requested a retrofit on a B2 or B4. The new fin of the A310-300 is mentioned later.

Like the horizontal tail, the main landing gears were another major item which it was considered merited complete redesign. In the early days of the B10 this was not thought to warrant detailed consideration, but, following much discussion with an enthusiastic Messier-Hispano-Bugatti, the main units were started again almost from scratch to achieve an absolutely optimized design, the chief objective being reduction in weight. Standard tyres are smaller than on the A300, though customers have the option of using A300 tyres at inflation pressure reduced to 8.9 *bars*, 129 lb/sq in. This is considerably less than anything offered by any other wide-body constructor, and is suitable for virtually all airport pavements. The nose gear is of A300 type, with tyres inflated to 9.0 *bars* (131 lb/sq in), lower than that for all A300s except early B2s. Thanks to Britain's rejoining AI, Dowty receives a 40 per cent share in landing-gear manufacture, and assisted in the design.

Brakes are standard Messier-Hispano-Bugatti, with a customer option of Bendix. As described later, the French company managed to qualify carbon brakes for the new A310-300, and these brought a massive saving in weight of about 544 kg (1,200 lb). Their adoption followed a sometimes bitter battle at the supplier level with the British company Dunlop, who on Concorde had been the world pioneer of carbon brakes and had far more experience in this field than any rival company. It was entirely because of Britain's withdrawal from the programme in 1969 that the French supplier was picked to supply ordinary steel brakes for all Airbuses. Despite Dunlop's greater experience with carbon it never succeeded in gaining even a toehold into the programme, and in 1986 Dunlop announced it would no longer try to compete. Today the French company's carbon brakes are standard on all A310s, not just the Dash-300, but PanAm specified Goodyear from Ohio.

Fuel capacity is not the least of the major variables on the A310 which went through various metamorphoses before settling at levels very different from those envisaged. At the 1978 launch of the A310 there were two models on offer, the Dash-100 with a gross weight of 268,000 lb (121.56 *tonnes*), with an already impressive fuel capacity, and the Dash-200 with a weight of 291,010 lb (132 *tonnes*) and fuel capacity of 54,900 litres (12,077 Imp gal). The 310 was described by *Jane's* as a 'short/medium-range transport'. What happened in practice is that, just as in the case of the A300, most customers were interested in longer ranges, and many had their eye on using the extremely efficient A310 as a replacement for long-haul 707s and DC-8s on routes where traffic did not justify a 747. Thus, the 310-100 was never built, and was soon deleted from the programme, while in its place came a new long-hauler, the Dash-300. But this was by no means the end of the story, and how the 310 has developed will be related later in this chapter and Chapter 5.

In its systems the A310 follows the very well established principles of the A300, except for the fact that it is a digital aircraft. In other words, all data, information, pilot commands, feedback and recording is done with discrete 'bits' or 'bytes' rather than by means of voltages or mechanical movements transmitted by cables and pulleys. From very early in the programme the decision was taken to use a digitial AFCS (automatic flight-control system). This provides computer-based flight guidance in all planes, stability augmentation and thrust control, suitable for Cat II landings. Prime contractor is SFENA of France. Addition of a second computer was then to be offered to give fail-operational capability suitable for Cat IIIB (almost blind) conditions. Today's A310 has a single FCC (flight-control computer) to Arinc 701 standard, a duplicated FAC (flight-augmentation computer) to the same standard, and a TCC (thrust-control computer) for aircraft speed and propulsion control to Arinc 703. In parallel is a duplicated FMS (flight-management system), comprising a computer unit and a display unit, to Arinc 702.

Functioning basically as an autopilot, the FCC drives the flight director and SRS (speed reference system), and can be set to function in any of the following modes: pitch hold; heading hold; roll/attitude hold; altitude capture and hold; flight-level change; heading select; vertical-speed select and hold; VOR select and homing; auto takeoff; and auto go-around. Installation of a duplicate FCC, requested by several (mainly European) operators upgrades the system to Cat IIIB weather, for automatic landing with rollout and ground guidance. The TCC provides the following functions: permanent computation and command of optimum N_1 (engine speed) and/or EPR (engine pressure ratio) limits; autothrottle functions; autothrottle command for windshear protection; autothrottle command for speed and alpha (angle of attack) protection; and a test function. A customer option is a DFA (delayed flap approach) mode in which fuel burn and noise are reduced by commanding flap angles much later than normal.

Most of the other avionics, including the unique and very advanced ECAM (electronic centralized aircraft monitoring) system, are similar to those of the A300-600. A standard feature is an AIDS (airborne integrated data system) to Arinc 717 which continuously monitors and records parameters in all parts of the aircraft, for maintenance purposes and also for parts-lifing, crash investigation and other functions. The standard AIDS covers 80 parameters (40 mandatory plus 40 chosen by the customer), but it is designed to be expanded into a 160-parameter system. Navaids include choice of the same weather radars as on the A300-600, with option of a duplicate radar, and with almost every major item duplicated (such as ILS, radar altimeter and ATC transponders) and some triplicated (such as the AHRS, attitude/heading reference system). Options include Omega, dual ADF and dual or triplex IRS (inertial reference systems).

Among several major improvements in the main ancillary systems is a completely new APU (auxiliary power unit). The Garrett GTCP 331-250 is smaller and lighter than the APU on the B2 and B4, burns less fuel, is quieter and cuts maintenance costs. Not surprisingly, it was later selected for the A300-600.

To return to the flight test programme, this began on 3 April 1982. From the very start it was clear that the new 310 was a winner, but not even its most ardent in-house admirers had any idea by how much it would exceed its design or predicted values. An absolutely crucial factor was the new wing, which with its 3D curvatures and completely clean external profile set standards never before attained in the industry. Before the end of April the drag measures had proved so low that optimum cruise Mach number was raised from 0.78 to 0.805, giving more operational flexibility in cruise speed and extra savings in aircraft-mile costs. Most remarkably, the buffet boundary proved to be even further beyond prediction than it had been in the case of the A300B. The margin was almost exactly 10 per cent, enabling cruise flight level to be set 900 m (2,000 ft) higher for any given weight, or, of greater immediate importance, enabling 11 *tonnes* (24,250 lb) more payload to be carried at a given cruise height.

Another important and rather unexpected bonus was the reliability and seemingly effortless ease of the new-generation avionics and cockpit. Many technical people, both within and outside AI, as yet did not comprehend these new hi-tech developments, and there was inevitably a slight tendency to regard it all as slightly 'gimmicky'. This was particularly the case with established *pilotes de ligne*—professional airline pilots—whose generally negative views have already been aired fully. From April 1982 they simply had no chance. The AI pilots flying the new 310, never numbering more than just two, simply loved every minute. Average duration of flight tests was increased from 2 hr on the A300 to 4 hr on the A310, yet crew efficiency remained at a higher level than before.

The No 2 aircraft, No 172 off the line, made its first flight on 13 May 1982. Powered by P&W engines like its predecessor, it was painted in the colourful AI house livery, and it was in all but one or two trivial respects a standard production aircraft. After making 22 outstandingly successful test flights, it took off from Toulouse on a route-proving exercise to the Middle and Far East. The author, who had been familiar with a few such trips since 1950, had never known anything quite so successful. It did not merely operate like clockwork: it knocked predicted values into a cocked hat. On the very first leg F-WZLI carried a load equivalent to 218 passengers and their baggage and flew non-stop 2,600 nm (4,818 km) to Kuwait. This was nothing. At Kuwait the new 310 took off, with the same payload, and bucked an average 45-knot headwind all the way to Singapore, covering in 8 hr 40 min an equivalent still-air distance of over 4,000 nm (7,415 km).

Boeing had led an army of rivals, and a few supposed friends, who had poured criticism on the A310's small and highly loaded wing. Many were the predictions of dire shortfall in performance, and these centred chiefly around very poor altitude capability and consequent severely limited range. On this route-proving exercise WZLI silenced such critics for ever. Again carrying a full payload, the sector from Kuala Lumpur to Bangkok was flown in a steady climb to 43,000 ft (13,100 m)! On return to Toulouse after flying 13,930 nm (25,815 km) in six sectors, in a total block time of 31 hr 40 min, the overall performance was such that people cast around for fresh adjectives. First, the performance of the wing was nothing short of fantastic. Second, the reliability was that of a long-mature aircraft. Third, at Mach 0.8 the cruise fuel burn averaged 6.5 per cent below the best prediction. With fuel of density 0.79 the average burn was 3.27 US gal (2.7 Imp gal) per nautical mile.

On the day after WZLI returned to *l'abreuvoir* (the cattle trough) at Toulouse it made a routine test flight of 4 hr 35 min. The general considered opinion in AI was that the 310 could be certificated two months ahead of the scheduled date of March 1983, but in fact the original schedule was retained because March was the date to which hundreds of equipment vendors were working. But there was a further and potentially very important outcome of the early test flying. The performance of the wing was such that there was clearly the possibility of revising upwards all the projected weights for future A310 versions, with all that this meant in terms of range with a given payload.

The immediate result, published in September 1982, was to offer the basic A310-200 with a fixed fuel capacity of 55,000 litres (43,100 kg, 14,530 US gal) but at two weights, 132 and 138.6 *tonnes* (291,010 lb and 305,560 lb), the latter having much enhanced payload/range properties, and also to offer an entirely new long-haul model, the A310-300. The latter was to have fuel capacity of 61,500 litres (48 *tonnes*, 16,250 US gal) and to have MTOW of 149 *tonnes* (328,490 lb). This new Dash-300 model promised to carry 218 passengers and baggage a remarkable 4,000 nm (7,415 km), compared with 2,800 nm (5,190 km) for the original Dash-200. Most customers were very impressed, but what not even AI then realized was that the actual Dash-300 would go far beyond these seemingly optimistic estimates. Just how far one can 'blame' AI for bad predictive arithmetic is hard to say; certainly the author cannot think of any previous commercial transport, of any kind or character, that started out as a short-hauler and ended up looking almost exactly the same externally but as about the best and most efficient long-hauler in the business.

It is perhaps worth just reiterating what we mean by the terms 'short-haul' and 'long-haul'. Until the 1960s a short-haul jet seldom had to fly a sector as long as 1,000 nm (1,853 km), while anything with a range in excess of 3,000 nm was very definitely a long-hauler. Today, thanks to the onward march of aviation technology on all fronts, and perhaps especially in the matter of large HBPR (high-bypass-ratio) turbofan engines, the numerical interpretations of these adjectives have been revised upwards. When the A310 was announced it was called 'short/medium' even though it was estimated to carry its full passenger payload about 3,000 statute miles (4,828 km). Today the A310-200 family are officially called 'medium-range', even though they can actually carry a full payload over sectors up to 3,800 nm (4,376 miles, 7,042 km). The official term for the remarkable new Dash-300 is 'extended-range', despite the fact that it has full-payload capability of 5,000 nm (9,266 km). As this is almost double the range that 25 years ago was called 'long', the mind boggles at what a modern long-hauler might have to do. The subject is raised again in the last chapter, which includes the specialized long-haul A340.

In August 1987 AI began flight testing an ACT (additional centre tank) in order to achieve certification in late September. First customer for the A310-300 with the ACT is Wardair, though the tank was actually fitted to the A300-600s of the Private Flight Department of the United Arab Emirates which were delivered in 1986. The tank occupies the space of two LD3 containers at the front of the rear hold immediately aft of the MLG (main landing gear) bay. It holds 7200 litres (1,900 USG) of fuel, and extends 310-300 range by 400 nm/750 km.

To run over the A310's payload capacity, it naturally has the same body cross-section as its bigger ancestor, but fewer rows of seats and shorter underfloor holds. More than half the customers for longer-ranged versions fit fewer than 200 seats; Kenya, for example, has a three-class configuration 12 + 39 + 144 which adds ups to 195, and the Swiss 310-300s have only 172 seats. Most 310s seat 210 to 242, and the aircraft is certifiable up to 280. Under the floor it carries standard LD3 containers, the normal load in the front hold being eight and in the rear hold six, plus an optional position for a seventh LD3 or LD1, making a normal maximum of 15 LD3s. Bulk cargo capacity is 17.3m^3 (611 cu ft), or 8.6 m^3 (303 cu ft) with a 15th LD3. The standard 106-in (2.69-m) wide door to the forward hold means that three 88-in or 96-in × 125-in pallets can be loaded, reducing turnaround times. The A310-200 and -300 are also available in C (convertible) and F (freighter) versions. Both these have the same large upper-deck cargo door as is fitted to the A300C and F, with a width of 3.58 m (11 ft 9 in). This enables a single operator to load up to 16 standard 88 × 125 pallets on to the cargo floor. Weight-limited capacity of the 310C is normally 36.8 *tonnes* (81,220 lb), and that of the F is 39.4 *tonnes* (86,860 lb).

The dramatically new cockpit, first put into service in an earlier form on the bigger A300s of Garuda and Tunis Air, has already been discussed at length. It is still worth repeating that, far from being a revolutionary collection of gimmicks, the A310 FFCC (forward-facing crew cockpit) was from the start designed as a totally integrated workplace in the most intimate collaboration with AI and customer pilots. At all times the basic design principle was to achieve the most perfect symbiosis, or communication, between the two pilots and the entire aircraft. Crew workload, with just two pilots, is actually very much less than with the former crew of three, though such a factor is hard to quantify in numbers. It is minimized by: combining the functions of control, visual feedback and visual malfunction alert by the simplest means possible (pushbuttons); eliminating all visual warning lights (the 'lights out' philosophy) except in times of real emergency; introducing basic system automation, whilst leaving the crew complete freedom to carry out any manual monitoring they wish; fully applying the 'need to know' concept via digital technology; reducing the need for pilot action by giving clear feedback information for flight-guidance and system operation; introducing an unprecedentedly comprehensive digital flight-management system; and providing six large colour CRTs (cathode-ray tubes) as interactive displays for flight guidance and data and also for total systems-monitoring.

So far the latest A310 sub-family are the Dash-300 series, already briefly referred to. When first announced in early 1982 as the longest-ranged member of the family, the 310-300 was slightly misconstrued by most of the media. To quote the British monthly *Air International*, for example, 'As the wing of the basic A310 is already full of fuel, Airbus had to find space for the extra capacity in a cargo hold, the fin or the tailplane, and has chosen the last-mentioned alternative.' This puts the cart slightly before the horse. Putting fuel in the tailplane is not a last resort but an excellent idea for other reasons, which in due course must become common jetliner practice.

To go back to 1958, in that year the author conducted a campaign, which at times generated more heat than light, to try to get designers of all aircraft, and especially of commercial jets, to remember that the traditional configuration has fundamental shortcomings. In cruising flight the aircraft CG (centre of gravity) is ahead of the centre of lift of the wings. Thus, the aircraft would enter a dive or outside loop, were it not for a continuous down-load applied by the elevators or, more often in the case of modern jets, by the trimming tailplane. Pushing down at the tail may hold the aircraft in level flight, but it is nonsense deliberately and continuously to make the aircraft 'heavier' than it actually is. Wing angle of attack has to be increased, adding to drag, and at all times more engine power is needed for a given cruising speed. Moreover, at takeoff and landing the aircraft is deliberately rotated nose-up not by lifting the nose but by forcing down the tail. Thus, a further (and very large) download is applied just when the aircraft most needs forces that lift it, instead of forces that try to push it downwards.

As long as we have tailplanes instead of foreplanes we can do nothing about the powerful downward force applied at takeoff and landing, but we certainly can do something about the downward force needed to trim the aircraft in cruising flight. Ironically, the first time anyone eliminated trim drag in a commercial transport the subject was the first airliner in service without a horizontal tail: the Concorde SST. This was a special case, because as an aeroplane accelerates from subsonic to supersonic speed the centre of lift of the wings migrates rearwards, sharply increasing the nose-down trim change. In Concorde it would have been intolerable to trim this nose-down pitching moment with continuous upward deflection of the trailing-edge elevons; drag would have been so great there would have been no possibility of carrying payload. Instead, and obviously, a fuel tank was built into the tailcone of the fuselage and the fuel system so arranged that, during transonic acceleration, about 12,730 litres (2,800 Imp gal) of fuel was pumped aft into this previously empty tank. At the end of supersonic cruise the fuel was pumped forwards

Right *First takeoff by the first Dash-300 of Dubai-based Emirates, featured on pp 84–85 of Osprey's picture-book* Big Jets

Centre *Another early operator of the wingtip-fenced A310-300 is Air India, previously a customer for the A300B and today waiting for a big fleet of A320s*

Below *Take off by* Albert Cuyp, *one of the ten 310-200s of KLM Royal Dutch Airlines. This fleet have CF6-80A engines*

again. This transfer of mass almost perfectly cancelled out the trim-change caused by migration of the centre of lift.

In a subsonic transport there is very little migration in wing lift, but there remains the continuous problem of the need for a downward force on the tail. In the latest fighters this drawback is eliminated, partly by using a foreplane thrusting upwards instead of a tailplane thrusting downwards, and partly by boldly throwing all previous notions of stability overboard and designing the aircraft to be inherently unstable. Suppose, instead of rotating the tailplane to give a downward force we instead add a heavy weight in the tail. We then get the download but without any extra drag. The obvious kind of weight to add is fuel, because this can be moved about to vary the CG position, and it is something we need to carry anyway.

The research into use of fuel as a trimming medium was carried out in a programme known as ACCTA by the German AI partner MBB, in collaboration with the German research establishment DFVLR. It involved careful computation of rearward shift in CG position, the resulting reduced stability of the aircraft, and the best way to arrange for the necessary changes in the fuel system. The objective was to move the CG to a point just aft of the centre of lift of the wing. In this condition the unaided aircraft would always tend to loop. To resist the tendency all we need do is reset the trimming tailplane to give just enough upthrust to keep the fuselage level. This upthrust helps lift the aircraft, and means that angle of attack of the wing in cruising flight can be reduced, thus reducing drag.

In the 310 the tailplane is a Spanish responsibility, but most of the new design work for the Dash-300 was done by MBB. The entire structural box of the tailplane was strengthened and sealed in exactly the same way as the wing box, to become an integral tank. Like the fin, this structural box is ideal for the purpose, because it is already there, needs very little modification, is far from the CG (thus having a powerful effect on trim) and outside the pressurized fuselage. There was no difficulty in installing the required electrically driven pumps, contents-measuring system and venting system, all inside the Dash-300 tailplane. Connections between the trim tank and the main wing fuel system are provided by double-walled pipes.

Usable capacity of the tailplane tank is 5 *tonnes* (6,200 litres, 1,363 Imp gal). The 5-*tonne* mass acting right at the tail shifts the CG over 12 to 16 per cent of the aerodynamic chord, or 80 per cent of the total CG range. Control of CG is automatic; a trim-tank computer controls and monitors the preset CG positions on the ground and in flight. The pilots also have the ability to monitor CG position, and effect manual control at all times. MBB UT (Transport Aircraft Group) in Hamburg estimate that a Dash-300 would, over an operating life of 20 years, burn 8,000,000 litres fuel less than a Dash-200 flying the same sectors. So detailed were the many calculations of improved efficiency and economy that the extra range seemed almost incidental, yet this is the factor that most people think of exclusively when considering this version.

Other partners made a contribution to the Dash-300, including Aérospatiale, who had experience with the only previous fuel-trimming system, that of Concorde. New software was written for the AFCS/FMS to ensure that trim would be optimized from takeoff to landing, without the need for pilot action. But many other advances were built into this new variant. A completely new CFRP fin was designed and produced by MBB, at the Stade plant in Lower Saxony. This is the first carbon-fibre tail surface to enter production on any airliner. It saves 22 per cent in weight (310 lb, 140 kg) and, as it has 96 parts instead of 2,072, it also effects an overall saving in cost despite the high price of CFRP. An even greater saving in weight resulted from the introduction of carbon brakes, which will become standard on all future Airbuses. The cockpit was further updated to what AI calls the ergonomically superior New World layout. And there was also a modification visible externally: winglets.

Winglets, or as AI calls them 'wingtip fences', are not aerodynamic crutches needed to improve airflow across an imperfect wing. Instead they are a means of extracting as much as possible of the energy otherwise wasted in generating powerful vortices which stream away behind the tips of the wings. In the largest jetliners the power in these vortices near the airport can reach several thousand horsepower, and they can pose a formidable and quite long-enduring wake hazard to aircraft following the big jet on the approach. The basic mechanism generating the vortex stems from the fact that pressure under the wing tends to be above that of the local atmosphere and to spill outwards, while that above the wing is naturally well below that of the local atmosphere and tends to draw airflow inwards across the tip. There is thus a powerful rotation around the tip from below to above the wing, and the higher the wing loading (aircraft weight divided by wing area) the greater the intensity of this rotation. It is especially acute in tight turns and other manoeuvres imposing positive G, and especially in the high-lift configuration at high angles of attack.

It is only in the past decade that it has become common to try to do something to minimize this energy loss, not so much to reduce the wake hazard near the airport but to reduce cruising drag, which in the ultimate has to be accounted for in extra fuel burned. There are several ways in which the vortex can be reduced, but the simplest methods involve adding one or more aerodynamic surfaces projecting from the tip. Sometimes the projection is a winglet, an extension of the tip curved sharply upwards and countering the vortex rotation. Sometimes there are several small fin-like projections from a streamlined pod on the tip. AI's initial answer was an elegant and quite small (30-in, 0.75-m) vertical tip fin looking rather like a delta wing on its side. It weighed very little, and on test with an A300-600 demonstrated a saving in cruise fuel consumption of about 1.5 per cent. For the A310-300 British Aerospace designed a larger and more effective tip fence, with a vertical span of 55 in (1.4 m) and a rear nav-light fairing. This reduces cruise fuel by over 1.5 per cent. It was first flown on the A310 on 1 August 1984. Standard on the Dash-300, it became standard on the -200 also from summer 1986. There are prospects for refining this tip fence, or winglet, still further.

All A310s from mid-1986 have the weight-saving carbon brakes, the pads and discs actually being made of a composite of carbon-fibre reinforced carbon! The weight saving is dramatic, equivalent to four or five passengers and their baggage. These new brakes also offer much greater life than traditional steel brakes. At the time of writing, one of the latest new features for the 310-300, and optionally for the -200, is the fitting of radial tyres to the main landing gear. Carbon brakes and radial tyres have performed admirably in the severest of all landing-gear tests routinely made on completed jetliners, the RTO (rejected takeoff) at maximum energy. This involves abandoning the takeoff at the last split second, at the highest possible speed, at maximum overload weight, in hot/high-altitude temperature conditions, all of which greatly augment the kinetic energy in the aircraft which must be entirely dissipated. Virtually the whole of that energy goes into heating the small mass of the carbon brakes and disc pads to almost white heat, though some is absorbed as heat in the deflection of the tyres which must transmit the severe drag force from the runway without slip.

The first 310-300, with 7R4E engines, began a brilliantly successful test programme on 8 July 1985. The first to be powered by the new CF6-80C2 engine flew on 6 September 1985. Certification followed in December 1985 for the P&W engine and February 1986 with the GE. It is unlikely ever to become available with Rolls-Royce engines, and this is particularly unfortunate because the latest installed D4D engine has the lowest fuel burn, and the best performance retention, of any of the big turbofan engines. Altogether the 'little' 310 has grown to have capability far surpassing that of even the earlier A300Bs. In the author's view, the Dash-300 is the most efficient high-technology twin-aisle transport in the sky today.

4

PEOPLE AND PLACES

THIS IS A BOOK ABOUT AIRCRAFT. To an exceptional degree it is also a book about the organization which created them, called Airbus Industrie, so it must also be a book about people and places. Unlike most planemakers AI is not just one giant manufacturing plant, where workers swarm like ants all speaking the same language. AI is lots of plants, scattered throughout Western Europe. Though the professional engineers tend to do nearly all their business in English, which happens to be the *lingua franca* of aviation, the people who actually build Airbuses speak English, French, German, Dutch, Flemish, Spanish, American, Australian, Italian, Swedish, Norwegian, South Korean and many other tongues, not forgetting Welsh.

This list covers 13 countries where things are built that go into each Airbus. Within the companies that make up AI one finds many more nationalities. On one visit to Toulouse the author sat down with Stuart Parker, the senior General Electric representative, and compiled a list of nationalities of people personally known to us at that one location. The total added up to 39, including a Chinese whose job was checking decals and stencils in that language. Obviously, the real total must have been higher.

At the start of the long haul to build AI its many detractors might have used this information to create a picture resembling a Tower of Babel. How could hundreds of 'foreigners', each with their own contrasting ideas, backgrounds, beliefs, working methods, working pace and language—to say nothing of bitter memories of past wars between their countries—possibly become knit into a tightly integrated computerized team able to rival the almost inhumanly efficient giants who are AI's rivals? Surely the principals, France and Germany, would try to score off each other? Surely the British would be on strike? Surely the Spaniards would enjoy their siesta in the sunshine, thinking that the next tailplane could always wait until mañana? Surely there would be trouble in Belgium, because of the bitter rivalry between the different language groups (and the AI work could hardly be shared out evenly between them)? Surely it would be economic nonsense to ship wing ribs all the way from Australia? Even more ludicrous, how could anyone hope to make money by rolling and stretch-levelling giant slabs of alloy in Davenport, Iowa, in the American Midwest, ship them to England, truck them to Chester, machine them into wing skins, truck them to Manchester, fly them to Bremen, fasten on movable surfaces made at Amsterdam, Brussels or Charleroi, fly the completed wings to Toulouse, bolt them on to the aircraft, and then use the wings to fly the 'green' aircraft to Hamburg for completion? And if Pratt & Whitney had an engine to ship from Connecticut, would they not always give priority to a US planemaker?

Even within AI there was a lot of rather lighthearted banter about whether or not all the parts from all the factories really would fit together. Underlying it was a nagging germ of a real problem. Making giant aeroplanes is a complex business. It makes a difference whether a wing skin or a keel member is manufactured lying east/west or north/south. It makes a difference if a door made in scorching Spain fits (or fails to fit) a door frame made in freezing Germany. And how can one be sure that slat sections 75 ft (23 m) long are going to fit *precisely* on to their powered arms along the very rigid front spar?

In the event not one of the real or imagined problems ever reared its head, though perhaps AI did try harder than absolutely necessary to avoid them. Despite universal use of computer-controlled NC (numerical control) machining, the decision was taken to put each wing box in a giant fixture and precision-machine right round the root to ensure a perfect fit on the centre section and fuselage side. With the A310 only the lower part of the root is machined, and it may prove possible to eliminate root machining entirely. But this is a mere detail. More important are the underlying management philosophies.

In the first chapter it was related how France tried to insist on 'design leadership on the airframe'. In those early days before 1970 not many people had much experience of international collaboration in aircraft design and development. Many—especially, the author felt, in France—genuinely believed that one of the partner countries, or partner companies, could or indeed should have such leadership assigned by mutual agreement. They would then no longer be an equal but a superior, able if necessary to order the other partners what to do, and to take unilateral decisions regarding almost any aspect of the programme. Today we can see that, had this been allowed to happen, while it might not have been a recipe for immediate disaster, at least it would have thrown away one of the greatest benefits of a collaborative programme. This benefit is to bring fresh minds to each problem, with contrasting answers, and to talk each problem through until everyone is agreed on the best course of action.

From the very start AI has held Chief Engineers' Meetings at which every thorny technical problem is thrashed out in this way. Depending on the agenda, the best brains available in the partner companies on the particular topics to be discussed can be flown in to each meeting—and they usually are. Roger Béteille has no doubt whatever that these concentrations of highly competitive brainpower were the main, if not the sole, reason why the A300B and A310 are the only big jetliners never to

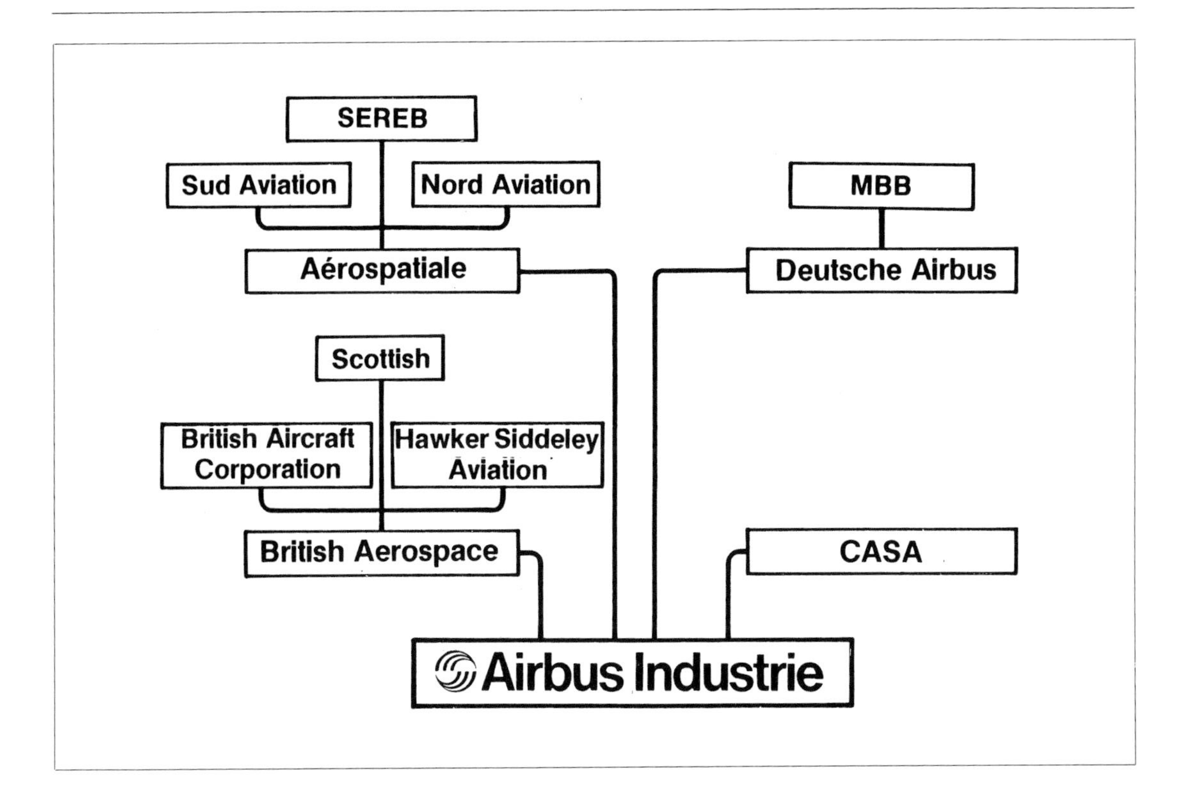

Above *The basic family tree of Airbus Industrie's main shareholders. Fokker and Belairbus are associates, some Deutsche Airbus work is subcontracted to Italy and some BAe work to Australia*

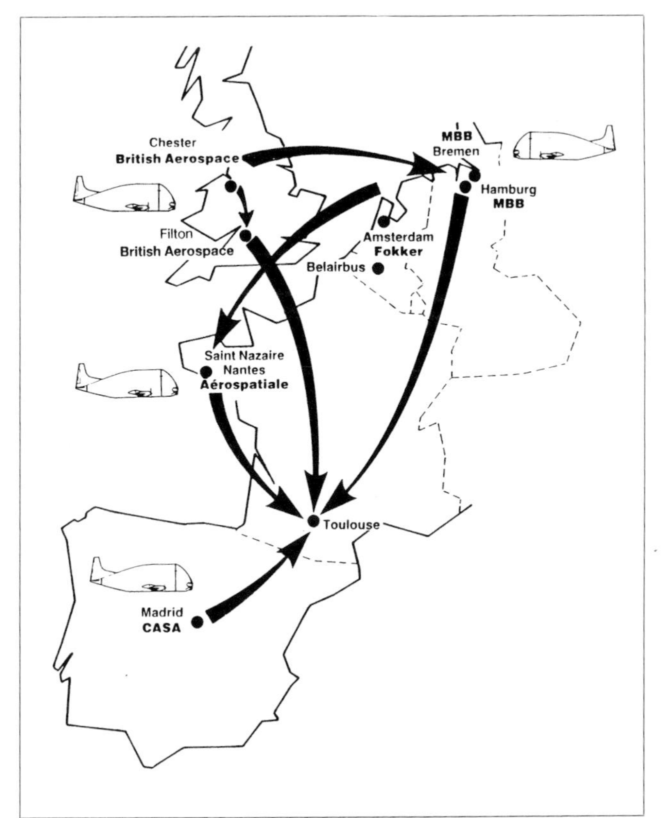

Right *Super Guppies shuttle the completed fuselage, wing, tail and other parts from the manufacturer to the Toulouse assembly line. Chester makes wing boxes, completed at Bremen or (for the 320) Filton*

have been grounded, nor hurt a single passenger. As an example, Béteille cited the case of an MBB engineer who reported in detail on the catastrophic consequences of explosive decompression of an underfloor cargo hold, resulting in downward collapse of the main floor and loss of control of the aircraft. As a result the A300B was made proof against such an event two years before the horrific DC-10 crash at the Forêt d'Ermenonville.

There is another and less weighty pronouncement by Béteille. At a time when he and Bernard Lathière had spent ten years together, respectively as Executive V-P and General Manager, and President and Chief Executive Officer, he said 'Bernard and I have only disagreed five times, and one of those was because he insists on red ties and I wear white ones'.

At the start of the programme the problems were bigger ones. It was a blessing in disguise that the ebullient French tried to call the tune, because by insisting on the final assembly line being at Toulouse they solved one potentially giant problem that never occurred to anyone at the time. Airbuses take up a fair amount of sky, and at almost all the other AI plants the sky above is full of lousy weather, criss-crossed by airways, and crowded with all kinds of traffic at all flight levels. At Toulouse-Blagnac each test flight climbs out, usually into a beautiful sky, with nothing much to get in the way until one meets the peaks of the Pyrenees and the Spanish frontier (where some of the best publicity photographs are taken, as this book shows). Bernard Ziegler said 'This is surely the only airspace left in Western Europe where we have such freedom to plan each flight without having to worry about conflicting traffic.'

Such a halcyon environment is certainly not the daily lot of the trucking crews who fly the Guppies. These are the vital swollen-bodied vehicles which spend their lives shuttling all the major Airbus bits between the various factories. These aircraft stemmed from the succession of grotesquely enlarged rebuilds of Boeing 377s (civil Stratocruisers and military KC-97s) created by Aero Spacelines, run by former Boeing test pilot A M 'Tex' Johnston. The purpose of the various Guppies was to transport the stages of giant space boosters between NASA contractors and launch pads, but they were soon found to have many other attractions in carrying outsize loads. Biggest of all was the Commercial Super Guppy 201, originally built to fly DC-10 fuselages from Convair and TriStar wings from Avco Aerostructures at Nashville. Stretched wildly in all directions, these machines are powered by four Allison 501-D22C turboprops, each rated at 4,912 shp with water injection, driving very broad-blade Hamilton propellers. The vast fuselage has a fairly short (32-ft, 9.75-m) section with a roughly circular interior with width and height of about 25 ft 6 in (7.77 m). This is considerably greater than anything available in any other aircraft, and it is amply big enough for a pair of A300B wings or sections of fuselage.

Though there are small doors low on the right side at nose and tail, all cargo is loaded through the nose. The entire gigantic front end of the Super Guppy hinges open to the left through 110 degrees, driven round by a small powered wheel which is lowered to the ground both for this purpose, and also to support the right side of the nose after the fuselage connections are broken. All the major airframe partners have built or purchased special trailers and tugs for ground-handling the giant Airbus components. In each case the sections of airframe are safely and securely held in cradles resting on a giant tray whose height can be varied through 10 ft (3 m) or more by scissors links and hydraulic jacks. This is necessary in order to match the platform height exactly to that of the lofty Super Guppy floor level.

Though fuselage sections may look bulkier, the heaviest loads are the wings. A ship-set of left and right wing boxes is loaded at the Chester factory on to a trailer over 15 ft (4.57 m) high. At the root the wings are over 18 ft 6 in (5.63 m) wide (considerably wider than two buses side-by-side), and the tractor and trailer have a combined length of over 94 ft 6 in (28.8 m), weighing 50 long tons. At Manchester Airport the massive load is precisely aligned with the Super Guppy and the wings are winched horizontally aboard as one unit. This is one of the heaviest loads, and CG position is much further forward than the ideal. Even with both pilots hauling hard back there is a virtual certainty that the monster will hit the Bremen runway nosewheels-first, so the nose gear is of 707 type.

AI began operations with a single Super Guppy, but soon acquired a second. Aero Spacelines went out of business, becoming Tracor Aviation, after selling AI the drawings and production rights of the Super Guppy 201. In the late 1970s the two Guppies were hard-pressed to carry the increasingly frequent loads, despite a sustained round-the-clock effort by the operator, Aéromaritime, the charter subsidiary of the French airline UTA to whom AI subcontract the whole trucking operation. Accordingly, AI contracted with UTA at Le Bourget, Paris, for the conversion of two more Super Guppy 201s in 1982 and 1983. There is no doubt that more 201s will be required in due course, especially when the smaller A320 is in full production.

Looking further ahead, the introduction of the A330 and A340 could well result in AI having an increased share of the twin-aisle market. Assuming the planned continuous updating of the A300 and A310, there will be a growing need for shuttling major airframe sections between the AI factories. Though basically a very old aircraft, with many features traceable right back to the World War 2 B-29 bomber, the Super Guppy 201 has an excellent record on AI business. This reflects great credit on Aéromaritime, who run a very tight operation with a minimum of fuss. It is extremely rare for any airframe component to be out of the production process for longer than 48 hours, and this is especially remarkable when one considers the often appalling weather in Northern Europe—and, incidentally, such factors as the short and narrow runways at some of the plants. It always surprised the author that British Aerospace never lengthened the main runway at Chester

Arrival of an A300B rear fuselage by Super Guppy from Hamburg. All the partners have broadly similar ground transporter trollies with scissors links to raise and lower the platform. The Super Guppy 201 is certified at 170,000 lb and cruises at about 250 mph

Super Guppies 1 and 4 together at Toulouse soon after No 4 went into action in August 1983. Looking almost like airships, they surely flout the laws of aerodynamics?

from the wartime 4,715 ft (1,437 m), to avoid the need to take wings by road to Manchester. Of course, despite the existence of the so-called EEC and 'Common Market', it is still necessary to clear customs when leaving or entering Britain and most other EEC countries. No duty is charged on, for example, Airbus wings leaving Manchester or arriving at Bremen, but national treasuries often like to inflate figures for trade and income, and the UK monthly return of export statistics does include the book value of Airbus wings, which is perfectly reasonable. Occasionally, however, the picture becomes slightly distorted, and one example is the appearance of West Germany as by far the biggest 'importer' of British 'aircraft and parts' every month for many years past. A large part of this flow of 'exports' is due to the fact that Airbus wings do not go direct to Toulouse but to Bremen, where the secondary structures and movable surfaces are added. This increases the value of each wing by over 60 per cent, thus enabling West Germany to claim even bigger 'exports' to France when the Guppies take the completed wings on to Toulouse.

To an exceptional degree, every major airframe section arrives at Toulouse in a virtually finished state. No part can be absolutely finished, because there are some pipelines and electrical cables which are installed on the final assembly line, even though almost all of these have to have disconnections to permit a wing, tailplane or other part to be removed. From the start of the programme it looked as if the assembly line at Toulouse would be the one place where the proverbial shoe would pinch. The St Martin assembly hall is an old and not wholly suitable building, and part of it is actually used for making the Airbus nose and cockpit sections—what Boeing call the cab section—and there is room for just one assembly line with nine stations. At the start it was predicted that a likely limit on production rate would be four per month; should demand exceed this rate, a second assembly line was expected to be needed in Germany.

It did not work out this way. Thanks to brilliant work by the AI design, planning and production engineers, the single short line at Toulouse-St Martin has coped with every demand made upon it, and at times the output has been close to eight per month. This has been made possible almost entirely because of the near-finished state in which everything arrives at Toulouse. The colloquial word is 'stuffed'; each major wing or fuselage section arrives complete with many thousands of wires, cables, pipelines, ducts and functioning parts such as valves, actuators and linkages. It would be grossly inaccurate to claim that all the Toulouse assembly fitters have to do is get things lined up and then insert a few bolts, but the fact that the whole process of final assembly accounts for only 4.0 per cent of the total man-hours and costs in building each aircraft speaks for itself.

From 1979 onwards all the AI partner companies have made exceedingly large financial investments in their design and manufacturing operations to improve efficiency and reduce costs. In every production programme there is always a learning curve which, by the inevitable process of education, familiarity and experience, brings down the time and cost needed to build each successive aircraft. There are no 'AI' figures, for reasons explained earlier, but each partner has published in the fullest detail how his own learning curve has progressed. MBB, for example, needed 340,000 man-hours to build the fuselage sections of the first A300B1. By the 75th aircraft the figure had dropped to 85,000, and the company nearly reached its ultimate target of 43,000, at which level it remains. Later in this chapter the remarkable changes that have taken place at all the partner factories will be examined in more detail.

From the start there was a conscious effort to restrict the number of AI staff. The AI partner companies employ well over 150,000 people, of whom some 23,000 work directly on AI production. Of the latter figure about 98 per cent are company personnel at company sites; only about 2.5 per cent are seconded to AI in Toulouse. A larger number on the marketing and support side have offices in different parts of the world. Special mention is also made later of Aeroformation, the AI training organization, and ASCO (Airbus Service Company Inc). There is thus a substantial movement of personnel between AI partner companies, the objective being always to put the best person into each slot at the right time. Durations of assignments vary, but because moving a whole family is fairly traumatic the period is seldom less than three years and may be much longer.

One of the ongoing problems has been personal finance. Houses and apartments vary considerably in price in different parts of Europe, and even within individual countries. So too do salaries, and varying inflation, especially in 1977–79 in Britain, threatened to make nonsense of carefully structured salary scales. In the case of a Briton assigned to Toulouse in the mid-1970s the simple rule was 'multiply his salary by three'. This compensated for the greater French cost of living, with a bit on the side that just about covered the removals expenses for the few who brought their household effects. After 1979 the differential was cut by half, but there are still major factors to be applied, the biggest being Spanish staff from CASA where the salary multiplier can be ×4.

Most of the early importees were fairly multilingual, though often with excruciating French accents. As the number of families built up, so did the problem of schooling become highly visible. By 1980 large numbers—fluctuating around the 100 level—of basically English-speaking children had nowhere to go but the Paul Bert II primary (junior) school and the Lycée International Victor Hugo. Without good command of French they found it hard to learn, and their parents were worried at the progressive erosion of their native tongue. This was the situation when in 1980 Alan and Mary Lee arrived from Hatfield. Soon they set up an organization from among AI parents for qualified teachers—almost all of them AI staff or wives—to hold classes in written and spoken English outside normal school hours, and this snowballed

Some idea of the enthusiasm behind every Airbus comes through in this picture of the first A320 wing coming out of its jig on 3 October 1983. Unlike other parts the 320 wing boxes go by road to Filton for completion

The A310 static-test airframe appears to be shouting with pain as its wings suffer 1.67 times the maximum design load without breaking in June 1984. This test programme was performed by CEAT Toulouse

rapidly. With the collaboration of the French education authorities this became formalized as system English 31, and it became fully integrated into both the schools just mentioned. Several hundred children from all sorts of countries, including Kenya, the USA, Venezuela, Israel and France itself, now receive a full-time French education plus reinforced English and other subjects related to British culture. A surprisingly high proportion of pupils also learn the other AI languages, especially German and Spanish. London University has accepted the Lycée as an overseas GCE examination centre, and so far over 80 of the first 100 examinations were successful.

This chapter has already indicated that 1979–80 was a turning point in the AI story. In that period the sales-famine at last came to an end, production rates began to increase to more sensibly economic levels, white tails (aircraft completed but unsold) began to find ready buyers, and firm plans could be made to invest the kind of money needed to go forward boldly through the 1980s. To a small degree the extra investment was needed to integrate the A310, though this was on a massive scale only at British Aerospace. In most of the plants the investment was needed to replace outmoded methods, increase production rates and introduce new technology and new materials.

Hawker Siddeley clinched a deal which restored their investment on delivery of wing set No 25. In 1978–84 British Aerospace invested a further £250 million, partly in increasing the number of A300 wing jigs from four pairs to eight and partly in increasing the number of A310 wing jigs from zero to six pairs. Further investment was needed to enable Hurn, near Bournemouth, to build the 310 leading edge (not the slat, of course), and Filton, Bristol, to supply the rear-spar shrouds which fair-in all the rear movable surfaces. Yet more investment was needed to bring in Brough on Humberside, Chadderton near Manchester, and Hatfield.

Aérospatiale's Aircraft Division builds major elements of all AI aircraft at Nantes-Bouguenais (rear cockpit and centre wing box) and at Saint Nazaire (lower centre fuselage), as well as the nose and cab sections and other small parts which are made at Meaulte, Les Mureaux and Bourges. In 1980 alone Aérospatiale invested almost 400 million FF in improved facilities for A300 and A310 production, and this has since been multiplied several times over to bring in the new A320 programme. The massive capital expenditures, paralleled by BAe and MBB, have largely been required for new NC (numerically controlled) milling and riveting machines, the Drivmatics being especially important to BAe, while surface-treatment installations have been another major area of expenditure. Not least, all partners have had to modernize existing buildings or, as at BAe Bristol, invest in new ones.

No partner has done more to streamline its operation than MBB's UT (Transport Group), which is today the effective operating element of Deutsche Airbus. UT has over 2,000 engineers and technicians working on the A300 and 310, with the 320 now also 'coming on stream'. In 1982–86 MBB totally rearranged its plants throughout northern Germany, several of which used to call themselves VFW, converting them into one of the most advanced, automated and efficient manufacturing complexes in the world. There are six plants, all in the Elbe/Weser area, employing 16,500 people. Each has become a specialist in one field: Einswarden for fuselage panels, Bremen for sheet-metal parts, Varel for machining, Stade (Lower Saxony) for CFRP and other composites, Hamburg Finkenwerder for all fuselage assembly and cabin furnishing, and Lemwerder for product support and modification retrofit. This rationalization, which has almost resulted in six new factories, avoids duplication and makes much better use of jigs and tooling, with a neat streamline flow of (at any one time) about 11 million separate parts within and between the six plants.

Each factory's facilities are applied to performing similar tasks for all the types of aircraft made by MBB. Einswarden, for example, has batteries of computerized machines which, depending on the software fed in, produce fuselage panels for A300-600s, A310s, A320s or Fokker 100s! Apart from initial positioning at the first station, all riveting is automatic. Each panel travels round the plant hung from a small overhead-rail carriage, semi-completed panels being housed in a computer-controlled buffer store. Completed panels go by truck to Finkenwerder, where they join an identical overhead-rail system until repeated joints have turned them into complete sections of fuselage which are so heavy they must be moved by semi-automated cranes which precisely position them in their jigs for further assembly, before going aboard the Guppy. Among many other developments at MBB's UT are automatic tape-winding and curing of advanced CFRP parts at Stade, which is now producing complete CFRP fins for 310-300s—largest composite primary structure in Europe—a computer-controlled flow system at Varel, and factory-floor robots at Bremen for transport of small parts between work-stations.

Fokker has installed a mass of totally new high-technology plant for the manufacture of the 310's CFRP main-leg doors and flap-track fairings, all-speed ailerons and wingtips. CASA, at Getafe outside Madrid, has gone even further in CFRP production facilities, but these are almost entirely for the A320 and are discussed in that chapter. On the A300-600 and A310 CASA supplies almost exclusively aluminium-alloy parts, many of the components of which are manufactured by the Spanish partner's other works at Seville and Cadiz. Among CASA's responsibilities are the complete horizontal tail, forward passenger doors and the undercarriage bay doors hinged to the fuselage.

Though Aérospatiale accounts for only a minor proportion of the actual manufacture of each Airbus, and a mere 4 per cent in final assembly, this major AI partner makes up its full quota with such tasks as final checking, painting, test flying and many related duties. The author was staggered when, one day in 1978, he blundered into the new paint shop at Toulouse. Previously aircraft painting had been rather a hand-to-mouth affair, but Aérospatiale built a new hall specifically for this purpose. A controlled atmosphere, moving past the aircraft at a controlled speed, and a high-voltage electrostatic attraction, ensure perfect working conditions in which virtually each microscopic globule of paint goes exactly where it is intended. The operators occupy cabs suspended from the lofty ceiling on vast telescopic arms about 66-ft (20-m) long. At the touch of a button, or if necessary under computer control, their cab can rise 30 ft, travel 100 ft sideways or rotate. Suppose the customer requires a red cheatline strip starting at a particular point on the nose and climbing in a curve along the fuselage to end at the top of the fin. This can be programmed so that it comes out right first time. Usually there are five different coats of paint, each of precisely controlled thickness adding up to 0.1 mm, yet weighing some 880 lb (400 kg) and with an outer surface like glass. Never were commercial transports, or any other aircraft for that matter, painted with such pristine perfection and lack of bother.

Curiously, while the new Airbus may be brilliantly coloured externally, it is still officially ‘a green airplane’. In other words it lacks all its interior furnishing, and probably lacks most of its customer-specified avionics, though it must have sufficient navaids and communications for safe flight in the worst weather and a final ILS letdown to the cramped runway at Hamburg Finkenwerder. Since aircraft No 21, the first A300 for Lufthansa delivered in February 1976, every Airbus has been flown from Toulouse to Finkenwerder for customer furnishing. This MBB factory stores some 300,000 parts ready to go inside otherwise completed Airbuses. Some 70 customers on every continent have rung the changes in every way possible, and many have asked for truly customized interiors.

In fitting out each aircraft Finkenwerder installs—apart from doors and windows—every single item that the passenger sees or touches inside the aircraft. The work starts with thermal insulation, noise insulation, wall cladding, door cladding, floor cladding, partitions, bulkheads and various kinds of ceilings. Then come massive lighting installations, overhead storage bins, individual fresh-air ‘punkah louvres’ and individual reading lights and call buttons, entertainment systems with music and films on 12 channels, and, not least, galleys, toilets and seat units. Numerous contrasting types of kitchen and toilet equipment have been specified by different customers. Nobody has yet asked for galleys or toilets to be below the floor, though in theory this has always been possible, at a penalty in reduced cargo capacity. Indeed, there have even been studies for underfloor passenger cabins. Each airline has its own ideas about fabrics, colour schemes, logos, seat design and on the desirability of a central row of overhead stowage bins. The A310s of Sabena, a typical member of the ATLAS group, has 18 First-Class seats at the front, 193 Economy in the main cabin (211 in all), four galleys, five toilets and nine seats for cabin crew.

The 310, incidentally, started off with an even higher standard of comfort than the

300, including 70 per cent more passenger headroom when opening overhead bin doors, considerably more capacious overhead bins on a per-passenger basis, and many other features giving greater comfort, resulting from a redesign of the entire cabin. The 310 was also the first aircraft in the world to anticipate the new and more stringent certification requirements for furnishing fabrics subjected to extremely hot flames. Long before any legislation made it mandatory, the first 310 was completed with fabrics throughout the cabin which easily meet all requirements for fumes and toxic-gas emission. It was also one of the first aircraft to make it virtually impossible for anyone to open a passenger door with the escape slide armed, unless they really mean it! Altogether, the process of furnishing a 300 or a 310 adds more than 27,000 parts with over 28,000 joining elements.

This is the point at which to take a look at another MBB operation, at Hamburg Fuhlsbüttel (which is the city's airport). This is Airspares, the AI Spares Support Centre. Here is a most impressive Airbus spare-parts warehouse; it is gigantic in scale (231,000 m^3, 8,200,000 sq ft), and appears to work with supreme efficiency. Over 500,000 types of spares are held continuously, and via satellite links to Washington and Hong Kong other sources can be tapped within minutes. The service operates 24 hours a day, 365 days a year. The whole operation is totally computerized, including the AIMS (Airbus Inventory Management System) and OTS (On-line telecommunications system) which provide the necessary management backups.

Two years before a new customer's first A300, A310 or A320 takes up service, Airspares recommends an initial spares inventory tailored to the airline's needs. This initial stock should permit as many repairs as possible to be completed without ordering parts, yet be as small as possible to keep investment at a minimum. With certain parts, providing 2 per cent greater probability of immediate repair can increase costs by as much as 20 per cent. In cases such as these, knowing which spares will probably be needed and which will not is the true art practised by the Airspares experts.

Flexibility and a wealth of experience are also mainstays of the AoG (Aircraft on Ground) Service, likewise manned 24 hours a day, 365 days a year, at Hamburg-Fuhlsbüttel Airport. Airspares guarantees that urgent requests for any part in stock will be filled within four hours of receipt, which means the part will be on its way to the customer in its prescribed special packing and accompanied by all the necessary documents within a few hours. The average time taken to fill orders at Airspares has actually been well below this limit for years.

Airspares is now equipping itself for future spares management tasks by adding another on-line telecommunication system to the Airbus Inventory Management System. This will enable computers from different airlines to place their spare-parts orders in direct communication with the Airspares computer. Further steps in order processing are to a large extent also automatic. For example, the semi-automatic multi-tier warehouse, which contains more than 90,000 different items, is equipped with a computer-controlled buffer warehouse which enables any item to be retrieved within three minutes.

At the very start of AI operations it was recognized that, not being American, the new group would have to 'try harder'. It was obvious—at least it was obvious to AI's farsighted people—that in such matters as provision for all-round support and training for customers the Europeans would have to be better than anything seen previously. Hardware support has already been discussed. Training is something else. Essentially limitless in its scope and diversity, it embraces flight crews, cabin crews, maintenance personnel, station staff and even people concerned with such areas as passenger or cargo services, marketing, stores management and safety provisions. Skin colour includes every hue known to humanity, and, despite the fact that every trainee is a well-educated selectee, language problems are often considerable.

Aérospatiale had wide training experience in the Caravelle programme, and AI could easily have just built on this. But by sheer chance in the early 1970s the company was linked with BAC of Britain in another programme, the Concorde. In almost all respects this aircraft was highly technical and very different from anything seen previously, and it was decided to form a special company to train Concorde customer personnel. Its name is Aeroformation, and as it is invariably pronounced in the English way it is written without an accent. The author has never managed to wrest himself away from the French pronunciation, because it is otherwise meaningless; the French *formation*, which sounds faintly like 'formassyon', means a moulding of character. The advice of Flight Safety International of the USA was sought, and for many years Aeroformation has been a GIE, like AI itself, owned 90 per cent by AI and 10 per cent by FSI. Almost from the start it was also involved with the A300B, and since the late 1970s AI products have pushed Concorde far into the background. Today it also handles training for the ATR 42 turboprop.

Aeroformation was planned by people with exceptional foresight, nerve and optimism. At a time when the only customer for its A300B services was Air France, which decided that Aeroformation should train just three three-man flight crews for each of its six aircraft then on order, the new organization was planned with an initial staff of over 150 housed in an impressive new building designed for the purpose at Toulouse-Blagnac. From the outset Aeroformation was as modern as the hour. Most of the instruction was done in individual student booths called Carels, equipped with the latest audio-visual aids enabling each student to work at his or her own pace whilst rapidly gaining in proficiency. Complex and often massive systems trainers duplicated every part of the A300B, sometimes to explain how things worked and often to permit 'hands-on' operator training. There were cockpit and maintenance panel procedures trainers, and a growing range of simulators, starting (where Airbus was concerned) with a six-axis LMT installation with external visuals which in those days were provided by a vidicon camera moving over a giant vertical landscape model reaching to the lofty ceiling.

It was found that each hour of a classroom course required about 150 hr of prior preparation by authors, draughtsmen and studio workers to prepare literature, slides and film, and this has increasingly extended to video and software specialists. Though there has seldom been a need for instant on-line translation, such as at the United Nations, there has always been a need for complete courses to be available in many customer languages. And, with the growth in AI's global success, Aeroformation's task has grown inexorably. Training has had to be made available in 17 languages so far, and from the A300B2 and B4 the number of aircraft types has grown to include the A300C and F, A300-600, A310-200 and -300, and A320. Various Airbus simulators have been bought (mostly from Thomson-CSF) by customer airlines, but the simulator centre at Toulouse has never ceased to expand, and the major simulators have played a central role in aircraft certification, being used to train certification crews and for the flight-deck workload analysis.

Of course, it is increasingly common practice for flight crews to be converted on to a new type of aircraft solely on the simulator, in what is often called the 'zero flight-time' technique. This was first done with closely related types, such as conversion from the 707 to the 727, and then perhaps from the 727 to the 737. Eastern, however, pioneered the zero flight-time method with the A300B, which was to a considerable degree unlike the 727, DC-9, L-1011 or any other Eastern type. The airline's very tightly timed introduction to the A300 was carried through entirely with training by Aeroformation. Then in 1980 Eastern's own A300B simulator became operational at Miami, initially as an FAA Phase I, but in March 1982 qualified as a Phase IIA simulator for total transition and upgrade training. Between March and September 1982 Eastern qualified 34 pilots on the A300 without any aircraft training whatsoever. At the time the airline's Director of Flight Crew Training was Capt Les Leech, who was also Chairman of the ATA Training Committee. In his view 'In the hectic introductory period Aeroformation provided what we needed, and all in the minimum time.' And, on the subject of zero flight-time conversions, he said 'We see no difference in proficiency between these pilots and those who are type-rated after actual flight training'.

Having got Eastern in intensive operation with 34 Airbuses, AI looked at its growing list of customers in the Americas and on 1 October 1985 opened its own Miami training centre run by ASCO (Airbus Service Co Inc). With Aeroformation's monitoring and assistance, it virtually duplicates Aeroformation's Toulouse operation on a smaller scale. It has all the expected aids, the main simulator being able to represent a B2 or a B4, with either GE or P&W engines, complying with full FAA Phase II standards for complete transition training within the simulator. The first courses were for PanAm flight and maintenance crews, but Miami has since supported many other A300B operators in both North and South America.

From 1980 Aeroformation has pioneered VACBI (video and computer-based instruction) in partnership with Control Data Corporation. This revolutionary development was introduced to support the A310, and at first comprised a large central computer linked to up to 90 terminals to provide individual self-paced instruction to any kind of trainee. Its software was based on Control Data's Plato (program logic for automatic teaching operations). It seemed futuristic, but the technology moved so fast that the last Plato-type VACBI was phased out in March 1986! In its place Aeroformation—initially for the ATR 42 turboprop transport, closely followed by the A310—worked with Control Data on a new-generation VACBI-C with flexibility never before approached.

Today the basic VACBI-C unit is a self-contained work station comprising an Ecrin-T microcomputer connected to a video-disk reader and TV monitor with full colour and animation, the interface being either a keyboard or a 'mouse'. Totally new software, called GSM (graphic simulation model) has much higher speed, is easy and attractive to use, and sets new standards of flexibility and efficiency. Thanks to a clear author language, no previous knowledge of computers is needed to write, modify or update a course. Thus each customer can have courses exactly tailored to his own aircraft. The new VACBI is arranged in three configurations. Stand-alone is for self-paced individual learning; trainees usually work one to a station for flight training and in pairs for maintenance courses. The cluster configuration consists of up to 15 stations connected to a file server. In late 1986 Aeroformation had 116 stations with five clusters interconnected to any of 20 terminals, three of the clusters being used for the A300-600, A310-200 and A310-300. In the third layout, the wide-angle VACBI, two giant concave screens are used for classroom instruction.

As this book was written, in late 1986, Kenya Airways and Air India were both deeply involved in A310-300 training, and—unusually—in both cases Aeroformation carried out extensive training in the customer's own country, using the actual aircraft. Kenya's base training was at Nairobi and Mombasa, involving OTJ (on the job) maintenance training and flight training of crews phased in with intensive scheduled flying. At Bombay Air India had to comply with special Indian regulations and not only do route-training but also night flying. In the author's view, it makes more economic sense to use Aeroformation's simulators and VACBIs at Toulouse!

People in Airbus naturally change all the time, but at the top there has been a notably happy and enduring management team. In 1986, however, important new appointments were announced, and today AI has a largely new 'first eleven' well equipped to take it into the 1990s. Chronologically the first new appointment was that of MBB's former V-P Engineering, Heribert Flosdorff, as AI Executive V-P and General Manager. A glider pilot for 30 years, Flosdorff held senior posts in the

Transall and Tornado programmes in addition to work on all the Airbus aircraft. In the same month Stuart Iddles was appointed AI Senior V-P Commercial. He was previously with Hawker Siddeley and BAe, notably on the 748 and ATP. On 1 March Angel Hurtado became AI Senior V-P Purchasing. CASA's first board appointee, Hurtado is an aeronautical engineer whose career has been spent instead in the fields of contracting and budgeting.

Finally, the two men who had led AI from the beginning, Lathière and Béteille, and who were unquestionably the architects of the whole enterprise, stepped down and welcomed their successors. Lathière's second five-year term as President ended on 4 February 1986, and for two months Béteille additionally assumed this office. Lathière's successor is Jean Pierson, previously Director of Aérospatiale's Aircraft Division and before that (1976–83) General Manager of the Toulouse plants. Lathière did not leave AI but became Supervisory Board Vice-Chairman, the long-serving Chairman being Dr Franz-Josef Strauss. Béteille's successor was Johann Schäffler, previously Managing Director of MBB's UT (Transport Aircraft Group). Both Pierson and Schäffler thus have for very many years had the closest possible managerial responsibility for Airbus programmes, and were the obvious choices, but Schäffler later left to become President of Dornier, his place being taken by Flosdorff. Dr Strauss commented that one of their first tasks would be to review AI's organization 'and to propose in due course such modifications as they may deem necessary'. There have not been many.

5

WIDEBODIES AT WORK

HISTORIANS MAY ONE DAY pin down the reasons for the utter failure of the world's airlines to evaluate either Airbus Industrie or its initial product until ten years had elapsed (1969–78). Then, and apparently entirely because of Eastern, AI at last began to be taken seriously. The author has only spoken to a few of the more obvious culprits, and none has yet come up with a convincing reason. There cannot have been anything wrong with the product. There cannot have been anything wrong with the organization behind it. Both have become tremendous successes.

Just to recap on the scale of the problem, AI sold four aircraft in 1974, nine in 1975, one in 1976 and only 41 from 1972 until early 1978. In the same period Boeing's jetliner sales exceeded 900, not one of these sales being of a short/medium-haul aircraft coming anywhere near the A300 in its ability to move people and cargo at low cost and with environmental acceptability.

The world's airlines are notoriously conservative and cautious—they have to be—and nobody wants to be first with an untried product from an untried manufacturer. Again, selling airliners is very much like selling silicon chips: in the latter business if you are selling a billion a week you will be deluged by customers wanting ten billion a week, but if you make only a million a week, sooner or later, you will go to the wall. In the same way, if you are Boeing, airlines will show no hesitation in queueing up to buy a new model. If you are anyone in Europe—before AI, that is—nobody would want to know, even if your new jet defied gravity and had no aerodynamic drag.

There is little point in speculating on this intriguing historical phenomenon. Any worries about the product, such as whether it was prudent to trust 300 people to two engines, have simply been answered by the past 16 years of unequalled technical success. Again, to regard AI as an 'untried manufacturer' (as it was described publicly by many airlines prior to 1978) is not merely ludicrously erroneous but insulting. Aérospatiale's Caravelle not only pioneered the whole idea of the short-haul jet but sold all over the world, including even mighty United, biggest airline in the non-Communist world and leader of those who today would pretend never to have heard of Toulouse no matter how good the product might be. As for British Aerospace, this has a proud record of jet and turboprop liners starting in 1948

(Viscount) and 1949 (Comet), in each case many years before any US manufacturer dared to move away from piston engines. The best answer must be that AI's first ten years were so conspicuously lacking in customer acceptance because of the cumulative effect of numerous real or fancied problems, all of which were later shown to be without foundation.

At the risk of belabouring the point, even the early 'sales' won by AI all too often turned out to be elusive. The first customers to be announced, in order, were: Air France, Lufthansa, Iberia, Sterling, SATA and Transbrasil, and of these all except the first two—in fact it was very nearly all except the first one—dropped out. Such problems continued to rear their head for a long time. Sometimes they involved purely political factors, sometimes the argument was over airline traffic rights, and sometimes it was over seemingly unrelated problems of international trade. Outstanding among the latter issues was Australia's government threat to withhold import licences for the A300s ordered by TAA in order to try to force the European Economic Community to allow more imports of Australian agricultural produce, especially of sheepmeat. This threatened ban was announced in July 1980 and was not rescinded until October, following an EEC promise that it would 'exercise restraint' in applying its trading laws. What this did to TAA's urgent A300 introductory planning can best be imagined, especially as the airline was spending A$7 million on an A300 hangar at Melbourne, 3.25 million for an engine test cell, 6.75 million for a simulator, 5.2 million for a new cabin services and support store, 6.4 million for A300 ground-support equipment, and many other infrastructure items which together came to A$36 million, quite apart from 12.5 million for CF6 engine spares and 11 million for engineering tools and equipment. Nobody today can simply go out and buy an airframe and start using it. Even if someone else pays for improvements at the airports, the capital costs of introducing a new type—especially one's first widebody—are astronomic. Uncertainty caused by inter-government hassle is simply not wanted.

Despite all the problems AI doggedly never gave up, and once it had captured Eastern the world airline community at last awoke. Curiously, operators the world over who had ignored the A300B performance on Air France and Lufthansa studied its performance with the US carrier with avid interest. Eastern's results could hardly have been better. Many figures have been given in earlier chapters. One of the toughest tasks was the even-hour operation by just two A300s of the NY La Guardia to Boston shuttle service. This began on 31 January 1980, and in its first four months (122 days) the two 280-seaters carried over 219,000 passengers in 1,506 flights. Though this is an average of just over 145 passengers, which could have been packed into a 727, there were 433 occasions when there were 178 or more passengers, saving the airline the cost of adding an extra section (backup flight) to carry the extra passengers. Jim Riordan of Eastern Air Shuttle said in summer 1980 'There's absolutely no doubt that the A300 has been a great aircraft for this type of operation'. The airline house magazine *Falcon* noted at the same time 'The A300 has won many friends' in a kind of operation perhaps nearer to the popular idea of an aerial bus than anything else.

By summer 1980 total deliveries of A300s exceeded 100, and in late June of that year total flight time exceeded 500,000 hours, in about 354,000 flights (which is far more gruelling than 500,000 hours of 747 operations, which would involve only about 70,000 takeoffs). The first four aircraft to pass the 10,000-hour mark were two B4s of Hapag Lloyd (one leased to Egyptair and the other being ex-Bavaria Germanair), the B1 of TEA and a B4-100 of Air France, while the first to pass the 10,000-takeoffs mark was a B2 of Lufthansa. In the author's view, after making a prolonged study of this question, no previous aircraft of any kind exhibited so few signs of age. No matter where you looked, at airframe fatigue, impact damage, surface scuffing and fretting, distortion of doors and hatches, all forms of corrosion, and wear and tear of systems, the A300s looked essentially 'as built' after passing the 10,000-hour mark. Of course, wear of cabin trim and furnishings is a different matter, depending on customer choice of fabrics and fitments and, to no small degree, on the behaviour of passengers and cabin crew. Even here the Airbuses showed up surprisingly well, considering that, compared with other widebodies, they took on fresh loads of passengers and cargo typically from three to six times as often. (With long-haulers such as the 310-300 the average sector distance is much greater.)

The largely ignored behaviour of the early B2s and B4s on Air France and Lufthansa was on the whole exceptional, almost all the major problems (such as inability of airports to process passengers on board to schedule) having nothing to do with the aircraft itself. Both these major operators quickly woke up to the tremendous cargo capacity, the underfloor bins holding much more than the total payload of an all-cargo 727, and the same was true of other early customers. In the calendar year from 1 April 1979 South African Airways' four B2Ks carried 16,772 *tonnes* of freight, as well as over 1.3 million passengers, while in the same period the six B2-100s of Indian Airlines carried 23,142 *tonnes* of cargo and 1.69 million passengers.

The million-flight-hours milestone was passed in March 1982. Unlike every other widebody—indeed, in all probability, unlike all previous civil transports—this point was reached without a single significant problem. From Day One on Air France the average technical dispatch reliability of all A300 operators has been 98.5–98.6 per cent, superior to that of any other widebody. As for costs, these are generally not published except in the USA, where CAB figures have consistently shown the A300 as having lower DOCs, and in particular lower maintenance costs, than all other widebodies in service. This influenced Capitol Air which in early 1984 began operating NY to Chicago, LA and Puerto Rico with two B4s leased from Hapag-Lloyd.

In 1984 AI began negotiations which were to lead to its biggest sale by far, and one of the biggest in the history of air transport. The customer was one of the world's most respected airlines, PanAm, and the deal involved three types of aircraft to be supplied under an interim lease agreement, a later purchase agreement and some very large options for further purchases altogether totalling 91 aircraft. Discounting options, the 44 firm lease and purchase contracts added up to a round figure of $1 billion (£834 million).

This was the kind of deal that Boeing, the arch-enemy, found difficult to explain away on a basis of 'predatory' or 'giveaway' financing, or 'government muscle' or any of the other excuses. The one factor in addition to the sheer quality of the products was that AI had readily available several white-tail A300s whose customers for political or financial reasons had been unable to take delivery. This made it possible for AI to offer very early delivery, but it should be emphasized that such a factor is a temporary one which played only a minor part in a transaction of the very greatest magnitude which will shape PanAm's future.

PanAm needed a lot of new equipment for domestic US routes, for services to and within the Caribbean, and for its European network including IGS (internal German services). The letter of intent was signed on 11 September 1984; press conferences to announce the deal were held in London, Paris and Berlin. On hand were C Edward Acker, the airline's Chairman and Chief Executive Officer, and Bernard Lathière. Acker firmly squashed any suggestion that AI had been selected for any reason other than merit. He said 'This order is a keystone in planning the PanAm aircraft fleet for the future. . . . The Airbus jets provide levels of cost-efficiency, passenger comfort, cargo capability, and latest state-of-the-art avionics unequalled in the industry.' The last item was new, reflecting the unmatchable cockpits, flight controls and other systems of the A310 and A320, but the other points were what had been obvious since about 1970. Like Eastern six years previously, here was a major US operator saying that it was all true, and backing it with a billion dollars.

The bones of the interim lease agreement were that AI would lease 12 A300B4s and four A300-200s, all to a very tight schedule, using aircraft already existing or nearing completion. In the second phase of the contract PanAm planned to purchase 12 A310-300s and 16 A320s, these completing the 44 aircraft costed at the round billion. In addition the second contractual phase included options on a further 13 A310-300s and 34 A320s, bringing the total to 91, representing a total investment by the airline of close to $2 billion, discounting support costs.

At the Press conference a big A310 model showed the airline's bold new livery, with the name written larger than any airline had ever used before. AI quickly got down to furnishing and painting the first four B4s to the PanAm specification, and these aircraft were delivered at Toulouse on 21 December 1984, flown to New York on the same day and, thanks to brilliant training and support, put into service

SCANDINAVIAN
SAS

Above *Alitalia's eighth B4-200, delivered in February 1982*

Top left *Eastern 'Whisperliner' N215EA pictured at New York La Guardia in October 1982, when 26 were in service*

Left *SAS was launch customer for the JT9D engine. Its B2s were upgraded to B4s, two then being leased to Scanair*

Right *Products of Stuttgart going aboard a C4-200 freighter of Hapag Lloyd*

immediately. Powered by CF6-50C2 engines, they have 24 First and 230 Coach-class seats, and went into service on routes from New York to Chicago and Minneapolis, and between NY and the US Virgin Islands, Trinidad and Barbados. Lathière said 'We are happy we could deliver the aircraft in December 1984 to meet PanAm's operating requirements . . . It was a complex transaction, entirely financed from commercial sources. It was finalized in the shortest timeframe; this was possible thanks to the excellent co-operation between the negotiating teams. We are proud of PanAm's confidence; they know they have our total commitment'.

The other eight B4s followed in short order in the first half of 1985, together with the four leased A310-200s. The latter, delivered in March to May 1985, were those originally ordered by MEA (Middle East Airlines), but unable to be delivered because of war-torn Beirut. Powered by JT9D-7R4D engines, they have 18 First and 207 Coach-class seats, and immediately went into service on PanAm's European network including the German services radiating from West Berlin. Later, as explained in the next chapter, these services will be taken over by A320s. As for the longer-range A310-300s, these are two-class 214-seaters with the new PW4052 engine. They were entering service as this book was being written in 1987, on US transcontinental, Caribbean and Latin American routes.

A new feature of the 12 A310-300s and the first 16 A320s for PanAm was the specification of wheels and carbon brakes by Goodyear, whose plant at Akron, Ohio, is the world's largest devoted to such products. Goodyear also retrofitted the leased A310-200s. This was the last straw for Britain's unfortunate Dunlop, the world pioneer of carbon brakes, which—entirely because of the British government decision to pull out of AI in 1969—had never been able to get even a toehold in the programme. Instead France's Messier-Hispano-Bugatti has been 'preferred supplier'. In February 1983 Messier installed part of a set of carbon brakes aboard an Air France A300B4. Three months later it put a full set into AI's A310 demonstrator. Messier carbon brakes entered service in September 1985 aboard the first A300-600 of Thai Airways International. They saved 1,100 lb (500 kg) per aircraft, and, despite much higher initial cost than steel brakes, last about three times longer and so also slightly reduce the cost per landing. Messier carbon brakes were from the start standard on the A310-300, entering service with Swissair in December 1985. From 1986 they have also been available as a retrofit on the Dash-200.

Scheduled service with the A310-200 began with Lufthansa on 12 April 1983, and with Swissair on 21 April. Just under two years later, by 31 March 1985, 56 of these aircraft were in service with 13 airlines. They had flown 103,400 revenue hours in 60,000 flights, giving an average sector of 1 hr 43 min, though British Caledonian's London–Lagos sector was timed at 6 hr 25 min. Considering the extremely short average flight duration the worldwide average daily utilization of 6 hr 10 min was remarkable, meaning an average of nearly four revenue sectors every day of the year.

Reliability had generally been excellent, with dispatch reliability of 97.8 per cent (with a high proportion of the delays being caused by factors unrelated to the aircraft) and an average of about three pireps per 1,000 hours. The pirep (pilot report) is the main trigger of component removal, and thus a good yardstick of line maintenance. To get right up alongside the 747 and big trijets in its first two years was creditable, and the incidence has since been lowered closer to the unrivalled 1.8 pireps per 1,000 hr of the B2 and B4 after 12 years in service.

A particular worry of many operators was that the new digital avionics would prove difficult and costly to maintain. To some degree this was fear of the unknown. In fact the hi-tech avionics have proved outstandingly reliable, and when anything does go wrong the system makes trouble-shooting almost simple. Two of the biggest subsystems, the EFIS (electronic flight-instrument system) and ECAM (electronic centralized aircraft monitoring) proved especially reliable, most of the hardware achieving MTBFs (mean times between failure) predicted after three years, not two. The actual displays themselves have hardly ever had to be removed from the aircraft, though the ratio of MTBUR (mean time between unscheduled removal) to MTBF is close on 80 per cent, compared with the 50 per cent which is typical of traditional electromechanical cockpit instruments.

Trouble-shooting of the all-digital systems proved no sweat at all, and very significantly simpler than with traditional analog systems. With the latter, airline maintenance staff can generally locate about 70 per cent of failed units without difficulty, the other 30 per cent needing fairly prolonged effort. On the A310, and on the similar A300-600, around 95 per cent of failed items are displayed in the cockpit and located immediately. Good design plays a part in this performance, but a lot of the credit is due to the easily interpreted BITE (built-in test equipment).

The new avionics played a central role in the clearance in November 1984 for A310-200 operations in the worst possible weather, so-called Cat IIIB (no decision height, and an RVR [runway visual range] of a mere 250 ft or 75 m). As in the A300-600 the key elements in such blind operations are the AFCS (automatic flight-control system) which controls the aircraft during blind landings, and the windshield guidance display which provides runway centreline guidance after landing and also on blind takeoffs. The A300-600 itself was certificated for Cat IIIB on 26 March 1985, following some 150 landings by the Dash-600 demonstrator during which its precision landings were measured in a variety of winds.

The A300-600 entered revenue service with Saudia in April 1984. A year later the Saudi Arabian airline had its fleet of 11 in service, while the next customer, Kuwait Airways, was operating three Dash-600C convertibles. Saudia's choice of engine was the JT9D-7R4H1, after wistfully recognizing the impossibility of launching a Rolls-Royce powered version. In its initial form these 'biggest twins in the world' could carry 267 passengers over a sector distance of 3,500 nm (6,500 km).

From the start the Dash-600 established an impressive dispatch reliability, seldom falling below 98 per cent and for the four weeks ending 31 March 1985 exceeding 99.0 per cent. Compared with the original A300B2 the Dash-600 at its entry into service offered productivity (payload × range) 2.5 times greater, and AI's aggressive product-improvement programmes have ensured that it is going to go on from there.

On 20 March 1985 the first improved Dash-600 version began its flight trials. Powered by the largely new CF6-80C2 engine, rated at up to 61,000 lb thrust, it also introduced the New World cockpit, carbon brakes and wingtip fences, the latter being of a slender short-span delta shape, less prominent than those of the later A310s. The first customer for this model was Thai Airways International, whose first aircraft flew on 1 July 1985 and entered service following certification two months later. Close behind them came Lufthansa. At the Paris airshow on 3 June 1985 Korean Air announced it was the fifth customer for the Dash-600, but using the 7R4H1 engine. AI was especially pleased, because this airline—in the pre-1977 period perhaps better able to form unbiased judgements than those of Western Europe and North America—had been its first customer outside Europe, and a most stalwart supporter from the entry of the A300B4-100 into service from Seoul in 1975. Chairman Choong Hoon Cho commented on the dramatic upgrading in capability of its new Dash-600s, despite their almost unchanged external appearance. They are some aircraft!

He particularly noted the unequalled cargo capability of all the A300 variants, which Korean was using to the full. By this time Eastern was also making excellent use of the cargo capacity, assigning seven aircraft to night cargo services operated in conjunction with CF-Airfreight. By summer 1985 this operation was breaking even on underfloor cargo carriage only, allowing the main-cabin passenger operation to be totally profit-producing. Yet another airline to enthuse about underfloor revenue in summer 1985 was A310-user Swissair, whose head of cargo sales, Fritz Arioli, said 'Give me a cargo-intensive route and an A310, and I will guarantee success by providing 20–25 per cent of the operation's total revenue from freight and mail.' He further added that Swissair's A310s were routinely loading side-by-side LD3 containers, as well as LD7 and LD11 containers and pallets, with direct interchange with its 747s and DC-10s.

Another welcome feature manifest by the summer of 1985 was acceptance of the FFCC cockpit. Belgium's Sabena, which inaugurated several quite long services the previous year (such as Brussels–Monrovia, 2,918 nm/5,410 km), in fact had no pilot dispute situation, and Capt Homble, V-P Operations, said 'The new technology in the A310 has significantly increased the regularity and punctuality of our operation. In addition, the spacious and efficiently designed cockpit makes flying the A310 a most enriching experience for any pilot'. [Author's comment: 'How about that?!!'] Even Lufthansa's Capt Robert Salzl, General Manager of the Cockpit Crews subdivision, said 'For all of us, the 310 plays an important role in the efficient operation of Lufthansa. It contributes in limiting costs, while offering enhanced reliability and comfort'. A purser (senior steward) with the same airline went on record with 'It's the best aircraft cabin in the Lufthansa fleet. Airbus has thought of everything, all the little things . . .' Lufthansa at that time operated the shortest A310 sector of all, Frankfurt–Stuttgart at 90 nm (160 km), while at the other end of the scale Singapore Airlines put its Dash-200s on the oceanic sector to Mauritius, 3,250 nm (6,000 km), though this is still considerably less than the distances now being flown by a few Dash-300s.

In autumn (fall) of 1985 manufacture began of upgraded A310-200s incorporating several features originally developed for the long-haul Dash-300. Among these features are carbon brakes, wingtip fences, the New World cockpit and, not least, the CFRP fin. First deliveries of these upgraded 310-200s were to Thailand and China in spring 1986. Moreover, the Dash-200 is now available with the PW4000 and CF6-80C2 engines, with clearance to an MTOW of 305,600 lb (138.6 *tonnes*) for a full-payload (typically 218 passengers) range of 3,700 nm/6,900 km, or to today's limit for this version of 313,100 lb (142 *tonnes*), extending full-payload range to 4,000 nm/7,400 km. Thus even this 'basic' version has in three years had its productive potential multiplied by 1.6! With the long-haul Dash-300 this measure has been increased to exactly 2.

From January to August 1985 the various A310 structure test specimens completed their three-year periods of torture, and were returned to the manufacturing companies for detailed survey. The tests, carried out mainly at the IABG (*Industrieanlagen Betriebs GmbH*) near Munich, subjected every part to more than 100,000 simulated flight cycles, or 2.5 times the number expected to accrue during 20 years in service. The tests helped to refine the design of the structure for future versions, and also assisted in establishing the inspection procedures. In mid-1985 tests began on the new CFRP fin and trim-tank tailplane, proving the static strength of these items before the Dash-300's entry to service in December 1985 and continuing to mid-1987 to prove their fatigue life. Apart from these two new items the IABG test facilities were immediately readied for doing the same with the smaller parts of the new A320.

In August 1985 AI began testing several unfamiliar subsystems. One was its first FADEC (full-authority digital engine control). This arrived with Pratt & Whitney's almost all-new PW4000 engine, similar in size to the old JT9D but, at immense cost, almost wholly redesigned to improve efficiency, reduce the number of parts (and thus costs) and enable the Connecticut company to compete against the formidable CF6-80C2. This new P&W engine was, like its GE rival, first flown aboard an AI aircraft; in each case this was the first time that a US airline engine had started its airborne life aboard a foreign hull. The PW4000 was hung on the right side of the AI A300 development aircraft, and successfully completed all major test goals in just four long flights between 31 July and 21 August 1985. AI and P&W packed the aircraft with test gear and engineers, and a world first on any airliner was the reprogramming of the FADEC computers during flight. This was instrumental in slashing the required flight-time from the original estimate of 40 hours to only 16. Launch customer for the PW4000 is PanAm, whose PW4052 engines are rated at 52,000 lb in the A310-300s delivered from June 1987. For the A300-600 the PW4000 is delivered as the PW4056 rated at 56,000 lb, available from May 1987.

Another major new subsystem to be tested was the A310-300 weight and balance system. All previous transports have their CG (centre of gravity) laboriously worked out by measuring average values of fuel density, passenger and cargo container weight, and then multiplying by quantities and by the distance of each parcel of load from the CG. Load and trim sheets are then written out by hand. For the A310-300 Weico in the USA and VDO of West Germany jointly developed a new system of a kind which seems bound to become standard on all except the very smallest commercial aircraft. By measuring the weight actually carried by each axle of the landing gear, by sensing small changes in magnetic reluctance, the new system automatically and immediately measures the total aircraft weight and the CG position, within an accuracy of 1.0 per cent. By detecting changes in the weight supported by each wheel of each bogie the sensor can also reveal an under-inflated tyre. In the first instance the new weight/CG sensor enables operators to realize the full potential for fuel-saving of the Dash-300 tailplane trim-tank. At present it is a customer option, but in due course it must become a standard fit. Later, in 1986 AI's Dash-300 demonstrator began flying a rival system developed by SFENA of France.

Another possibly unexpected development was triggered by several serious incidents, including fatal crashes, to various kinds of airliner caught in violent air movements whilst near the ground. One danger is windshear, in which, by flying through a region of rapidly changing horizontal wind, the airspeed of the aircraft—vital for its continued flight—can fall swiftly away until AOA (wing angle of attack) is forced up beyond the stalling angle. Another hazard is the microburst, in which the direction of air movement is violently downwards; aircraft flying through such a 'burst' are virtually flung downwards at the ground.

From the start all A300s have had two basic defences against windshear: alpha-floor and the SRS (speed reference system). The most dangerous form of windshear is clearly to encounter a wind which changes rapidly from a headwind to a tailwind. Assuming wind speed to be 40 kt, and approach airspeed to be 145 kt, this would in a few seconds knock 80 kt off the airspeed, reducing it to 65 kt, or around 60 kt below the stalling speed! The only way to fight this is to open the throttles quickly and fully

Right *Pratt & Whitney's PW4000 first flew in AI's trusty demo aircraft, BUAD, on 31 July 1985. Later BUAD became the fly-by-wire testbed for the A320*

A300
Airbus Industrie
F-BUAD

and increase the wing AOA to the safe maximum, just below the stall. When doing this manually, and in conditions of severe human stress, the possibilities for error are enormous, and the consequences catastrophic.

AI's alpha-floor system automatically applies full power if rate of change of airspeed and groundspeed (as measured by Doppler) exceed a preset threshold. Thus, it can detect windshear long before it is noticeable by the pilots. The SRS provides visual guidance on the flight director instrument on how much the pilot should pull the nose up to reach the point at which the stalling-AOA stick shaker—added to comply with certification authorities, such as that of Britain, who insist on clear warning of the onset of a stall—is just about to be fired. Thus, even the oldest A300B has more protection than most other airliners.

From 1982, AI began to introduce further safeguards, all of them displayed on the EFIS (electronic flight instrument system) in front of each pilot. First, there is speed trend, showing what airspeed/groundspeed will be 10 seconds hence, in the absence of pilot action. Second, the EFIS displays the speed margin remaining until the stick shaker is fired, giving clear guidance on how to fly at the optimum unstalled speed. Third is the flight-path vector, displayed on the EFIS and forming a sure indicator of windshear almost before it is encountered. In addition, a clear approach procedure based on groundspeed was devised. These methods have since been refined and automated in the later A320.

By October 1985 AI was ready to make firm proposals on a further upgrade of the A300-600, the extended-range Dash-600R. This was a natural synthesis into the bigger aircraft of new features developed for the A310-300. The two main advances are the fin and tailplane, the former being entirely of CFRP construction and thus considerably simpler and lighter than the multi-part metal fin, and the tailplane being the same trimming fuel tank as used in the Dash-300. This tailplane saves drag throughout each flight by minimising the need for aerodynamic download applied by the tailplane and elevators, whilst at the same time it houses additional fuel. The latter increases MTOW to a new high, for any twin-engined transport, of 375,900 lb (170.5 *tonnes*). To maintain flight performance at the higher MTOW the most powerful engines can be used, the CF6-80C2 or PW4056 or 4058, all of 58,000 to 61,000 lb thrust.

AI's almost unbelievable ability to turn an avowed short-hauler into a long-hauler naturally resulted in a changed approach to the interior furnishing. The so-called 'air bus' had originally been seen as a vehicle in which passengers were packed like sardines, for maybe 30 minutes. Now the 300-600R and 310-300 were carrying people for eight or more hours at a stretch, and a wholly new level of comfort was called for, at least as good as that on the 747s and big trijets. Thanks to their generous fuselage diameter there was never any problem, and today large numbers of users of long-haul Airbuses have very comfortable interiors configured for three classes of seating, something not expected back at the genesis of AI. Swissair, first operator of the long-range Dash-300 in December 1985, fitted these superb aircraft with only 172 seats: 22 in First-class sleeperettes, 61 in Business and only 89 in Economy. Air India's are equipped for 181: 12 in First sleeperettes, only 28 in Business and 141 in Economy. Kenya's Dash-300s seat 195: 12 in First sleeperettes, 39 in Business and 144 in economy. As for Lufthansa's A300-600s, five of the initial seven have an unusual three-class layout seating an eminently spacious 200: 18 in First sleeperettes, no fewer than 91 in Business and 91 in Economy. Clearly, further range extensions to the 310-300 and 600R will accentuate this move towards greater comfort and customer choice.

Back in autumn 1983 AI had rather tentatively and in a low key flown its A300 demonstrator with the captain's yoke (main flight-control handwheel) removed. The effect was electrifying, and visitors did not immediately notice that, ahead of the left armrest, there was a tiny SSC (sidestick controller), or 'ministick'. AI invited 25 pilots (ultimately 48 accepted) from 12 airlines to try it, and 'none had the slightest problem in piloting the aircraft'. The author would have welcomed the chance, because he is strongly right-handed, and hated flying with his left hand when his right was needed to work old-fashioned pumps and levers, usually immediately after takeoff. Such tasks are no longer required, but this ministick was for the left hand only. Capt Udo Günzel, AI Manager of Future Projects, considered that no ex-military pilot seemed to have any problem, and that the only real comment from visitors had been 'a feeling of being exposed, because there is no yoke in front of them'.

On 30 November 1985 the demo aircraft began a 40-hr test programme with dual sidestick controllers. Though aimed in the first instance at supporting the A320, the results were so positive that it seems highly likely that, on AI aircraft at least, traditional control yokes will soon be part of ancient history. Each one removed saves 123 lb (56 kg), gives a perfect view of the instrument panel, and makes possible a pull-out chart table in front of each pilot. The 1985–86 trials used autopilot throughout, to simulate the man/machine interaction in the computerized flight controls of the A320. The demo aircraft autopilot was specially programmed to offer total protection against upsets, stalls and other hazards, just like an A320. Another objective was to evaluate the laws governing how a pilot may override the inputs of his colleague, thus providing total routine safety following pilot-incapacitation. As the sidesticks are not interconnected, priority is allocated according to sidestick pushbuttons. Indeed, it will no longer be possible for an incapacitated pilot to 'freeze' on to and jam the flight controls, but there are still unresolved problems. AI pilots and engineers have already spent over a year with sidesticks in the simulator. They were soon judged to be the ideal way to communicate pilot demands to the A320 FBW system in the form of electronic signals, quite apart from being smaller, lighter and offering an unimpeded view of the instrument panels. Each controller incorporates the radio and

Above *PanAm's first A310-300 was delivered in June 1987. It was the first aircraft to enter service with the PW4000 (PW4152) engine*

Right *Seen loading at Jakarta Kemayoran, Garuda's first B4-200 introduced the two-man flight deck in February 1982*

Top right *First operator of the superbly efficient A310-300 was Switzerland's Balair, in March 1986. The engine choice was the General Electric CF6-80C2*

Right *With 20, Thai Airways International is one of the biggest A300 operators. This is one of its new Dash-600s, with CF6-80C2 engines*

BALAIR
HB-IPK
BALAIR
HB-IPK

Thai

intercom switches normally found on the left side of the yoke, but nosewheel steering on all Airbuses is done via the pedals. Rotation is achieved with firm backward pressure; if this pressure is maintained on the climbout the A300 maintains the correct attitude and airspeed automatically, the FBW system taking care of all turbulence and inflight disturbances. The author felt Günzel was being overcautious when he suggested that problems might prevent the sidestick from being introduced. The only problem not fully resolved in 1986 was how to assign priority to one stick in the event of the two pilots firmly insisting on doing different things. After all, is this any more serious a problem than the situation that has existed ever since two pilots first sat side-by-side with two handwheels mechanically linked together?

One quite complex aspect of airliner furnishing not often discussed is the inflight entertainment. AI was the first to equip twin-aisle twins with passenger entertainment, beginning with Eastern in early 1977. Those aircraft initially used projectors and screens with Super-8 film, but modern installations are based on simpler projectors and remote videotape players. Today at least 28 Airbus operators have entertainment installed, most of them selecting traditional videotape projectors with separate projectors and screens to serve First class, Business and Economy. But by 1985 two new schemes were available: retractable TV monitors and dual projection. The retractable monitors each cover only about 40 passengers (say five rows of eight) instead of 80 (ten rows), but give a brighter and sharper picture and also occupy less overhead baggage space than a projector and screen. First customers for monitors are PanAm's 310-300s and Lufthansa's 300-600s. Dual projection leaves baggage space untouched, because the projectors and screens—seven in an A310—are suspended above the aisles. They also provide a much better picture, but on the ground all seven have to be retracted upwards to leave the aisles clear for emergencies. First customers for dual projection are Air France and KLM.

The three millionth flight hour was logged on 27 November 1985, almost 2.75 million hours having been logged by the 239 A300s delivered by that date. The 70 A310s added 210,000, and the few Dash-600s another 45,000. At that time the number of takeoffs was very close to 2 million, and the number of passengers just over 300 million. Of the 326 A300s and A310s in service at the end of 1985, 123 were operated from Europe, 88 from the Asia/Pacific area, 57 from the Americas, 41 from the Middle East and 17 from Africa, but these totals were soon to change considerably. The number of carriers was 51, and destinations served about 260.

As already noted, assembly of the first A310-300 began in January 1985, the aircraft flew on 8 July and was certificated on 5 December, entering service with Swissair in the same month. Longest-ranged Airbus yet, the new aircraft was surprisingly upstaged by PanAm who, long before it got its first Dash-300, coolly announced that from April 1986 it would put its earlier A310-200s on the route between Hamburg and New York, 3,300 nm (6,110 km). Many airlines had wanted to use the A300 on the North Atlantic and on several other transoceanic routes, but they had run up against the certification rule for twin-engined aircraft that they must never be more than 60 minutes away from an alternate. In round figures this means that no twin could ever be more than 400 nm (740 km) from land. Such is the political strength of the USA that nobody even bothered to challenge this until US manufacturers began to be hurt by it. AI knew they did not have the right kind of clout, but Boeing did; and when the 767 was marketed in its ER (extended-range) form the political machinery creaked into action. The FAA formed a panel to study what at first was called ETOPS (extended-range twin operations) and later became EROPS (extended-range operations), and by 1985 all airworthiness authorities were agreeing on a range of measures which, when complied with, make EROPS legal for particular operators on certain specified routes.

Experience with the AI big twins, and especially the 11 years of troublefree operations by the A300, confirmed that they were the safest aircraft in history. Nevertheless, for EROPS it was still prudent to guard against particular in-flight failures, of which the most important was loss of adequate electric generation capacity. In January 1986 AI successfully demonstrated to the DGAC, the French airworthiness authority, its EROPS kit for the A310 and A300-600. Its chief item is a hydraulically driven generator, which can be cut in by the pilots or, following loss of generation capacity, automatically. To the author's knowledge this was an industry first, all previous emergency generators having been driven by a RAT (ram-air turbine) extended into the airstream. Other items in the EROPS kit are extended fire protection in the cargo holds and guaranteed ability to start the APU at maximum cruising altitude.

As already noted, Singapore was the first airline to fly an EROPS route, this being to Mauritius. On this 3,250-nm (6,000-km) route there are absolutely no alternates over 90 per cent of the sector, the Cocos Islands helping slightly at the eastern end. Singapore began flying it with 310-200s in June 1985. In April 1986 PanAm opened its Dash-200 operations under EROPS rules on the North Atlantic, starting with Hamburg–New York (3,300 nm, 6,110 km). Both airlines will be flying the Dash-300 by the time this book appears, Singapore putting it on non-stops to the Middle East with sectors comfortably beyond 4,000 nm (7,413 km).

In February 1986 Thai announced purchase of four more Dash-600s, bringing its fleet of A300s up to 20. It also announced conversion of one of its B4s into a C4 freighter. MBB, design authority for the C4, carried out the conversion between September 1986 and March 1987. As well as fitting the large door and semi-automatic cargo loading system, the work entailed structural clearance to an MTOW of 165 *tonnes*, up from the original figure of 157.5. MBB's UT (Transport Aircraft Group) has, with little publicity, also rebuilt more than 30 early B2-100s into B4-200s with productivity (payload multiplied by range) approximately doubled.

AI's position in the most difficult of all markets to penetrate, the USA, was strengthened in early 1986 when Continental, the eighth-largest US carrier, announced the A300B4 as its choice of widebody twin. It received the first two of six on 1 and 6 May 1986, two of the later aircraft being secondhand. With two-class seating for 272, these are the first Airbuses to be equipped with air/ground telephones for the use of passengers. President Phil Bakes said 'Continental is one of the fastest-growing of the US major airlines, with an extensive Pacific route network as well as new routes to Europe. We are excited about adding to our fleet the A300B4s . . .' Where they replaced 727s they have brought a dramatic increase in underfloor cargo revenue, as well as improved passenger comfort.

In the course of 1985–6 AI delivered a fleet of seven A310-200s to THY, the Turkish airline. Powered by CF6-80As, they seat 18 First and 192 Economy passengers, making First-class available on all THY's main routes for the first time. The success of the new 310s was such that the airline phased out its DC-10s, as well as many smaller types, rationalizing its fleet into the 310s for trunk routes (including a new service to Bahrain and Singapore), nine 727s and nine DC-9s. Later, in July 1986, THY signed for three Dash-300s to fly long hauls to Australia and Japan.

It is doubtful that any operator in history has ever achieved such a turnaround in economy and environmental appeal as Danish IT operator Conair. Part of the great Spies Group, Conair flies package holidays to 37 destinations in Europe and Africa, and its five Boeing 720s shuttled between Copenhagen and Billund in Denmark to resorts in Spain, Greece and other Mediterranean areas. These are now being replaced by three ex-SAS A300B4s, the first with JT9D-59A engines, which have been refurbished to seat just over 300 passengers in one-class layout. As well as eliminating the previous severe noise problem the B4s have reduced fuel burn per seat by 148 per cent!

In March 1986 AI's A300-600 demonstrator began simulating the tailplane trim tank of the Dash-600R by using water pumped up and down the fuselage. As explained earlier, the new tailplane—the same as that on the A310-300—not only holds more fuel but also reduces fuel burn by at least 1.5 per cent by maintaining CG at its most efficient position as far aft as possible. Taking off at the increased MTOW of 170.5 *tonnes* (375,900 lb) the Dash-600R can carry a full load of 267 passengers on sectors up to 4,400 nm (8,154 km), enabling it to fly heavy loads on EROPS routes such as Amsterdam–Miami or Honolulu–Tokyo. The Dash-600R was to fly in the fourth quarter of 1987 and be certificated around Christmas after some 50 flight hours.

Deliveries of upgraded A310-300s began in spring 1986. On 21 March the Swiss charter company Balair received the first Dash-300 to be cleared to the new MTOW of 153 *tonnes* (337,300 lb), and this was also the first to be delivered with the EROPS kit to permit long flights over oceans and other remote areas. Powered by JT9D-7R4E engines, it seats 242 in one class, and has a maximum range close to 4,600 nm (8,500 km). Four weeks later, on 14 April, Air India received the first aircraft to go into service powered by the outstanding CF6-80C2 engine. Thanks to a deal which also involved the Rolls-Royce 535E4 the British engine company had a 15 per cent share in the 80C2, so to this extent it is possible to claim that Rolls-Royce had got aboard the Airbus at last, but it is not quite what the people at Derby had hoped. Air India's Dash-300s replace 707s on routes from Bombay to the Middle East, East and West Africa and the Soviet Union.

The quality of the A310 is demonstrated by the technical dispatch reliability figures for the top three operators for the calendar year 1985. Air France achieved 99.1 per cent, PanAm 99.0 per cent and CAAC (Civil Aviation Administration of China) 98.9 per cent. The Air France A310-200 fleet, powered by CF6-80A engines, are configured to seat 32 passengers in First class and 214 in Economy. Frequently seen at virtually all European capitals, they reach out to Athens and Moscow. By 31 March 1986 total A310 time passed 250,000 hours, the highest daily utilization being a remarkable 10 hr 12 min by British Caledonian (which nevertheless, because of changed routes, is selling its 310s to THY).

As for the 'big brother' A300, this more mature aircraft has reached levels of reliability unequalled by anything else in the industry. In calendar years 1983, 1984 and 1985 Korean Air maintained its record with top technical dispatch reliability, the 1985 figure being 99.8 per cent. Runners up in that year were Toa Domestic of Japan with 99.5 and China Airlines of Taiwan with 99.3. The world average for the A300 is about 98.8 per cent. A new and very intensive operator from May 1986 has been Dan-Air, with a B4 chartered from Hapag-Lloyd. Seating some 300, it doubles capacity without requiring extra slots at often overcrowded Gatwick, and the British charter operator looks certain to become an AI customer in due course.

Orders arrived at a healthy rate in mid-1986. On 12 May Alia, the Royal Jordanian airline, signed for six 310-300s and six A320s, plus options for a further three 310s and four 320s. Powered by CF6-80C2 engines, the long-haul Dash-300s will seat 18 First, 35 Business and 138 Economy, and are to replace 707s. Chairman Ali Ghandour said 'The Airbus aircraft will constitute the cornerstone of our long-term fleet renewal programme. They offer an unbeatable combination of economy and passenger-appeal . . .' On the following day, 13 May, CAAC of China announced purchase of two almost identical aircraft, but seating 12/52/143, for EROPS routes within China and to Europe, backing up the Dash-200s previously purchased. On 3 June Finnair became a new customer, for two B4-200s. Replacing DC-8s on long holiday flights to the Canaries and Mediterranean, they will each have over 300 seats, CF6-50C2 engines and the FFCC cockpit. Chairman Gunnar Korhonen said 'The economy and payload/range are tailor-made for us'.

While most customers find the tremendous underfloor cargo capacity as much as they can fill, a few have opted for the Convertible versions, which are available in each of the twin-aisle types. The pioneer A300C4 operators were Hapag-Lloyd and SAA. A300-600C convertibles, which can be equipped as pure freighters in 20 hours, are in service with Kuwait Airways and the Private Flight Department of the President of the United Arab Emirates. Martinair of the Netherlands operates a convertible A310. The pure freighter A300F4 was certificated on 6 June 1986. In this all the passenger furnishing features are absent. This gives a bigger, and especially a higher, interior able to accept taller loads on 96 × 125-in pallets. The reduced basic-operating weight of 79.75 *tonnes* (175,818 lb) enables cargo payload to be increased to 46,653 kg (102,852 lb). The first F4 went to Korean.

Kenya Airways, which had been operating a leased A310, took delivery of its first long-range A310-300 on 16 May. Powered by CF6-80C2 engines, it seats 195 in a three-class layout, and if its first day is typical it will earn its keep. After being accepted at Toulouse it flew to London, took on a full passenger load and continued non-stop to Nairobi. Another new operator, from August 1986, is Wardair of Canada, but using B2Ks previously with SAA. Seating 30 First and 220 Economy-class passengers, these much-travelled aircraft now fly with high load factors from Toronto to Calgary, Edmonton, Vancouver, Florida and the Caribbean. Another sale in mid-1986 was two of the latest type A310-300s for Singapore, the pioneer EROPS operator using six Dash-200s. Configured for 191 passengers in three classes, the new aircraft were to be delivered in June 1987 and March 1988, and are likely to fly some of the longest routes yet assigned to any twin-engined aircraft.

During 1986 the performance of the well-used A300s so impressed Wardair that the Canadian carrier decided to make the A310 the backbone of its rationalised fleet, and on 30 January 1987 it signed for 12 of the latest Dash-300s, with tankage for 5,000 nm/9250 km. Seating 30 in 'Big Seat' and 166 in 'Wardair' class, the fleet was priced at $Can 915 million ($US 670 million), including spares. Their routes include Vancouver non-stop to the UK, France and Germany. An even bigger contract followed on 3 March 1987 when Robert L Crandall, Chairman and President of American Airlines, announced a contract for 25 A300-600Rs, the famed US carrier becoming launch customer for this version, biggest and longest-ranged of the A300 family. To be powered by the higher-thrust version of the CF6-80C2, the 600R fleet will seat 267, including 16 in First Class, and will be operated on American's network between the USA and the Caribbean.

By 30 June 1986 AI had delivered 350 aircraft to 54 operators, this total comprising 263 A300s and 87 A310s. The widebody, or rather twin-aisle, order book stood at 463, for 60 customers, in October 1987. Total flight time at that date was close to 4 million hours, of which 3.5 million were logged by A300s. This time has not come easily, because on predominantly short-haul operations it required considerably more than 2 million flights. The untroubled nature of these flights speaks for itself.

aerospatiale
A320
A320

Above *No other airliner even comes close to the A320 in all-round use of advanced technology. Captains converted on to this smaller twin have to a man become enthusiastic converts to large colour electronic displays and sidestick controllers, and appreciate the ability to pull out a small table on which to spread the FT or* Wall Street Journal

Previous page *About 2,000 invited guests watched the first A320 emerge through a silver curtain on 14 February 1987 into a world of artificial mist and son-et-lumière by laser. It survived this, and being christened by HRH The Princess of Wales, to make a flawless first flight eight days later*

Right *After the A320's 3 h 23 m maiden flight are (from left) Jürgen Hammer, Gordon Corps, Gérard Guyot, Pierre Baud, Jean-Marie Mathios and Bernard Ziegler*

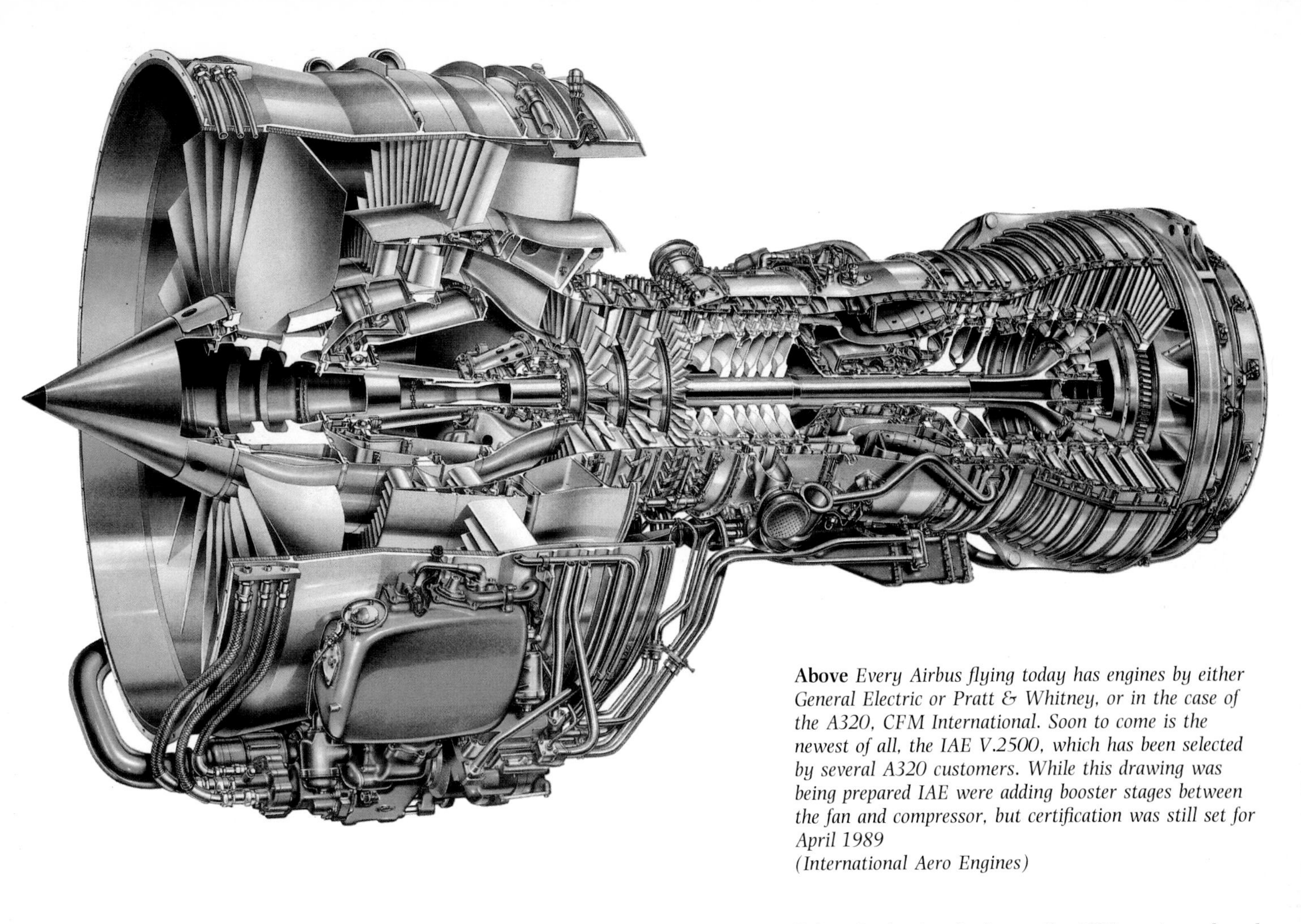

Above *Every Airbus flying today has engines by either General Electric or Pratt & Whitney, or in the case of the A320, CFM International. Soon to come is the newest of all, the IAE V.2500, which has been selected by several A320 customers. While this drawing was being prepared IAE were adding booster stages between the fan and compressor, but certification was still set for April 1989*
(International Aero Engines)

Below *Production sharing on the A320; engine pods and landing gears are supplied by specialist contractors*

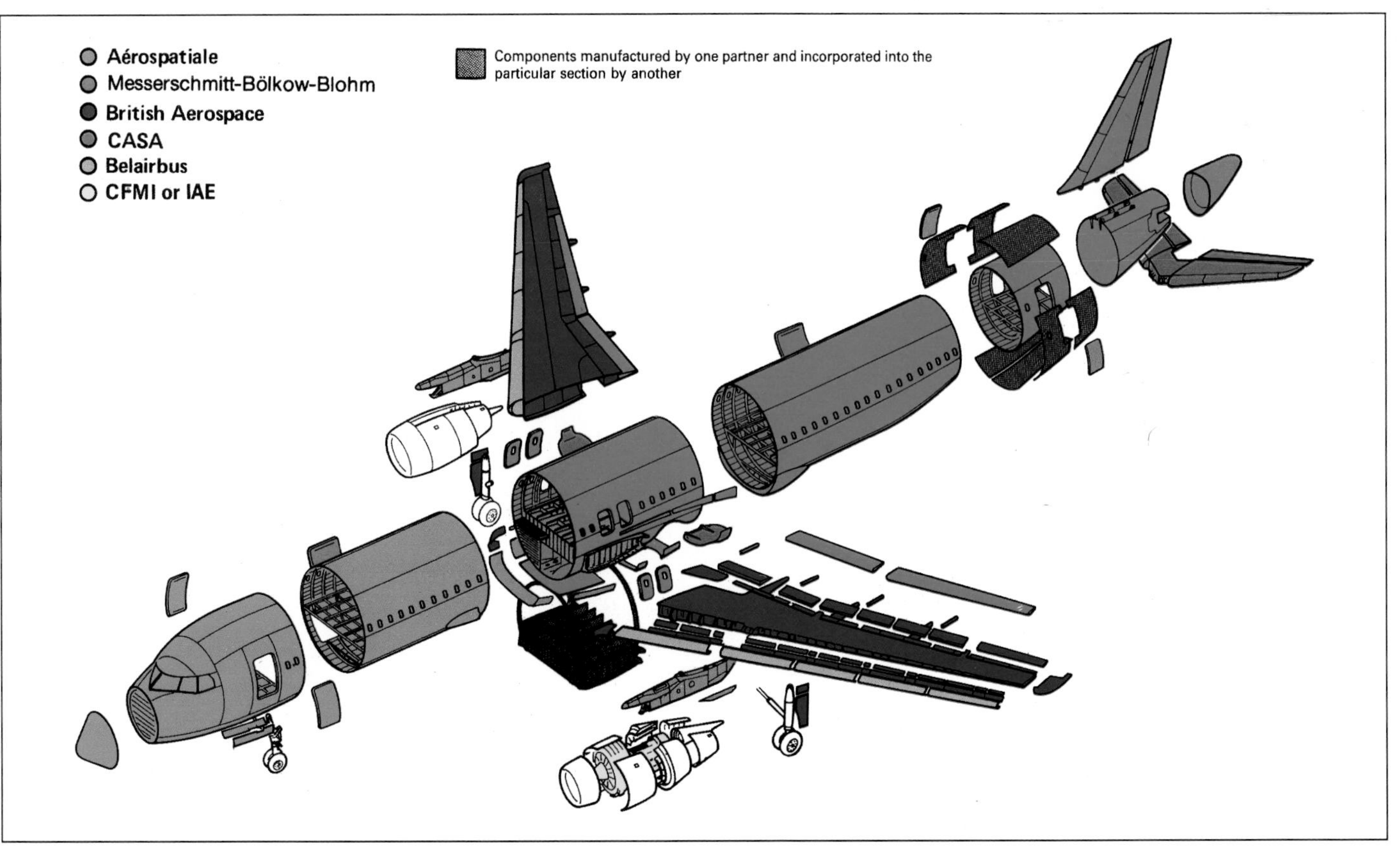

A330
A330

A March 1987 artist's impression showing the A330 and A340-300 as they were expected to look at that date. Since then both aircraft have benefitted from an increase in span and refinement of the wing, and the appearance of the ultra-longhaul A340 has been altered by switching to CFM56 engines of smaller diameter than the SuperFans seen here. In due course engines with a bypass ratio of about 15 will almost certainly become available

Above *The first A320 on an early test flight, formating on the photographic aircraft at low level with slats open. As this book went to press most of the 1,500-hour certification programme had been completed, and the aircraft depicted had been subjected to severe simulated lightning strikes to prove the integrity of the avionics and fly-by-wire flight control system*

Above right *As described on page 130 Aeroformation makes extensive use of VACBI-C (video and computer-based instruction), and this is what it looks like. Just visible at the right is one of the FCOMs (flight crew operating manuals) which have everything written down in the traditional way on paper—like this book*

Right *Computer graphics are also extensively used by Airbus Industrie as a design tool. This particular program can portray the interior of the A320 from any angle. At the touch of a key or light pen a designer can change the seats, or a customer can change the fabric*

The third A320 is painted in the livery of the French domestic airline Air Inter. Its chief task is to test the avionics, including the autopilot and flight-management system. Certification of this version, with CFM56-5 engines, is due in February 1988. Air Inter receive their first aircraft in May

6

THE A320

THE NAME AIRBUS HAS BEEN so closely identified with TA (twin-aisle), or widebody, aircraft that many people may find it hard to regard the A320 as an 'Airbus' at all. But such an aircraft simply had to happen if AI was to survive and prosper in the longer term. While the A300 and A310 complement each other perfectly, and have already carved out a major market base throughout every part of the world, AI needed to offer a greatly broadened range of products. Two routes to this broader range have been studied for a dozen years and are featured as the A330 and A340 in the final chapter. These are derived designs, stemming from the A300/310 but with yet another completely new wing. In contrast, the A320 is a totally new and uncompromised aircraft. It is, in fact, the only completely new jetliner flying developed, or even being considered, anywhere in the Western world.

Any builder of commercial transports will confirm that it is not merely desirable but essential to be able to offer a family of aircraft covering a broad spectrum of range and capacity. Only two companies today can do this. British Aerospace has the 125, Jetstream, ATP, 146, and a share in the Airbuses. Boeing has a family whose links are much tighter and more strategically planned, with the 737 and 737-300, 757, 767 and, out by itself with never any hint of competition, the 747. It is not possible to rival Boeing's product-range, even in the long term, and Boeing's great and increasing warfare against AI is not because it has any fear of being dislodged from its position as No 1 builder of jetliners to the world. About half the world market for such aircraft is in the USA, where any non-American builder finds it very hard to compete. Despite this AI has successfully penetrated this market, and the quality of its two big widebodies is such that in the particular sector of big twins it has pushed Boeing into the No 2 position, and has almost made a clean sweep of several large and important geographical areas. But, as in making cars, cameras and many other products, it helps to offer a range of different models. The obvious new AI model was seen almost from the start around 1970 as a significantly smaller twin, with a narrow body, of SA (single-aisle) layout.

Today the 320 seems so exactly right that it is hard to see why it took so long. The answers become clearer when we study history. For one thing, the airline market suffers traumatic ups and downs, with deregulation, soaring traffic growth followed by stagnation and bankruptcies, and fuel prices which soar and then unexpectedly slump. There are even rather childish matters of pure fashion, which around 1958–60 regarded turboprops as archaic mistakes, so that the Electra and Vanguard were marketing disasters; then, 20 years later, propellers came back into fashion as by far the best answer for all local service and regional airlines, so that about half the world's aircraft industries are today making rival propliners seating up to about 80. AI has never thought much about propellers, apart from future propfans for jet speeds as described in the next chapter. It has always concentrated its search for a new SA aircraft on efficient new jets covering the range of sizes from 70 to 200 seats, and concentrating on 140-180. Two of the studies were derived from existing aircraft, the baseline types being the French Mercure and British One-Eleven. Most were all-new, and the reasons why progress was slow and halting were that almost every European planemaker wanted a piece of the action, had formed himself into one or more industrial groups which mostly had a short life, and had his own ideas about how the aircraft should be designed.

At the start of the 1970s BAC at Weybridge was busy with its single-aisle 2-11 and the twin-aisle 3-11 project to rival the A300. On the side, another Weybridge team was studying the prospects for a QSTOL (quiet, short takeoff and landing) aircraft. To be powered by four geared-fan M45S engines of 14,525 lb thrust each, this high-wing machine was a larger ancestor of today's BAe 146, seating 108–140 and being designed to operate from runways only 2,000 ft (610 m) long. This May 1971 project was the basis upon which in 1972 BAC linked up with MBB of West Germany and Saab-Scania of Sweden, forming Europlane Ltd. Later in 1972 CASA of Spain also joined, forming a really good four-nation team. Europlane's board of directors read like a who's who of European top management (technical director was Heribert Flosdorff, today AI's Executive VP), and intensive studies suggested that the specialist QSTOL was all wrong. It gradually turned into the Europlane QTOL, a jet sized for 180/200 seats and able to fly at 600 mph from a 4,000 ft (1,219 m) runway, and with appearance resembling a giant One-Eleven.

A few months later Hawker Siddeley linked with Dornier and VFW-Fokker to look at its own QTOL. By this time, 1973, the dominant objective was not short field capability but quietness. This second grouping had 95 engineers at Hatfield and Bremen, yet it had nothing to do with AI. They soon called themselves and the project the CAST (Civil Aircraft Study Team), and they studied twins and trijets with 150–195 seats, generally favouring a narrow SA aircraft of Airbus layout. In France Aérospatiale studied the AS.200, an all-new 150-seater with the same configuration, while Dassault-Breguet stretched its existing Mercure into the Mercure 200 seating up to 176. CAST, AS.200 and Mercure 200 all looked almost identical, and they also had to have the only available engine: the newly announced CFM56, whose builder

CFM International had been formed on a 50/50 basis by SNECMA of France and GE of the USA in 1974. This was the only engine planned in the ten-*tonne* (22,000-lb) class, so almost everyone selected it for their paper aeroplanes. In 1975–76 BAC picked it to go on the rear fuselage of its X-11; basically a wide-body derivative of the unbuilt One-Eleven 800, the X-11 seated up to 160, yet used the wing, tail and many other parts of the One-Eleven, and seemed a better bet than a costly all-new design.

There was a vague feeling that there might be some safety in numbers, and in September 1974 at the Farnborough show the Group of Six was announced: BAC, Hawker, Aérospatiale, Dornier, MBB and VFW-Fokker. A few months later, March 1975, this had become the Group of Seven with the inclusion of Dassault-Breguet. This seemed to rule out the possibility of any formal connection with AI, whose A300B was by this time in airline service. Indeed Dassault soon became group leader when its Mercure 200 was chosen as the basis for further development—to the chagrin of the teams still ardently working on the AS.200 and X-11.

By 1975 Boeing had published numerous different forms of its proposed 7N7, the distant ancestor of the 757. Joe Sutter told the author 'We have British Airways—especially British Airtours—100 per cent behind us. So are Rolls-Royce. With their help there is every chance the 7N7 wing will be built in Britain, and maybe get your industry back in the civil planemaking business.' This was a low ebb for Europe. Despite the galaxy of technical talent beavering away on studies and committees, the politicians and top management appeared to doubt Europe's capability of actually doing anything. BAC and Hawker were diverted into trying to fend off, or minimize the effects of, their enforced merger and nationalization. Dassault talked with McDonnell Douglas, but the French government backed the 150-seater as a national project and handed it over to Aérospatiale as main production contractor.

To try to get something launched, McDonnell Douglas and Dassault-Breguet threw a giant shindig at Long Beach in October 1976 to launch the ASMR. None of the brochures mentioned the fact that this, the Advanced Short/Medium Range, was merely the Mercure 200 under a different name. At the eleventh hour Aérospatiale arrived as prime contractor for manufacture, Dassault remaining responsible for the design. The ASMR was basically a stretched Mercure 100 with turned-down wing trailing edges with better flaps, a longer body and CFM56 engines, with the Pratt & Whitney JT10D as a slightly vague alternative. Not much happened, despite the presence of 240 executives from 55 airlines. A year later the Mercure 200 had grown a new supercritical wing and been joined by the Mercure 300 trijet, but by this time Dassault-Breguet had reluctantly begun to despair of ever getting into the big jetliner business. Likewise, McDonnell Douglas went on to do its own thing called ATMR (Advanced Technology Medium Range) and further developed this by 1980 into the DC-XX, which looked almost exactly like today's A320 but was actually bigger and intended to compete head-on with the 757.

Yet one more strong contender was to emerge, at the Japan International Aerospace Show in November 1979. Having spent years trying to stretch its F.28 Fellowship, Fokker announced the F.29 as a largely new aircraft with a fuselage brought up to the same width as the 727/737/757 to seat up to 150. CFM56 or RB.432 engines were to be hung under the wings, yet the tail was of T-type. Chairman Frans Swarttouw said he was confident he would beat AI and tie up a collaborative manufacturing programme with Japan that would permit an early F.29 launch. The Airbus studies Fokker wanted to beat were called the SA (single-aisle) family, and unlike the F.29 these were in fact the aircraft that were in due course going to be built.

The SAs had their genesis in one of the happier acronyms, JET, from Joint European Transport. This study group was set up in June 1977 by the leaders of the AI companies: Aérospatiale, MBB, VFW-Fokker and, by virtue of Hawker's important subcontract role, BAe. To a man, they felt there had been too much talking and too many committees, so they formed one more to get something done. JET had several subgroups, one of which was the JET Engineering Team, headed by AI's Derek Brown and based at Weybridge. Its baseline aircraft was the 160-seat Jet 2, but careful study was also made of a smaller Jet 1 and larger Jet 3, though the only visible engine was still the CFM56 of 22,000 lb thrust which fitted the Jet 2. After so many years a sense of unreality creeps in, and it is doubtful that many of the team at Weybridge fully comprehended the great importance of what they were doing. This was the crunch time, when in the absence of any hardware or visible motivation, decisions have to be taken that will be so exactly right that the result will be a worldbeater for at least the next 20 years.

How do you accomplish such a thing? In part, you state your objectives clearly. In March 1978 someone in JET wrote 'The central design concept and philosophy is to provide a new long-term genus that will replace current first-generation short/medium-range transport fleets and bring a new order of quietness, fuel efficiency and operating economy'. He might have added that the time was also ripe for the across-the-board introduction of the very latest digital avionics and many other new features which would make this all-new aircraft by far the most advanced and attractive ever offered to the airlines. Apart from this, the crucial decisions taken by this time included fixing the fuselage diameter at 154 in (3.91 m) (later increased to 155.5 in, 3.95 m), basic design of the wing, with wing-hung engines seen as uprated CFM56s, and a conventional tail.

By 1979 BAe's acceptance as a full member of AI enabled an MoU (Memorandum of Understanding) to be drawn up between all parties, describing their exact responsibilities for design and manufacture of parts for the A300, A310 and the SA

Right *Like AI, CFM had to endure many years almost without customers before being swamped with orders. This is a gleaming CFM56-5A-1 for an A320. An advanced version of the same engine will power the A340*

CFM56-5
CFM56-5

family (formerly JET), the SA-1, -2 and -3 having different lengths of fuselage to seat from 130 to 180 passengers. At the 1980 Hanover show Béteille commented that SA-1 and SA-2 were 'already very competitive with the 737 and DC-9-80', and would 'have active controls'. Lathière confirmed discussions with Fokker, but made it clear that AI wanted to go ahead with its own design. Fokker hit back in July 1980 with an improved F.29 wing of reduced chord, claimed to give a margin of some 5 per cent in fuel burn over the SA family. This was really the bold Dutch builder's last throw, because in the first quarter of 1981 the AI board hardened against even considering other people's designs, recognizing for the first time the enormity of the prize they could grasp and the enormity of the margin by which their totally uncompromised all-new jetliner would exceed the standards of the aircraft it would replace. It also promised to do the same in competition with such derived part-new aircraft as the MD-80 and 737-300, though these were from the start correctly judged to be powerful competitors which, until at least 1987–88, would continue to grab a major share of the market despite their inability to come close to A320 standards.

In 1980 AI carried out a prolonged study of propfan propulsion for SA 150-seaters of various configurations. The work was done in collaboration with the propfan technology leader, Hamilton Standard, and Pratt & Whitney. The conclusion was to stick to turbofans, and AI has never had cause to regret this.

The designation A320 was first used in late February 1981, and even though a 'go-ahead in principle' was not announced until the Paris airshow in June of that year, there was no doubt whatever after February 1981 that it was 'all systems go' on the 320. But there were several major stumbling-blocks, one of which was deciding which AI partner was going to perform assembly and flight test. Most AI executives favoured BAe, which was enthusiastic and had ample available capacity, notably at Filton, Bristol. But BAe could not itself find the money for increased shareholding and for financing the tooling, and because Toulouse was bursting at the seams and MBB lacked floorspace and skilled manpower, Lathière said the job might even have to go to Fokker. He disliked the idea of bringing in an additional partner and immediately handing it a major prize; he preferred AI's existing structure.

At this time the A320 was offered in two body-lengths, closely similar to the SA-1 and SA-2 lengths, the Dash-100 seating 154 passengers at 32-in (813-mm) seat pitch and the Dash-200 seating 172 at the same spacing. First firm details were announced at the Paris airshow, and it was at that show on 6 June that the go-ahead was announced. This was made possible by Air France's public commitment to 25, plus 25 on option, the total of 50 being split between 16 short Dash-100s and 34 Dash-200s. This was the best possible beginning, and any objective observer who really did his homework could not fail to see what a tremendous advance the 320 would be over the aircraft it would replace, but AI continued to be held up by political delays, notably in Britain, and merely said it had decided 'in principle' to go ahead.

One of the uncertainties was the engine. Clearly the thrust had to be in the range 20,000–25,000 lb. The obvious candidate was the CFM56, produced by CFM International, the GIE formed in 1974 by SNECMA and General Electric. These partners had worked together on CF6 engines to provide power for every major version of the A300 and A310, and from the start of the SA project had done their utmost to ensure that they had the inside track on the engines for this aircraft also. By 1981 the initial production engine, the CFM56-2 family, was coming off the assembly line for civil and military customers. It looked well suited to the A320, though to keep their options open CFM offered a paper growth version rated at 27,000 lb, the CFM56-4. Other possibilities were the Pratt & Whitney PW2025, the proposed 25,000-lb version of the PW2000 series which had previously been known as the JT10D, and a possible growth version of the RJ.500 being developed by Rolls-Royce and Japanese Aero Engines, but these rivals to CFM were theoretical rather than existing.

Lack of an obvious certificated engine, and continued tinkering with the specification for the aircraft, combined with political and financial considerations to delay the true launch for almost three years until March 1984. In true British form it was indecision at the British government level that really held everything up, but on Thursday 1 March 1984 BAe was able to announce that the Department of Trade and Industry had at last agreed to provide £250 million of repayable assistance to cover all development and launch costs. BAe Chairman Sir Austin Pearce said 'The package covers the early years, when there is no income from sales [author's note: not quite true]. The latter part of the programme will be funded by resources generated internally by BAe . . .' He privately said BAe could have funded the whole participation, but only by depriving all the other BAe projects of funds. It was not really unfortunate that British procrastination delayed the project for so long, putting back the in-service date from 1986 until 1988, because the time was put to very good use. Each day the design became more refined, and by 1983 it had almost reached the definitive stage. A major development in October 1981 was to reject the idea of short and long bodies, though this was filed away for possible resurrection later. Instead the standard overall length started at the 128 ft 9 in (39.24 m) of the Dash-200, shrank to 126 ft 1 in (38.43 m), and then in 1983 to only 120 ft 1 in (36.83 m), and finally settled at 123 ft 3 in (37.57 m), without significantly changing the cabin length. There remained the choice of the Dash-100 or -200, but these now differed only in fuel capacity and MTOW, and hence in range for a given payload. Both versions were to be powered by engines 'in the 25,000-lb class'.

In 1982–3 consideration was given to the SBP-8 project with twin pusher single-rotation propfans on the rear fuselage. It scored many minuses as well as pluses, and AI were certainly right to adhere to the known and proven design of A320.

Both at the 1982 Farnborough and 1983 Paris airshows AI put out unusually hard-hitting literature really making the case for the A320. Unlike its rivals, AI was 'the only manufacturer whose 150-seat programme is completely uninhibited by any need to protect intermediate or other products. AI has no stop-gap aircraft on the market and as a result has pushed vigorously ahead with a completely new-technology project . . . which will be a truly economic replacement for the obsolete, fuel-thirsty, narrow-bodied aircraft now in service, and an attractive alternative to the short-term solutions provided by derivative updates of yesterday's technology'. Ten years earlier this would almost certainly have fallen on deaf ears. Even as it was, many airlines, especially those in the USA, committed themselves to a further 20 years of 'derivative updates of yesterday's technology' with massive orders for MD-80s and 737-300s, but by the 1980s AI had arrived as a major force on the world scene. Today its rivals have wondered what they can do to stop the A320, which in spite of the long delay is now clearly seen as the right aircraft at the right time.

During the 30 months of refinement the aircraft changed quite dramatically, and not a lot remained the same. In metres the span of the wings moved from 34.02 to 34.48 and 34.59, and finally settled at 33.91 (111 ft 3 in). Aspect ratio measured by the harsh European criterion is 9.396. At the 1983 Paris show AI had almost completed the process of refinement, and announced that, since 1981, the A320 had achieved: 'significant improvements in aerodynamic standards, a 2.4-*tonne* (5,290-lb) reduction in airframe weight, a full revision of systems standards aimed at higher efficiency and lower cost, and the incorporation of major technological advances that are now feasible'. The claims were real ones.

With Britain at last funded, the AI board took the full go-ahead on 4 March 1984, followed eight days later by the sanction of the responsible ministers of France, West Germany, Britain and Spain to provide funds to assist the launch. Total non-recurring costs were estimated at US$1.7 billion, and this was expected to be recovered through the usual levy on sales by the 600th delivery. Wistfully, one recalled the original estimated launch cost of the A300 at £190 million, or little more than one-tenth as much; but then Boeing's original investment in the 707 was $15 million, and at the board meeting in Seattle on 22 April 1952 that seemed a desperate gamble!

This is the point at which to break the history and describe the A320 as it finally matured. At all times it was planned as the absolutely uncompromised single-aisle vehicle, and, while its size initially fluctuated, it was to no small degree the uncompromising opinion of Delta Airlines in 1981 that the correct seating capacity was to be '150 plus or minus zero' that tipped the balance in favour of a fixed body length. Again, from very early in the project it was certain that the cabin width needed to be greater than the 128 in (3.53 m) of the 727/737/757, but as nobody would dream of putting more than six seats (3 + 3) into one row on a single-aisle aircraft there soon comes a point at which greater width just means extra weight and drag. Almost all the precursor projects, including the JET studies, had circular-section fuselages. These are structurally efficient and tend to have minimum weight, but even in single-aisle sizes they often make poor use of available volume and also lack underfloor height. In winter 1980–81 AI changed the cross section, reducing the diameter of the underfloor lobe. The resulting faired double-bubble looks almost circular, but increases the underfloor depth so that LD3-compatible containers can be loaded.

A320 fuselage width is 155.5 in (3.95 m), giving an internal cabin width of 145.5 in (3,696 mm). This is noticeably wider than today's single-aisle Boeings, while the contrast with the MD-80 series (which are only 121-in, 3.07-m) is pronounced. AI worked with seat suppliers to refine the design of an outstanding triple seat 62 in (1,575 mm) wide and with exceptional capacity underneath for extra carry-on baggage. The latter factor is seldom likely to be needed, because in all seat configurations the capacity of the overhead lockers is greater per passenger than in 'any previous aircraft of this type', a typical figure being 2.1 cu ft (0.06 m^3). The body cross-section also makes for minimum weight and drag for a given shoulder-height in the cabin, and aisle width is unequalled by any other 3+3 cabin. Customer acceptance of the furnishing mockups has been exceptionally positive. Lufthansa calculates the wide aisle, matched with engineering design for fast turnaround, will be worth 'an extra sector a day on Frankfurt–London'.

A totally new feature of the A320 is CIDS (cabin intercommuncation data system). Modern passenger jets need up to 75 miles (120 km) of cable to wire up the public-address speakers, lighting, reading lamps, entertainment system, crew intercom and the cabin safety and sign system. Any change in the seating classes and cabin sizes requires extensive recabling, with precise documentation in the handbooks, costing a great deal of time and money. MBB created the CIDS as a centralized digital system with microprocessor control. Operators of the A320 will be able to alter the class distribution almost entirely by changing the software. This will take only a few minutes, the cost being trivial.

While the correct body is crucial to the success of any transport, in an era of intense competition the wing is also vital. Just as the A300 and A310 had their success based squarely on the use of a super-efficient wing, so has the A320 had the benefit of what is by a very wide margin indeed the best wing on any single-aisle fast jet, the 757 notwithstanding. And, like its big brothers, the 320 rides on a wing of British origin. The difference, apart from size, is that the 320 wing began not at Hatfield but at Weybridge. Its origin can be traced to the stillborn BAC Three-Eleven, for which six wings were studied, known as W1 to W6. Valuable help in test facilities came from the RAE Farnborough and ARA (Aircraft Research Association) at Manton Lane, Bedford, and the RAE also suggested aerodynamic refinements. All had quarter-chord sweep of 25 degrees, with a kinked trailing edge, and W1 to W6 featured progressively more advanced and efficient supercritical profiles representing the ultimate in the aerodynamic art. In 1982 a scaled-down W6 wing was adopted for the A320, and finally by March 1984 this was refined into the W6-4 with maximum thickness surprisingly far aft, and root thickness/chord ratio of no less than 15.3 per cent, tapering to a more expected 10.8 per cent at the tip.

Weybridge also developed the high-lift system, which is commendably simple and effective, reaching C_L max of 3.2. The flaps are of the tracked slotted type, and most unusually they run without a break past the rear of the engines. Left and right wings have just two sections of flap each, made of composite material (almost entirely CFRP) by MBB. Each section travels aft and down on two tracks, the three outboard tracks being enclosed in CFRP fairings which are among the numerous secondary parts made by BAe. On the leading edge are the slats, which represent the 2 per cent contribution made by Belairbus. These are the only wing movables of aluminium alloy, and unlike the big twin-aisle Airbuses are broken by the pylon strut, there being one section inboard and four outboard.

Roll control is by conventional outboard ailerons, assisted by four sections of spoiler ahead of the outboard flap on each wing. The inner pair of spoilers on each wing serve also in the symmetric mode as lift dumpers. Further inboard, ahead of the inboard flaps, are two-segment speed brakes. All these movable surfaces are of CFRP construction and driven hydraulically by the FBW (fly by wire) flight-control system as described later. One of many new features of the A320 is load alleviation. With flaps retracted and speed over 200 knots, automatic signalling of the ailerons and the two outboard roll spoilers on each wing, triggered by accelerometers in the fuselage, reduces peak wing-root bending moment in turbulent air by 15 per cent, thus prolonging airframe life and giving a smooth ride.

The tail is outwardly conventional, comprising a fixed fin, one-piece rudder, trimming tailplane (horizontal stabilizer) and one-piece elevators, the horizontal surfaces being mounted just above the mid position on the rear fuselage to give 6 degrees dihedral. For the first time in a commercial transport, the entire tail is made of CFRP, the vertical surfaces being made by MBB and the horizontal by CASA, whose 5.4 per cent share includes the fuselage-mounted main landing-gear doors and aluminium-alloy skins for MBB's rearmost section of pressurized fuselage.

Structurally the A320 is designed to the very latest standards, promising fully to uphold the unequalled service record of its big brothers. Though it has finally emerged as quite a long-ranged aircraft, carrying its full payload up to 3,627 miles (5,837 km), the design criterion was absence of any accrued damage or corrosion during 60,000 flights of one hour each. Thanks to integrally stiffened machined skins, honeycomb, composite construction and such new techniques as SPF/DB and TEM (both explained later), it has an extraordinarily small number of joints between separate parts. Great efforts were made in the design stage to make inspection easy, eliminate sources of corrosion and generally enable the airframe almost to be a 'fit and forget' item. A particular problem in the design stage was how far to use Al-Li (aluminium/lithium) alloys. Though very expensive, these have high strength and might save 10 to 20 per cent in structure weight, but AI was anxious not to run into Al-Li problems of the kind suffered by rivals who expected too much, too soon. In the event these alloys could at an early stage be used for some highly stressed items in the fuselage and the nose ribs and skin of the wing, and research continues at Aérospatiale, BAe and MBB.

Turning to the engines, the only visible engine in 1981 was the planned CFM56-4, intended for 27,000 lb thrust but derated for this application to 23,000. However, Delta's requirement shrewdly demanded 'half the fuel burn per seat of the 727', and CFM felt they could try harder. Via the CFM56-2000 the group derived the CFM56-5, which retains the same diameter of fan as the original Dash-2 engine (though with part-span instead of tip shrouds), but incorporates new features throughout, most of them stemming from GE's E^3 (energy-efficient engine) and CF6-80C2 but on a reduced scale. Among the major advances are a new three-stage LP booster, redesigned combustor, roller/ball No 3 bearing, precision aerofoil struts, new details throughout the engine to reduce leakage and improve aerodynamic efficiency and, not least, a FADEC (full-authority digital engine control) and a new accessory gearbox. On a typical short-haul mission CFM at first estimated the Dash-5 to burn 13 per cent less fuel than the original CFM56-2. Later this was improved to 19.4 per cent. In July 1986 CFM announced an uprated Dash-5 to be rated at 28,600 lb in 1989.

Unfortunately for CFM, in March 1983 Rolls-Royce and Japanese Aero Engines stopped working on the RJ.500, previously seen as a rather vague A320 engine, and formed a completely new company, IAE, International Aero Engines, in partnership with Pratt & Whitney, MTU and Fiat. It was the first time since 1947 that Rolls-Royce and Pratt & Whitney had collaborated on an engine, and the result could hardly fail to be important. Called the V2500 (a contrived designation, the V meaning in Roman numerals the five partners and the number signifying 25,000 pounds of thrust), the new IAE engine clearly outperforms the CFM56-5. Just as AI can claim the A320 to be superior to old-technology derived aircraft, so can IAE claim that its V-2500 must be superior to the derivative CFM engine. But it is not as simple as that. The V2500 is being developed later, in a more expensive fiscal environment, and CFM claim that their inherently older engine has 'a more proven base' and 'during the first 10 years of A320 service offers maintenance savings of $1.5–2.0 million per aircraft compared to 320s powered by the "all-new" competitor engine'. Of course, it is not as simple as this either. One of the tricks of aerospace marketing is to try to have your cake and also to eat it, by convincing customers that, whilst your product is as modern as the hour and packed with the very latest technology, at the same time it is so well proven that it will never give any trouble or incur any unexpected costs.

Suffice to say that both engines are firm, both are running very well on test as this book is written—though the V2500 has had a year of worrying problems which have tended even to damage the image of the group—both have secured a good customer base aboard the A320, and there seems no reason to doubt that both will prove to be excellent engines. On paper the V2500 is naturally more efficient; it has to be. Brochure sfc (specific fuel consumption) in typical cruising flight at 35,000 ft (10,670 m) is only 0.560, compared with 0.591 for the CFM56-5. It should also have lower installed drag, since the fan diameter is only 63 in (1,600 mm) compared with 68 in (1,727 mm). On the other hand the CFM engine is somewhat lighter, at a brochure figure for the bare engine of 4,734 lb (2,147 kg) compared with 4,943 lb (2,242 kg). One reason for the greater weight is that the HP (high-pressure) turbine of the all-new engine has two stages. CFM launched a particularly strong campaign aimed at convincing customers of the advantages of having a single-stage HP turbine, as in their engine; but the HP turbine of the V2500 is a P&W responsibility, and that company has equally convincing reasons for dividing the work between two stages. There is seldom a dull moment in competitive marketing.

In the case of the CFM engine the French partner, SNECMA, is responsible for installation. Most details of the pod cowl have been subcontracted to the California specialist Rohr Industries, already experienced on the A300 and 310. The fan reverser discharges forwards through four large petal doors, each hinged at the rear and opened by an internal hydraulic jack. This is an unusual arrangement, the more common method being to translate (bodily move rearwards) the whole surrounding rear section of fan duct and case, this action uncovering rings of cascade vanes which deflect the airflow forwards whilst simultaneously closing off the fan nozzle by a ring of blocker doors. In the case of the V2500 the IAE team offer a complete installation. Again, the pod has been subcontracted, and this time Rohr shares the work with another specialist pod builder, Shorts of Belfast.

Standard fuel capacity of the A320-100 is 15,906 litres (3,500 Imp gal, 4,203 US gal), housed in three integral tanks in each wing, with a small dry bay behind each engine. The A320-200 has a centre-section integral tank of 8,035 litres (1,767 Imp gal, 2,122 US gal) bringing capacity to 23,700 litres (5,213 Imp gal, 6,190 US gal).

In general the A320 systems are representative of the very latest traditional practice, if that is not self-contradictory. There are three independent 3,000 lb/sq in (207-*bars*) hydraulic systems, any one of which is more than adequate for complete flight control. Again, there are three 90-kVA electric generators, one on each engine and the third on the APU. The latter, in the tailcone as in previous Airbuses, is the extremely efficient new Garrett GTCP 36-300. This drives the third generator directly, at constant speed, the others having integrated hydraulic drives. The APU also provides ground air-conditioning. The bleed pipe for this purpose runs forward to the main pressurization and environmental control system, which is based on left and right packs in the bottom of the flat centre section. Main contractors are ABG-Semca

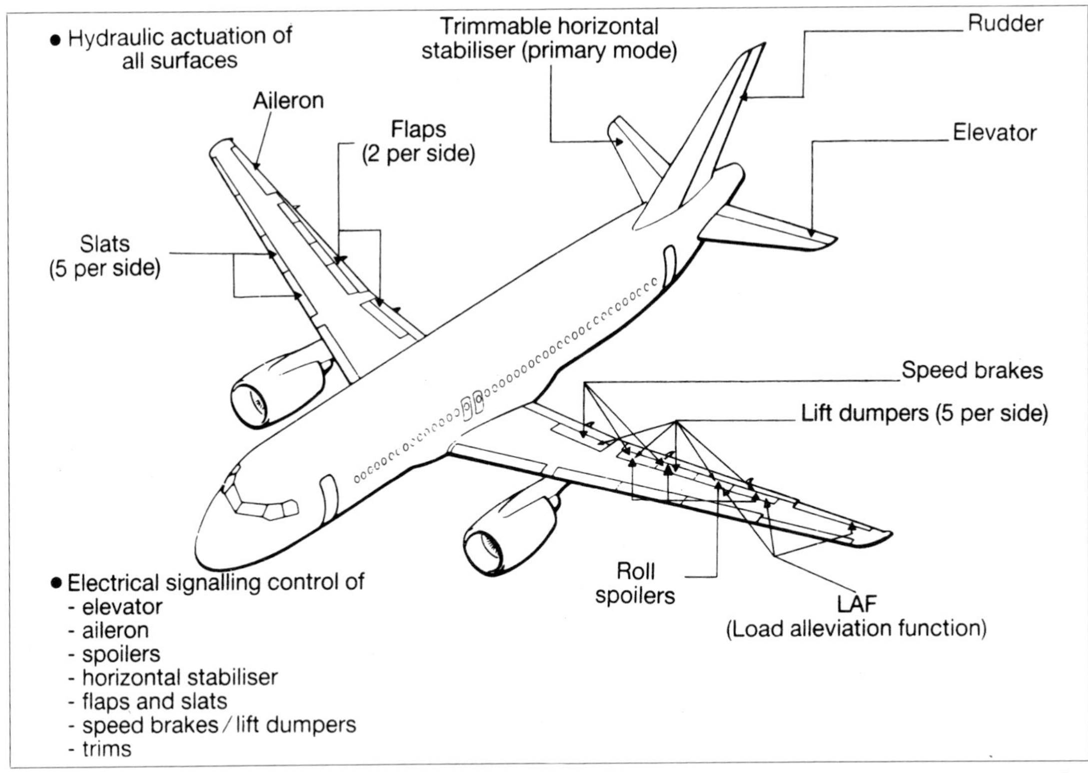

As the only all-new jetliner in the sky today the A320 shows the latest thinking in aerodynamics. Conventional ailerons were retained partly on LAF grounds. Pitch can be controlled by tailplane (horizontal stabilizer) or elevator

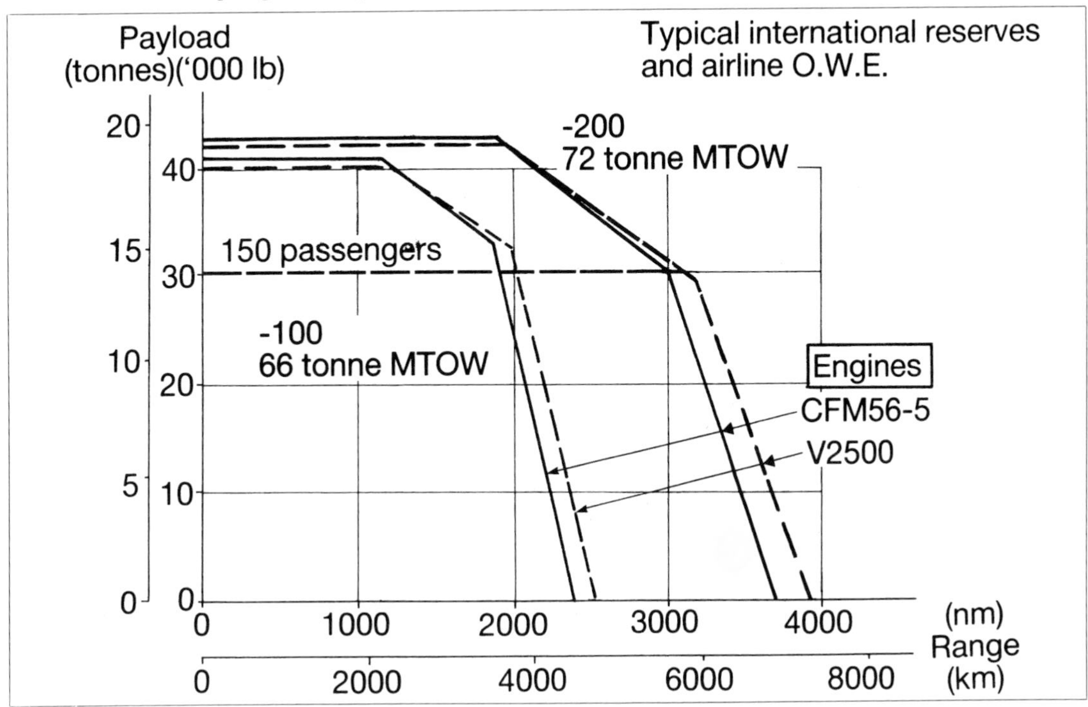

AI just can't help delivering roughly double what it originally aimed at! OWE, operating weight empty; MTOW, maximum takeoff weight

of France and Liebherr-Aerotechnik of Germany, but main AI partners helped design the external aerodynamics which make this the most efficient cabin air system ever installed. It operates at a dP of up to 8.25 lb/sq in (0.57 *bar*), and the fuel-burn penalty of the engine bleeds which drive the packs is minimized by carefully arranged ram inlets for the incoming cold air, and outflow valves which give propulsive thrust. The digital avionics also minimize fuel penalty in icing conditions, with raw AC for the windshields and air-data sensors and very hot bleed air for the engine inlets and the four outboard slat sections, the latter incorporating piccolo tubes along the leading edge.

A British firm, Dowty Rotol, at last secured a major item as contractor for the main landing gears, which are extremely neat inwards-retracting units with twin wheels. Standard tyres are 46 × 16–20 in radial-ply, but crossply are an option, as are two larger sizes for operators wanting a bigger footprint with reduced inflation pressure. Messier supplies the carbon brakes except when, as in the case of PanAm, a customer specifies a US company such as Bendix or Goodyear. Messier also provides the forwards-retracting twin-wheel nose gear, which again can be fitted with oversize low-pressure tyres.

Unquestionably the most significant advances made in the A320 are in the areas of digital avionics with FBW (fly by wire) flight controls. The one thing the basic aircraft designers shrank from doing—and they were probably wise—was to make the aircraft longitudinally unstable in the way that is now universal for air-combat fighters. Use of CCV (control-configured vehicle) technology enables such unstable aircraft to be not only more agile but also physically smaller, and thus to have reduced weight and drag. This is immediately equated with reduced fuel burn. Another new technology is the FSW (forward-swept wing), which again can show aerodynamic advantages translatable into reduced aircraft size, weight and drag. In due course CCV and FSW technology may be introduced to commercial jetliners, but not in the timescale of the A320. Indeed Boeing, which since 1981 has lost no opportunity to try to find some way of technically leapfrogging past the 320 in its future projects for the 1990s, has made no mention at all of either technique.

Thus the A320 is fundamentally a conventional stable aeroplane, but with exceedingly clever flight controls. As already described, the actual surfaces are entirely conventional; indeed, unlike its big brothers the 320 even has normal ailerons. Where it differs is in the cockpit, the interfaces between the pilots and the controls and, above all, in the new digital computer capacity to fly the aircraft better than humans can.

Certainly, though the 320 looks ordinary on the outside, once the pilot goes up front he is in a new world. The cockpit—which was made beautiful by the Porsche Industrial Design Bureau—is unlike anything he will have seen before, though over the coming decade it will become quite normal. The two obvious differences are that there are no control yokes and almost no traditional instruments. Instead each pilot has an uninterrupted view of two colour displays bigger than any seen before (7.25-in, 184-mm, square), with two more superimposed on the centreline. All six displays are identical, but all can be programmed differently. There is almost no limit to the scope and diversity of the information that can be displayed, though normally each pilot will have one in a horizontal-situation mode and the other in a vertical mode, with the central displays devoted to engines and systems. The 'horizontal' picture forms the ND (navigation display) and the vertical one the PFD (primary flight display). Together they make up the basic EFIS (electronic flight instrumentation system) which for the first time gives the pilots a feeling of uncompromised symbiosis with the aircraft. Indeed, in 1986 it was difficult to imagine how the system could be improved, though doubtless by year 2000 it will appear outmoded!

The EFIS is integrated with the two central displays which together form a major part of the ECAM (electronic centralized aircraft monitor) system which continuously displays everything the pilots need to know about the hardware. Any desired information can be called up by touching a button or the particular printout line on the screen, and any malfunction, or incipient malfunction, is displayed instantly. Three management computers drive the six displays, and any one computer can handle the entire flow of information. No possible on-board malfunction could fail to leave fewer than two displays operating normally and programmable as before.

Even the few 'instruments' are often not what they seem. A traditional electromechanical instrument has a dial and a needle, and these are rudely uncompliant and unalterable. The A320 instruments are in many cases analog displays generated electronically, and thus often alterable in various ways, besides being more reliable and precise in operation. The total count of 'instruments' on the A320 is in fact 12, compared with 42 on the 737-300 and 43 on the MD-80. Further examples of modern interfacing are seen in the RMPs (radio management panels) which flank the throttles on the central console. In an area smaller than this page these not only control a mass of communications and navigation avionics—the usual HFs, VHFs, VORs, ADF and ILS—but also faultless pre-dialling of frequencies and many other functions. Ahead of the RMPs are the usual MCDUs (multifunction control display units) as on the big Airbuses. Another difference is that the throttles are not connected mechanically to the engines but to the FADEC already referred to, which improves engine performance and response whilst significantly prolonging the life of the hot parts. Among other things, and on both types of engine, the FADEC allows for VSV (variable stator vane) scheduling for both transient and steady-state operation, and provides fully modulated feedback for the most efficient microscopic clearance round the HP turbine blades.

The most startling feature of the cockpit is that there are no control yokes. Instead, in front of each pilot there is a big pull-out chart table! To fly the A320 the pilot takes hold of the small SSC (sidestick controller), conveniently positioned ahead of his outboard armrest. Pulling a selector knob on the FMS (flight-management system) glareshield display gives him control; pushing the knob in transfers control to the FMS. As in the big Airbuses this interface provides for immediate digital selection of heading, flight level, airspeed and vertical speed (rate of climb or letdown). Integrating the FMS into the aircraft's AFS (automatic flight system) results in the A320 coming under the complete control of an FMGS (flight-management and guidance system). In this mode the pilots, and up to two supernumeraries, have nothing to do from takeoff to touchdown but take an active interest.

Apart from a very much earlier analog system on Concorde, the A320 is the first commercial transport to have an FBW (fly by wire) flight-control system. The system is quadruplex, with safeguards which in the author's view make total failure something one need not consider. Special 'raceways', which in future may be made by advanced metal plastic-forming methods, keep the cable bundles separated yet accessible, and make provision for earthing lightning strikes. FBW cuts the number of mechanical components in the system by about 90 per cent, and eliminates the need for autopilot servos. In a 150-seat aircraft this saves about 300 lb (136 kg) in weight, besides almost eliminating maintenance. The A320 also makes limited use of what may be the next generation, FBL (fly by light), mainly to link duplicate 'black boxes', but the introduction of optical fibres to airline service must be a gradual process.

The FBW system sends the electrical signals, originated in the SSCs or the FMS, to the hydraulic power units driving the elevators, ailerons, spoilers, speedbrakes, flaps, slats and, when the spoilers are thus used, gust alleviators and lift dumpers. The rudder and tailplane are excluded and are always drivable manually, to guard against the impossible happening. As explained in an earlier chapter, the SSCs are connected electronically into the FMS computers so that, in normal flight, the signals from the two SSCs are added together to give the FBW output. An instructor can correct a pupil's action by reducing its effect by moving his own SSC in opposition beyond a given threshold (each pilot is warned what is happening). Alternatively, the actions of the other pilot can be augmented. In emergency either pilot can press a takeover button on his own SSC, which then flies the aircraft regardless of the position of the other, to handle the incapacitated-pilot case.

Such an eventuality is unlikely to occur in the nominal 60,000 flights to which the aircraft has been designed, but other kinds of emergency can happen frequently: dangerous situations arising from incipient stalls, overspeeding and overstressing. Like the latest fighters, the A320 gives its pilot so-called carefree handling. Try as he might, he can never hazard the aircraft, and even the dread spectre of windshear is no longer a problem. Basically, the FMS computers are programmed to know the aircraft's permitted flight envelope, the limitations on its indicated airspeed, angle of attack and vertical acceleration (G). Thus, so long as the pilot's commands stay within the flight envelope they are relayed without modification; should they go outside it they are instantly inhibited, and those that approach the boundaries are progressively modified by being electronically shaped to preserve safe flight.

Suppose the A320 encounters severe windshear. The future-speed sensors detect its onset at an early stage and increase engine power and angle of attack. Should the sensor be inoperative for any reason, the pilot flying the aircraft can immediately slam on full power and haul back on the SSC as hard as he likes. Nothing dangerous will happen, he will immediately get full power and the AOA will rise to the safe limit and stay there to give maximum lift. On the approach, which is one of the crucial times when windshear is important, the MGS (minimum groundspeed system) continuously calculates the correct approach regime by using the airspeed, groundspeed and the known surface wind entered by the pilot into the FMS. Any deviation from the entered wind automatically triggers a change in engine power to maintain the correct speed.

Basically the A320 flight-control system is a logical extension of that flying on the A310, but with FBW and incorporating considerable extra capabilities which in due course will probably be transferred to the bigger Airbuses. Of course, there is no need for artificial feel; the SSCs merely incorporate light springs tending to restore them to the neutral position. Apart from eliminating all known sources of danger, the FBW/FMS is lighter than a traditional system, more enjoyable to operate, and appreciably less demanding in maintenance. Altogether it is probably the biggest single plus in the entire aircraft, and something that could never economically be built into such derivative aircraft as the MD-80 and 737-300.

Of course, such an advanced system did not happen overnight. Development of the final system began six years before first flight, and involved many research tools. The SSCs were first flown in the A300 demonstrator, and the control laws of the FBW computers were refined by flying the same A300 via a specially programmed autopilot, simulating the A320's protective software which guards against stalling, overspeeding or overstressing. Not least, Aérospatiale built an 'Iron Bird' at its Blagnac plant, next to the AI headquarters. Incorporating a complete A320 flight-control system, with FBW-signalled hydraulics, the Iron Bird was switched on in April 1986 and has operated virtually non-stop ever since. Its three main tasks are to verify the design before first flight, aid certification by demonstrating tolerance of component failures, and serve as a platform for endurance testing. In the same building are three A320 simulators, one of which is at the nose of the Iron Bird and permits pilots and engineers to 'fly' the rig directly, complete with aerodynamic and visual effects. Such manual flying has taken up more than half the total test time, the rest being controlled by computer programs that simulate hundreds of flights every few hours to keep the Iron Bird far ahead of any real A320 in terms of flight-control operating time.

Another aspect in which advanced avionics will make life much, much easier is in maintenance. This has been described by AI's Dennis Little: 'BITE (built-in test equipment) has developed in a haphazard manner. In the A320 we devised CFDS (centralized fault display system); we thought about what we want to achieve, and set out to exploit available technology to achieve the most cost/effective solution. CFDS provides line maintenance personnel with a central checking facility for all electronics and for systems with electronic control. It replaces the multitude of individual BITE indications which today are carried on the front face of each item, in widely differing formats. Two MCDUs (multifunction controller display units) on the flight deck enable one mechanic to follow up defects reported by the flight crew. An unambiguous message identifies the item to be replaced, and any tests to be performed subsequently. No documentation is required, and in the few cases where a test is required this is done via the MCDU. For simplicity we use the CDUs of the FMS (flight-management system) for the CFDS function, also.' Fantastic!

Clearly many features of the A320 flight-control and avionics systems, developed with the help of A300 and A310 aircraft, will in due course become available on AI's larger transports, and it could happen in a relatively short period thanks to AI's background of experience. So too can many of the other advanced features of the A320, including new constructional methods and protection against corrosion. AI have from the start been industry leaders in the battle against corrosion, which can make young aircraft quickly grow old, and costs unbelievable sums in such rectification programmes as reskinning. Though the twin-aisle Airbuses are built to a standard which exceeds the IATA and FAA requirements, the 320 sets even higher standards. For example, its fuselage sections are primed before assembly and not after, and the primer is a new epoxy which will remain throughout the aircraft's life, instead of being stripped off on each repainting.

As for new structural techniques, no commercial aircraft before the A320 has made such extensive use of so many different types of composite material. The latter include radome and fairings in glassfibre, the entire tail unit and many other parts, including most of the engine pods in CFRP, and Kevlar and other aramid-fibre composites in various areas outside the pressurized fuselage. BAe pioneered SPF/DB (superplastic forming and diffusion bonding) of titanium, which among other parts is used to make the manhole covers along the underside of the wings and some of the slat-track cans. Using 6Al4V (6 per cent aluminium, 4 per cent vanadium) alloy, the parts are made just like glassblowing by inflating with argon gas at about 990°C inside a precision mould. Despite the high alloy cost, SPF/DB parts are cheaper as well as lighter, and technically superior to parts made by fastening various pressings together. Exactly the same technique was pioneered by a division of Texas

Instruments using aluminium alloys, the name in this case being TEM, from thermally expanded metal. TEM is for the first time being introduced in various selected parts of the A320, and promises in the longer term to transfer to metals the production-cost advantages of composites.

As finally agreed, the work-split on the A320 differs both from the original scheme and from the shareholding by the partners in AI itself. Aérospatiale has 34.0 per cent, and not only handles assembly and flight test but also makes considerably more than it does on the 300 and 310, the main extra items being the complete forward fuselage, passenger and service doors (the forward passenger door having the option of integral airstairs) and various pod and pylon strut parts. MBB has an even greater share, 34.6 per cent and makes all centre and rear fuselage sections, the vertical tail, flaps and cargo doors. BAe has 24.0 per cent, and contributes the wings outboard of the fuselage, including (unlike the 300 and 310) the secondary and movable structures apart from the slats and flaps, as well as the main-gear leg doors. CASA (5.4 per cent) makes the horizontal tail, main-gear bay doors and rear-fuselage outer skins. Belairbus (2.0 per cent) makes the slats. BAe subcontracted the wingtips to FAF at Emmen as part of an offset deal with Switzerland.

As noted earlier, Air France was launch customer, with a total requirement for no fewer than 50 to replace all the airline's old-technology 727s and 737s. There followed commitments from British Caledonian and Air Inter. All three airlines selected the CFM56-5 engine. Next came Inex Adria of Yugoslavia and Cyprus Airways, who deferred choice of engine. Then came the massive order from PanAm, for 16 firm and 34 on option; this was the crucial launch order for the V2500 engine, which was then also picked by Inex Adria and Cyprus. In June 1985 Lufthansa announced it was buying 15, but for delivery from 1989, with an option on 25 more. These aircraft will have V2500 engines, will seat eight First-class and 126 Business, and will initially replace 34 B.727s. In the same month Ansett of Australia announced selection of the 320 for its fleet modernization programme, with eight firm and nine on option. Sir Peter Abeles said Ansett would call the A320 the Skystar. Seating 140 in two classes, these aircraft are being delivered from July 1988 with the CFM engine.

For many years British Aerospace had been gradually selling vast factories, and in 1985 it still had a surfeit of buildings and even complete sites. Despite this the economic demands of the A320 programme were such that in June of that year BAe announced that it would build a completely new A320 wing completion centre at Bristol. Costing over £4.5 million, this was in full operation just one year later, with wings moving on air-bearing 'hoverpallets' down the central area 350 ft long.

In August 1985 work began on testing A320 airframe sections for both static strength and fatigue. Five parts were assembled for the latter programme, which will continue long after this book appears. The nose and forward fuselage are on test at

CEAT, Toulouse, a few kilometres from AI's assembly line. The wings and fuselage centre section are at IABG in Munich. The rear fuselage and CFRP fin are on test by MBB at Hamburg, and all AI experience to date indicates that CFRP parts have an indefinite fatigue life. The complete tailplane is being tested by the maker, CASA of Getafe, Madrid. Also in August 1985 AI completed the vital A320 maintainability review, in which the entire aircraft is studied by maintenance engineers; in 1985–86 a further review was attended by staff from customer airlines.

A major milestone on 1 July 1985 was transfer by Super Guppy of the No 1 wing centre section from Aérospatiale Nantes to MBB Hamburg, the first of thousands of such transfers. In September Aérospatiale St Nazaire completed the first front fuselage, and a month later BAe Chester took the first pair of wing boxes out of their jigs and in early November trucked them to Bristol, the first time that major parts of an Airbus aircraft had routinely travelled between sites by road. Also in November MBB mated the first centre and rear fuselage sections at Hamburg.

Another early journey was transfer of the first nose and forward fuselage from St Nazaire; this became the first bit of A320 to reach Toulouse, on 31 January 1986. It was immediately taken over for further systems installation at the head of the A320 assembly line in the Toulouse St Martin factory which once assembled French Concordes. Unlike the big A300 and 310 the A320 fuselage is delivered to Toulouse in only two parts, the front from St Nazaire and the rest from Hamburg. A lot more happened in January 1986. On the 7th the first complete centre/rear fuselage came out of its jig at Hamburg, while a complete cockpit structure for birdstrike tests was delivered to CEAT Toulouse. On the 14th SONACA at Gosselies, part of Belairbus, dispatched the first slat sections to BAe Bristol. On the 20th James M Robertson, President of the leasing giant GATX Air, (whose Chairman J Warren Samborn signed for ten 320s), said 'The appeal is its advanced technology; we are buying an airplane that will have a lot of value to us in the future'. On the same day the No 2 set of wings was completed at BAe Chester, to go via Bristol (with only limited systems) to the static-test aircraft at CEAT. And on the last day of the month SNECMA at Villaroche, south of Paris, pushed the button for the automatic FADEC-controlled start of the third CFM56-5 engine, the first to be built to A320 production standard.

On 4 March 1986 Alia Royal Jordanian signed for six A320s, followed 13 days later by a massive contract, valued at over US$1 billion, for 19 aircraft for Indian Airlines. In addition the Indian domestic carrier signed for 12 on option; its aircraft will seat 167 all-economy, and will be powered by the V2500. On 28 March final assembly of No 1 began when the centre/rear fuselage arrived at Toulouse and was joined to the forward section soon after. At this time MBB Hamburg had fuselage parts in jigs for the next ten aircraft, while three days later St Nazaire trucked the No 2 forward fuselage to CEAT for static testing. The St Nazaire plant was by this time completing No 4 forward fuselage, in a building previously used for the Dassault-Breguet Falcon

20. Toulouse St Eloi contributes the windscreen surround, Nantes a 'slice' of fuselage incorporating the forward passenger door, and the former Potez works at Meaulte, near Paris, the keel section. St Nazaire is another plant that uses hoverpallets to move the large sections between work-stations; to make the main hall relatively quiet the first three stations, where rivet guns are active, are encapsulated in a soundproof room.

Exactly on schedule, on 30 April 1986, Bristol delivered the first pair of completed and tested wings to Toulouse. Much lighter at 9 *tonnes* (20,000 lb) per pair than A300 wings, the 59 ft (17.67-m) wings went aboard a Super Guppy straight from the interim assembly hall where they had been made; indeed the Guppy came right inside the building, where Sir Peter Masefield, never one to miss an opportunity, had laid on BCal's Highland pipe band for the occasion. AI's A300 demo aircraft made a flypast at Bristol to demonstrate the foolproof safety of the A320 flight-control software. Flown by the SSCs, it came by at 17 degrees AOA at an IAS of only 95 knots—and then slammed into a 25 degree banked turn and departed in a climbing spiral, still at the same AOA and IAS. At a height of 300 ft no other jetliner could have done this. A watching captain said 'Very impressive. We will have to ensure that any equipment we buy has at least this capability' (but nothing else does). Other captains had been equally impressed by flying the same A300, BCal's Capt Hallett noting 'There is a psychological link with the aircraft which I had not expected to find'. AI was happy to let visitors do just as they wished; for example, make a violent avoidance manoeuvre at V_{ref}, pulling 1.5G and holding this to max-alpha (maximum AOA) where the aircraft is automatically stabilized. The A320 realizes the dream of many certification pilots: expensive and prolonged test and modification programmes to cater for extremely rare but dangerous events are no longer needed, as the A320 will never be able to get to the borders of its flight envelope.

While the first production-standard CFM engine reached full power a week from first run, the all-new rival V2500 made its first run at Pratt & Whitney's East Hartford, Connecticut, main plant on 4 March 1986, followed by the first run of a European-assembled engine at Rolls-Royce Derby on 13 April. Later in 1986 a third IAE partner, MTU, commissioned a V2500 testbed, and as this book went to press the very advanced engine looked on schedule for certification in April 1988, with entry into service due a year later. This was the engine specified by another important customer, Australian Airlines (previously TAA, Trans-Australia Airlines), which signed for nine Dash-200s with the centre-section tank to give transcontinental capability despite being able to use the smallest airports on the airline's jet network.

On 10 June 1986 CASA delivered the first tailplane. The Getafe plant has enormously expanded and automated its CFRP facilities, to include computer-controlled 'clothcutters' which automatically slice out tailplane skins, and five autoclaves (high-temperature presses), two of the latter being able to bond a whole left or right tailplane. Each tailplane is about 21 per cent lighter than a metal one, and has fewer than half as many parts. On 17 June MBB Stade delivered the biggest CFRP part, the fin. These tail surfaces were added to the No 1 aircraft just after it had moved down the line to Station No 2, rolling on its own wheels. Engine pylons arrived from the factory next door on 16 June, and in August vibration testing began with dummy CFM engines installed. Flight CFM56-5A-1 engines were installed in December, the rollout took place on 14 February 1987, and the first flight went like a dream eight days later. This aircraft flew at the 1987 Paris airshow in June, after which it went to MBB Hamburg for interior completion, resuming testing in August with hot/high trials at Madrid. Certification is due at the beginning of 1988, by which time the first four aircraft should have flown 440, 360, 200 and 180 hours, a total of 1,180. Air France, BCal and Air Inter receive the first six customer aircraft in March–May 1988.

As this was written, in mid-1987, 15 airlines and three leasing companies had signed for 287 A320s, plus 160 on option, a total of 447. Current plans call for 100 to come off the line in the first two years, and the peak production rare of 8 per month, to be reached in late 1989, is likely to have to be increased. This outstanding customer acceptance 'off the drawing board' is of the greatest importance to AI, as it confirms the rightness of all major decisions taken on the A320, including the choice of derivative turbofan engines. For the first time, Boeing is seriously worried, and so far the market has not believed the US rival's propaganda that in 1992 the propfan will suddenly make jets obsolete. There could be no more telling proof than this of the way AI is shifting the centre of gravity of the world's commercial planemakers.

On 1 October 1986, after this chapter had been written, statements were issued in Minneapolis/St Paul and in Toulouse which confirmed the rightness of the A320. NWA, Northwest Airlines, announced a trial lease of ten, plus an option to purchase a further 90. The total of 100 would constitute one of the biggest orders in airline history, worth getting on for $3 billion. There are several reasons why this sale is of particular importance. From the emotional viewpoint, NWA is the chief airline of the northwest part of the United States, and the No 1 operator through Seattle, home of Boeing. Thanks to deregulation, NWA has purchased Republic Airlines to become the third biggest carrier in the Western world. Deregulation inevitably means that US airlines will tend to order new equipment not in small increments but in widely spaced single gigantic orders, which will re-equip the airline, or a major part of it, for at least a 20-year period. NWA is as technically advanced and perceptive as any operator in the world, and it has been subjected to more than most in receiving the sales arguments of those who claim that the A320, with so-called traditional engines, will be 'obsolete after 1992'. NWA's decision has been to re-equip its single-aisle fleet with A320s whose deliveries will stretch beyond 1992, and which will certainly be in service in the year 2000. This is bad news for the propfanners, and it will certainly exert a very powerful influence on many other potential A320 customers.

7
COMPLETING THE FAMILY

CHAPTER 3 OPENED WITH THE COMMENT that, while AI envisaged nine variations on the A300 at the start of the project, some 20 years ago, the first one to become reality was a tenth variation invented much later. Indeed, ten years back there were also two further derivative projects, the B11 and B12, later restyled TA11 and TA12 to show that they were twin-aisle widebodies. Few builders of aircraft have ever had a better basis for derivative aircraft than the A300, and right from the start AI recognised that it had to ring the changes as far as its tight funding would permit.

So far, an outside observer might say that AI has produced no derivative aircraft except the A310. This would give a misleading impression, because continuous 'product development' has over the years transformed the A300, and indeed the A310 also, to the point where the widebody aircraft seen round the Toulouse cattle-trough in 1987 are each equal to at least two of the early A300s, in terms of range and payload. But the fact remains that for almost 15 years AI has consistently *not* built two derivative aircraft which it has dearly wished to build, and which at times have seemed imminent. In 1973 Phil Smith at Hatfield said 'The A300B no longer seems "too big", and I would like to see the stretched B9 get the go-ahead'. Only a year later Béteille said 'The B9 remains our most immediate prospect for several potential customers', while, also in 1974, Gilbert Pérol of Air France said 'We must replace our fuel-thirsty 707s at the earliest possible time, and for 18 months we have viewed the Airbus B11 as the best candidate aircraft'.

Thus, to lay the cards on the table, right back in the early 1970s AI saw the B9, B10 and B11 as the A300 derivatives which would complete its widebody family. The B10 became the A310. The B9 was to be a stretched A300 with the original wing and the most powerful engines available. The B11 was to be a true long-hauler to replace the 707 and DC-8 on 'long thin routes' with insufficient traffic to support 747s. It was to have a new wing of increased span, the shorter fuselage of the B10, and four new engines in the 22,000-lb (ten-tonne) thrust category. Altogether the A300, B9, B10 and B11 were planned to form a formidable and integrated family which, with ongoing development, could see AI's widebody production through to beyond the year 2000. But the B9 and B11 remained paper projects year after year until 1987.

This was chiefly for the good reasons that AI was never in a position to go ahead, or to try to scrape together the massive funding needed, and launch customers did not appear. Put another way, AI's energies were more profitably channelled into the 310 and 320. But it should not be thought that the long delay was in any way a disaster for AI, because a handful of project engineers kept on refining both the '9' and the '11', and today they are dramatically superior to their original conceptions, besides being more closely related. Advanced technology keeps on happening, and today these two projects have become the A330 and A340, respectively, and no more advanced subsonic transports could possibly be devised without introducing unacceptable technical risks. At the same time, AI exists in the most competitive of all worlds, where billions can ride on a technical decision that might at the time seem rather unimportant. At the conclusion of this final chapter AI's more distant future is examined, and the prospects are exciting. At last, these two big derived aircraft are about to become reality.

By 1977 the B11 had become a well-defined project based on the B10 fuselage and powered by four CFM56 engines hung 747-fashion along the long-span wing. Béteille told the author in that year 'I do not have the slightest doubt about it; we simply have to do it'. Two years later Lathière even said 'A decision on the B9 will be made within a year'. Well, it wasn't; but again this stretched A300, offering the range/payload of a DC-10 whilst burning 25 per cent less fuel, was always seen as another must for AI. The new designations TA9 and TA11 came in 1980, a year in which several TA11 studies had three engines of Rolls-Royce 535 or Pratt & Whitney JT10D-232 type, to see how these stacked up against the four-CFM56 versions. Indeed in that year's *Jane's* the TA11 was said to have 'Four underwing turbofan engines in the 30,000-lb class', well beyond anything then offered by the CFM56. Actually the thrust requirement for the four-engined project went as high as 35,000 lb at times, before the moment of truth came with the prospect of an imminent go-ahead, when the advantages of using proven engines—the CFM56-5 or V2500, as on the A320—were fully recognized.

Of course, few things in aviation stay the same for two days together. Prospects, timing and costs have for many years been deeply affected by the soaring price of fuel followed by its unexpected decline, by massive variations in exchange rates between major world currencies, and by other factors which have affected traffic growth on AI customer airlines. A further complicating factor was AI's dramatic development of its own A300 and A310 to carry more and fly much, much further than anyone had believed possible. A minor influence was the substantial re-engining programme on the DC-8 with CFM56 engines, which went a little way towards pre-empting the TA11 at less cost.

Certainly one of the biggest positive factors was the recognition in 1977 that both the new projects could share the same wing. As the long-hauler could also use the fuselage of the A310, the total bill for design and development began to look not unreasonable; a ballpark figure in 1981 was $1.5 billion, or slightly less than that for the smaller but wholly new A320. It was also clear by 1981 that natural competition between the engine builders would ensure the availability of growth versions of the current Airbus engines suitable for the stretched twin, the TA9. In the event, General Electric was by 1985 offering the CF6-80C2 at 61,000 lb, while the Pratt & Whitney PW4059 could be rated at 59,000 lb, either of which seemed to suit a very capable TA9.

At the 1982 Farnborough show AI published revised specifications for the two projects, emphasizing for the first time the stretched TA9's tremendous underfloor cargo potential: 16 LD3s or five pallets in the forward hold and 14 LD3s or four pallets in the aft hold. 'This', said AI, 'adds up to nearly twice as much as current trijets and 18 per cent more than a 747 using LD3 containers'. With a fuselage stretched by some 27 ft 9 in (8.48 m) over the A300, it would seat 326 mixed-class or up to 410 in all-economy, with fuel burn per seat about 22 per cent lower (later improved to 28 per cent lower) than current trijets. Two models were envisaged, the TA9-100 for sectors around 1,500 nm (2,780 km) and the Dash-200 for full-payload operations up to 3,300 nm (6,110 km). The market was expected to open up—for example, as a DC-10 replacement—from the late 1980s, with a potential by year 2000 of some 3,000 aircraft.

At the same time details were given of the shorter-body TA11 and a related twin, the TA12. These were seen as 220-seaters, mixed-class, with 17 underfloor LD3s, using the same wing as the TA9. The 11 would have 'four engines in the 30,000–34,000 lb category' while the 12 would have 'two engines in the 62,000 lb category'. With nothing much changed from the TA9 except 40 per cent fewer seats, it was not clear how the TA12 would beat the trijets by 24 per cent on seat-mile costs, or the 747SP by 35 per cent—bigger margins than the TA9, but over longer ranges up to 5,000 nm (9,200 km). The four-engine TA11 was intended for oceanic sectors up to 6,830 nm (12,650 km). It was accepted that 'because of the depressed state of the airline industry and the glut of long-range trijets on the secondhand market, the emergence of a strong market for the TA11 and TA12 has been pushed back to the early 1990s'.

By the 1983 Paris show things had been somewhat rationalized, AI explaining that all three projects would have maximum commonality, use proven engines, and be assembled building-block fashion from as many existing parts as possible. 'In practice', the press release stated, 'this will mean that the new aircraft will have largely in common a new wing, centre fuselage, main landing gear and tailplane. The TA11 and 12 will both use A310 front and rear fuselage sections, and the TA9 those of the A300-600 plus two simple new segments. The fin and rudder will be the A300-600's, and the nose gear an adaptation of that on the same aircraft.' The TA9's fuel burn per seat was improved to '30 per cent less than . . . trijets and about 25 per cent less than the proposed stretched version of the competitor twin-aisle twin' [the 767-300]. The TA11, envisaged as being powered by four 34,000-lb Rolls-Royce 535 or Pratt & Whitney PW2000-series engines, was being studied with two lengths of fuselage, the Dash-100 seating 230 mixed-class plus 17 LD3 containers, and the longer Dash-200 seating 270 with 24 LD3s.

By 1985 the new long-span wing had been given an important new feature: variable camber. For 70 years aircraft designers have tried to introduce polymorphism—the ability to change shape—into their aircraft. In recent years the 'adaptive wing' has been seen as a desirable goal. This attempts, in a crude way, to emulate the flexibility of a bird's wing, which throughout flight keeps adapting itself to changing aerodynamic requirements. Of course, fitting flaps makes a wing mildly adaptive, but these are usually not used in cruising flight. The variable-camber wing does a little better by making the whole area of the wing flaps pivoted, and able to hinge slightly downwards by varying amounts throughout each flight with no sudden discontinuity in profile. Introduced to the new long-span wing, variable camber promises at least a 2 per cent gain in aerodynamic efficiency, together with about a 1 per cent improvement in buffet onset in terms of lift coefficient at a cruise Mach number of around 0.82. (Diagram, page 196.)

It will be recalled that improving the wing profile of the A310, with inbuilt downwards camber along the trailing edge, was worth some 11,000 lb (5 *tonnes*) in extra payload or fuel by pushing out the buffet boundary at a given altitude and manoeuvre load factor. Again, lift in the landing configuration was increased by some 8 per cent despite simplifying the flaps and removing their trailing-edge tabs. Since 1980 continued work by the AI partners, notably by BAe at Bristol and Hatfield, has further refined the wing profile for the new projects until they can be made significantly deeper in profile, for any given sweep angle and drag-divergence Mach number. Making the wing deeper means that it can be skinned with thinner sheet, and thus be appreciably lighter; and obviously it can also accomodate more fuel. These are very important advantages for a long-haul aircraft, and this aerodynamic refinement has led to significant improvements in the TA11, in particular. Not least, AI has intensified its studies of laminar flow.

All today's aircraft are surrounded by a boundary layer of violently turbulent air. Most of the whirlpools and eddies are very small, but they add up to greatly increased drag, and hence increased fuel burn, as well as to impaired flight control and reduced peak lift coefficient. Making wings and other parts truly laminar, surrounded by air flowing perfectly smoothly from front to rear, has been the elusive goal of aerodynamicists for over 40 years. Most schemes have sought to keep the flow laminar by sucking away the boundary layer through fine sieves or porous wing skins. This is not difficult to do, but the slightest surface imperfection makes the flow

A 1/44 model by MBB of the as-then-planned A340, on test at NLR Amsterdam in April 1986. Many other models have been tested by BAe and Aérospatiale, as well as the German partner

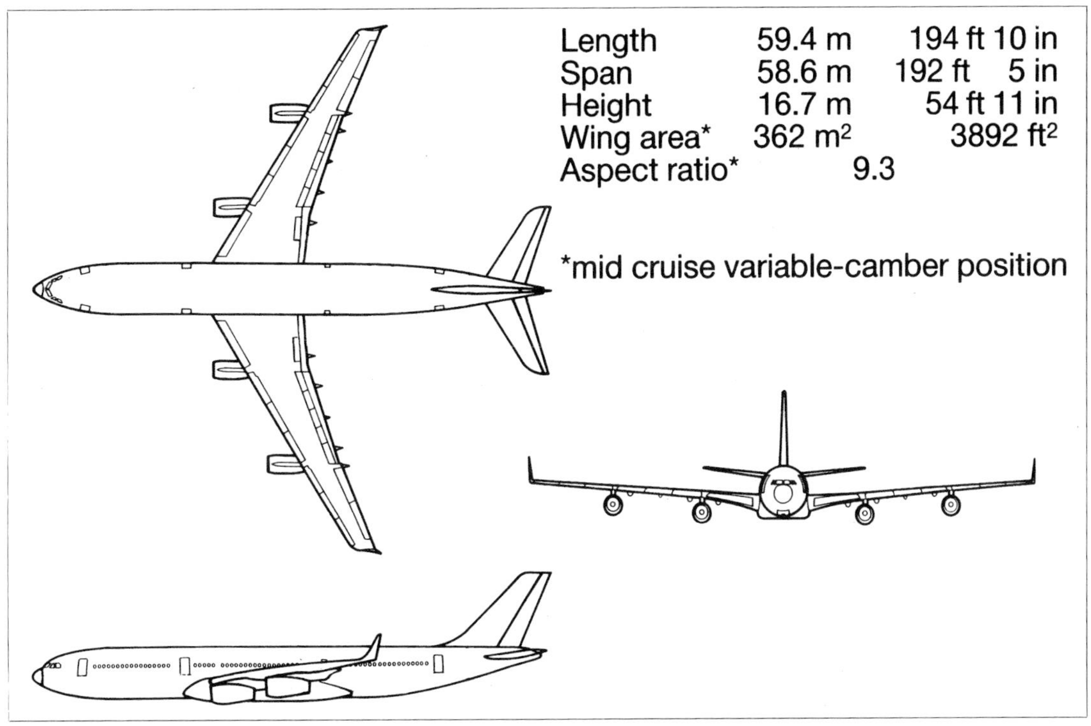

A fairly definitive three-view of the A340-200, with CFM56-5C1 engines. A comparative drawing of the stretched Dash-300 appears on page 196

In the author's view the A330 ought to be one of the biggest smash hits in the history of air transport. This May 1987 artwork shows GE CP6-80C2A6 engines, though not only P&W but also Rolls-Royce, with the RB.211-524L in the 70,000-lb class, are fighting to get aboard

A March 1987 impression of the A340-200 in Lufthansa colours, as it would have looked if powered by the V2500 SuperFan. Common sense suggests that an aircraft looking very much like this will get into production eventually, but not by 1992. Note the small wingtip fences

turbulent. A tiny skin dent, or a fly squashed against the leading edge, make laminar flow impossible. But today AI is not only working on traditional sucking and blowing methods but also researching tantalizing new possibilities.

According to Dennis Little, Assistant/Deputy to V-P Technology and New Product Development, 'AI is looking at new aerofoil sections as a means of achieving natural laminar flow, and we would envisage testing a large component at some stage. However the chordwise pressure distributions and the aerofoil sections are quite different from those of today's advanced transonic wings. There are also restrictions on the angle of sweepback that can be used . . . We cannot expect to see this sort of development in airline service before the second half of the 1990s. Of more immediate interest is the possibility of limited natural laminar flow on specific components such as the engine nacelles. We are working closely with the engine manufacturers in this area, and we could expect to see such a development producing benefits of 1 per cent to 2 per cent in cruise fuel burn in service in the early 1990s.'

AI is also studying ways of providing the wing's upper surface with narrow suction slits aft of the point of maximum thickness. By cutting two such slits from tip to tip, air can flow automatically from the higher-pressure region downstream of the shockwave into the region ahead of it. This weakens the shock, reduces flow separation and improves drag, lift coefficient and buffet boundary, at almost no cost.

Thus by 1985 various possible new ways of improving the vital aerodynamics were being examined, while market forces continued to bend and reshape the new projects. AI widened the circle of airlines whose opinions influenced these aircraft, while partner companies began committing increasing sums to tunnel testing and other forms of research. Among many factors which kept the projects fluid were the falling price of fuel, the trend towards three classes of seating on long hauls, the generally rising standards of passenger comfort and amenities demanded, and the growth in size of the B.747 with the Dash-300 and Dash-400 versions, widening the gap between it and the trijets which the new Airbuses aimed increasingly to replace.

At the 1985 Paris airshow AI did not mention the TA12 but said the new wing for the TA9 and TA11 could be the same externally, but could have a 'tailored' interior. Varying metal (or composite) thicknesses could suit the different fuel capacities and wing bending moments, the TA11 having fuel from tip to tip. Target for this four-engined machine was now seen as achieving 'the seat-mile economy of the latest 747, whilst being almost 50 per cent smaller'. Flying 250 passengers in three-class layout over sectors up to 6,500 nm (12,050 km), it would have no overwater limitations and would also have 'significantly better performance from hot and high airfields' than competitors such as the 767ER. Meanwhile, the big twin TA9 was described as a 330-seater for 3,200 nm (5,900 km), confirming inexorable growth in the range demanded.

What AI did not say at Paris was that the building-block philosophy had taken a remarkable further step forward, and both projects now looked externally almost identical, apart from one having twice as many engines. Indeed, apart from the engines, fuel capacity and such details as some skin thicknesses and systems design, they had become the same aircraft. By late 1985 both looked very attractive indeed, the only real problems being the magnitude of the investment needed and the fact that if you polled 34 airlines on their opinions—as AI did—you got almost 34 different answers, not the least feature being the overwhelming US preference for a long-range twin. Not so long ago the same eight American airlines not only forced Lockheed and Douglas to put three engines in their previously proposed widebody twins but also scornfully criticised AI for sticking to 'only' two engines!

On 27 January 1986 the AI Supervisory Board met in Munich and approved the future strategy for completing its product range. It announced 'Airbus Industrie is now in a position to finalize the detailed technical definition of the TA9, which is now officially designated the A330, and the TA11, now called the A340, with potential customer airlines, and to discuss with them the terms and conditions for launch commitments.' The statement was put out by Board Chairman Dr Franz-Josef Strauss. President Jean Pierson added 'This will be the last major investment to be made by the partners in helping AI achieve a strategy of offering a complete family of aircraft. It will range from 150 to 400 seats, optimized for stage-lengths from 300 nm (550 km) to 7,000 nm (13,000 km), addressing the various airline requirements.'

In the same month AI's Senior V-P Engineering and former Chief Test Pilot, Bernard Ziegler, read a paper in Singapore in which he touched on four new technologies. One, variable camber, he considered virtually certain to be a feature of the A330 and 340. He commented on the efficiency advantage of being able to adjust wing camber to achieve aerofoil profiles matched to each flight condition. Obviously, the basic wing would have a profile matched to the ideal cruise condition, but important gains accrue from being able to use slightly different computer-controlled trailing-edge angles when forced by air-traffic control to fly lower, or slower, or in any other off-design condition. Another likely development was active controls. The author made the comment earlier that nobody has yet dared to design airliners like modern unstable fighters. With active controls the stability comes not from the weathercock action of big tail surfaces but from fast-acting computers driving small powered control surfaces. Ziegler emphasized the long time needed for certification authorities to build up confidence with such systems, none of which are yet even planned for civil aircraft (late-model TriStar 'active ailerons' are used to reduce bending of an extended-span wing on a conventional stable aircraft). This problem was discussed in connection with the A320s.

As for the other two new ideas, Ziegler guarded against expecting too much too soon. In the intensely competitive world of big jetliners there is a natural tendency to want to be 'fustest with the mostest'—to introduce more new technology quicker than one's rivals. In fact, Boeing at least has an excellent record of not promising what they cannot deliver, but to some degree that is because as world No 1 jet builder, by a very wide margin, they do not have to. When Boeing talks, people listen. The competition from AI, especially with the A320, has suddenly jolted Boeing into searching for ways of presenting the European aircraft as not really advanced at all, and this can only be done by finding technologies that are newer. Two of these newer technologies are propfans and all-electric controls. Both have been increasingly well understood since about 1975, though it is only very recently that results of full-scale hardware testing have become available. It is certainly too early to be dogmatic. In the author's view Boeing will risk losing its conservative reputation if it pushes new technology too hard while there are still unanswered questions. It has already burned its fingers to some extent with a too-early introduction of aluminium-lithium alloys, and this has made AI naturally cautious.

At the same time, AI has to guard against ever getting a reputation for scorning new technology. It is very unlikely to do this. As this book goes to press, AI has quite the reverse reputation; it is world No 1 builder of advanced-technology transports, as many of its recent customers—including six in the USA—have publicly confirmed. Nevertheless, it is clearly undesirable for AI's top people to make a habit of saying 'Watch it, world airlines! This exciting new technology, that looks so attractive in competitor brochures, may contain hidden problems and is likely to prove the proverbial can of worms'. So far AI has trodden a carefully charted middle course. The new technologies it has introduced have worked brilliantly. The even newer ideas it has doubted may indeed contain as-yet not fully comprehended problems, and airlines really do have to be cautious.

The two things Ziegler picked on were propfans and the all-electric aircraft. Propfans, which have many other names, are extremely advanced variable-pitch propellers, with typically eight to 11 thin scimitar-like blades, which give something like turboprop fuel economy but at jet speeds. Efficiency gain over a typical turbofan for a single-rotation propfan might be about 20 per cent, and for a counter-rotating double propfan it might be 25 per cent (these are not AI figures, but typical of those generally assumed). There are many ways of arranging a propfan, including a geared tractor, a geared pusher and GE's UDF (unducted fan) answer in which extra turbines downstream of the core engine carry the propfan blades on their outer periphery, forming a double contra-rotating ring round the middle of the engine pod. The chief problems, which as AI points out are still to some degree unknown, are noise inside the aircraft, vibration fatigue on the airframe, protection against shed blades, engine damage tolerance and, above all, the costs of maintenance, which are bound to be relatively high.

Thus, for the present, AI is pushing propfans much less enthusiastically than Boeing. Indeed, Fokker of the Netherlands recently published a cost analysis of a 100-

seater on a 300-nm sector (1985 AEA cost formula) in which the regular turbofan aircraft, such as the Fokker 100, was the baseline, a derivative aircraft with advanced propfans showed overall DOC (direct operating cost) 6 per cent *higher* and an all-new propfan aircraft came out 13 per cent higher! Thus, AI are very far from being a lone voice in the wilderness. In place of the unshrouded propfan, AI considers a preferable answer, at least for the early 1990s, to be the very high-bypass-ratio turbofan. This should overcome noise and containment problems, and avoid various other dangers, whilst offering fuel burn roughly 15 per cent below the best attained by contemporary engines. If fuel prices rise again, such engines will certainly be developed. At the same time, for the big new A330 and A340 AI had no doubt whatever that these should initially be marketed with proven existing engines, as already described. Indeed, there seemed to be no alternative in the timescale.

As for the 'electric aircraft', this would use nothing but electricity to bring power to every place on board. Today's massive hydraulic systems, with many miles of high-pressure piping, costly non-inflammable fluids, large linear and rotary actuators, and countless spool valves, seals, accumulators and other auxiliary devices, would all be swept away. In their place would be more extensive direct-current electrical systems of advanced conception and possibly using a voltage of 200 or more. These could either be all-electric—so-called EMAS (electro-mechanical actuation systems)—or electro-hydrostatic. In the latter, electric power drives a self-contained hydraulic actuator or motor. In EMAS a speed-reducing gearbox is usually required, but these can be quite light. What makes it all feasible, and indeed attractive, is the fantastically increased performance of the latest electrc magnetic machines, using rare-earth (usually SmCo, samarium cobalt) magnetic materials. On a recent visit to Fairey's advanced design centre at Claverham the author was deeply impressed at the prospects, but AI have yet to take the plunge and offer the all-electric jet. So has everyone else.

Through 1986, definition of the A330 and A340 proceeded at an increasing pace, with growing R&D at AI and the partner companies, as well as the efforts of a 50-strong Integrated Task Force at Toulouse comprising technical and industrial core teams. It was evident much earlier that both aircraft would have an advanced 'second-generation' digital avionics system, with FBW flight controls even more sophisticated than those of the A320, CFRP tail surfaces (the horizontal tail being a trim tank), and almost all the advances pioneered with previous AI aircraft as well as several new ones. The one giant new feature is the wing, originally designed with a span of 56 m (183 ft 9 in). In 1986 most tunnel testing concentrated on the high-speed cruise regime, with considerable effort at Hatfield and Filton (Bristol), Bremen and Toulouse.

Certainly the wing poses by far the biggest new design and development effort. Most of it was originally designed by various BAe sites. BAe Civil Aircraft Division

Technical Director J W H 'Tommy' Thomas expects the BAe work share to be 'between that on the A310 and A320, with responsibility for the complete wing'. Hatfield might handle the main box and systems installation, but overall project control is vested in Bristol, which is also responsible for the leading and trailing edges movable surfaces, fuel systems and main landing gear configuration. Overall boss is Sid Swadling, BAe Chief Engineer (Airbus) at Bristol, with his assistant, Jeff Jupp, in charge of design; Andy Carlile is Chief Designer at Hatfield. Obviously this is a massive programme for BAe, and the biggest production wings ever built in Britain, or anywhere else in Western Europe.

Accompanying diagrams emphasize the advanced technology of the new wing of the A330/340. One (page 91) shows the way AI has been able to make its wings thicker and thicker, whilst maintaining the same M_{DIV} (divergence Mach number), and thus the same high cruising speed capability. Increasing the thickness/chord ratio, to a remarkable 12.8 per cent in the new wing, means that span and aspect ratio can be increased without the severe penalties in weight which would be inescapable with a thin wing. For example, the wing of the rival McDonnell Douglas MD-11 has a t/c ratio of between 8 and 9 per cent over the main panel outboard of the engines, and there is no way the span could have been increased without making the skins thicker and heavier..

A wing of greater aspect ratio has inherently lower induced drag and greater aerodynamic efficiency than rival wings, and the fundamental Breguet formula shows that aircraft range is directly proportional to L/D (lift divided by drag). Other factors being equal, L/D depends on aspect ratio, the basic slenderness of the wing in plan. No rival airliner comes close to the A330/340 in this regard, but, as a further diagram (page 196) shows, AI has a second trick up its sleeve in variable camber. As explained earlier, ordinary wings have to be designed for best L/D at one particular condition, such as point B. In any other condition the drag increases sharply, so that the drag polar (lift plotted against drag) might follow a curve such as A-B-C. With the A330/340, for the very first time, AI can make the wing camber vary from takeoff to landing, so the drag always stays very close to the ideal minimum value (curve B_1-B-B_2). The shaded area shows the reduction in drag in off-design conditions, such as when heavy at the start of a flight and at a weight some 70 *tonnes* lighter near the destination.

This diagram also shows the principle of the variable-camber operation. Within each of the flap-track guides is to be found not one track but two, with totally different profiles. One track guides the nose of the flap and the other a point on the flap further aft, so that the two tracks together define the flap's position and incidence. Initial movement of the flap is directly to the rear, the undersurface of the flap remaining aligned with the wing undersurface so that there is no effect but an increase in effective chord and wing area. Continued movement results in slight rotation, to increase camber, the flap nose staying inside the wing profile. Further movement then brings a sudden change: the flap ceases rotation but moves bodily downwards away from the main wing, to give a low-drag high-lift setting. The final part of the flap travel pushes the main trolley down and the nose trolley up to give a rapid rotation to high incidence, for the final landing.

There has never been a major problem in the wing design; the wing has simply been progressively refined until today it is certainly the ultimate attainable with available technology. But in the matter of propulsion, for the A340 only, an almighty hiccup occurred which left a lot of people with egg on their faces, and damaged the credibility of a multinational engine company comprised of some of the most famous names in the business. It need never have happened; it should have been handled with more perception and sensitivity.

The engine company was IAE (International Aero Engines), which comprises Pratt & Whitney, Rolls-Royce, MTU (West Germany), Fiat (Italy) and Japanese Aero Engines, itself a three-company consortium. IAE have a potentially very efficient and attractive engine in the V2500, whose only application is that it is one of the two engines offered on the A320. IAE dearly wanted to get on the A340, but found it difficult to offer more than 27,500 lb thrust. Thus, though inherently more fuel-efficient than the CFM56, the A340 could actually fly further with the latter engine because it could climb more rapidly to high cruise altitude. One alternative would be, at high cost, to give the V2500 a bigger fan, driven by a larger LP turbine.

In parallel with such studies, the members of IAE spent 1986 playing with ideas and concepts for super-efficient engines in the UHB (ultrahigh-bypass) category, a generation later than the V2500. The most powerful members, Pratt & Whitney and Rolls-Royce, independently decided that the greatest merit attached to the ducted, geared, front-fan type of UHB engine, and the obvious core to use was that of the V2500. After detailed study the decision was taken at a meeting of the IAE board on 3 December 1986 to continue engineering studies of an engine known as the V2500 SuperFan. This comprised a V2500 core with augmented LP turbine power driving through a 3:1 reduction gearbox to a variable-pitch fan with a diameter of 110 in (2,794 mm), compared with the existing V2500 fan diameter of 63 in (1,600 mm). IAE proposed certification in April 1991, the same month planned for the first flight of an A340.

Compared with the regular V2500 the SuperFan promised a takeoff thrust increased from 25,000 lb (111.25 kN) to 30,000 lb (133.5 kN), with typical specific fuel consumptions reduced by around 15 per cent. This was just what AI wanted for the A340, and when AI was given a formal briefing and proposal on the SuperFan shortly before Christmas 1986 the AI management took everything on board with considerable excitement. IAE promised 'reasonable' development costs, and AI found no new landing gear would be needed. By this time McDonnell Douglas had announced the launch of the MD-11, which though rather bigger and basically a warmed-over DC-10 is nevertheless in very much the same category as the A340. AI suddenly saw in the SuperFan a 'next-generation' engine that they could use and the MD-11 could not. Though it was aware that the SuperFan was subject to various 'gates'—technical, political and financial—so is every other new technical development in modern aviation. AI was perhaps a little precipitate in making firm offers to airlines, and it was on the basis of these that the launch commitments for the A340 were signed in the first weeks of 1987. AI had stated that, for a launch decision on the 330/340 programme, it required 40 commitments from five customers. It did better than this, and at a meeting of the supervisory board on 13 March announced that it had obtained 104 commitments from nine customers. 'Therefore', AI stated, 'the board has decided to take all necessary steps for a formal launch decision by mid-April 1987 to ensure first deliveries of the A340 in May 1992, to be followed by first deliveries of the A330 a year later'. Soon afterwards, on 3 April, one of the world's most respected airlines, Northwest, announced a commitment for up to 20 A340s with an option on ten 330s. The future looked bright. It was then the bombshell arrived.

IAE had also briefed Boeing on the SuperFan. Boeing was looking for an engine for its 7J7 aft-engined 150-seater, and carried out a detailed comparison of the SuperFan and the rival unducted GE36. There are many reasons why the SuperFan should be preferable, and indeed pose lower risk, but GE's engine had already been flying a year in a 727 and was about to fly in a fairly definitive form in an MD-80. On 3 April, just as Northwest said it had signed for SuperFan 340s, Boeing Commercial Airplane's board decided to pick the GE engine. It made the decision public four days later, and on the same day, 7 April 1987, IAE's board announced what the media took to be the cancellation of plans to develop the SuperFan!

IAE assured the author that the decision was neither influenced by the Boeing rejection of the engine nor the rather protracted problems experienced by Rolls-Royce on the V2500 HP compressor, which by April 1987 were largely solved. According to IAE, 'The reason for this decision is that it was felt premature to launch the SuperFan programme at this stage, in the light of the technical and programme risks of meeting an entry-into-service date of spring 1992 to satisfy the airlines' desires. The SuperFan concept is not in question, and engineering evaluations for a variety of applications will continue to be pursued.' To the author the image generated by the whole saga seemed unnecessarily inept. That some kind of problem existed must be accepted, though this in itself is surprising. The fan itself was to be based closely on known technology, such as that of the RB.211D4D but with variable pitch. The gearbox was based closely on the proven technology of the Tyne. It seemed a reasonable comment when the magazine *Flight International* said in a leading article (6 December 1986), 'Subject, of course, to small development problems being

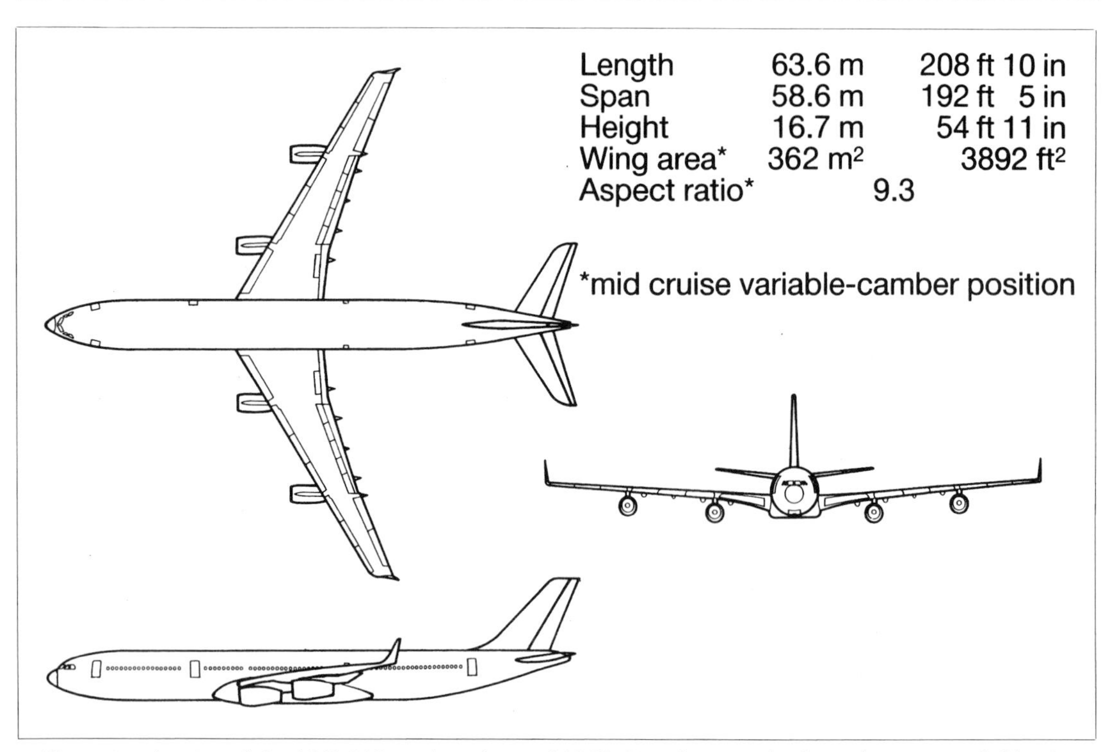

Three-view drawing of the A340-300 as planned in mid-1987. Two things strike the author as remarkable: the superficial similarity to the 707 as designed 35 years ago, and the amazing difference in transport efficiency (in the conversion of chemical energy into payload moved a given distance)

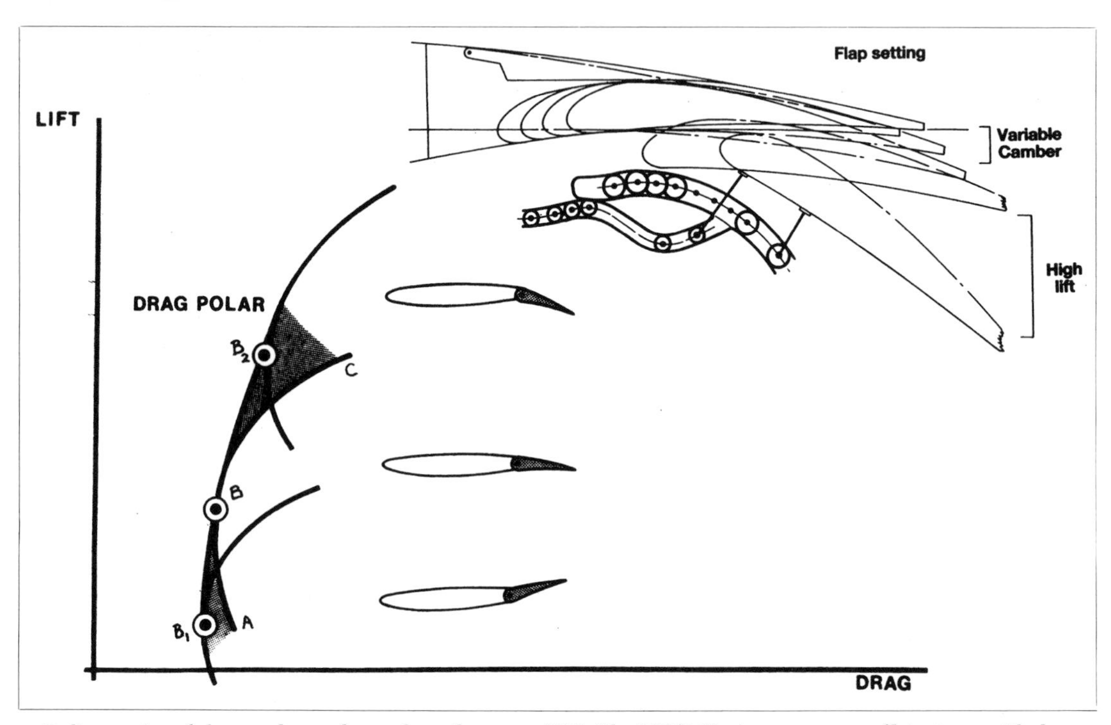

Ordinary aircraft have a drag polar such as the curve ABC. The 330/340 pioneer a more efficient era with drag polars such as B_1BB_2. The inset shows how the flaps move

solved, SuperFan has the advantage of employing mainly existing proven technology, and thereby offers a relatively inexpensive solution when compared with the clean-sheet development now being pursued in the United States'.

To say that the IAE announcement that it was backtracking on the SuperFan caused reverberations around the world is an understatement. Rivals, colleagues and customers vied with each other to criticize the decision, and point out the degree to which it damaged the credibility of IAE. Reinhardt Abraham of Lufthansa, whilst reaffirming his commitment to the A340, said 'When I negotiated with IAE I assumed I could rely on their information, as I have in the past when I worked individually with their members. . . . I took it for granted that when they told us about performance and scheduling that we could count on the information'. He noted that IAE had said the V2500-A1 engine for the A320 would be on time, but 'I cannot be sure whether I can be confident any more in what the consortium is promising'.

These comments, which were typical, inevitably rubbed off on AI. In any case, AI had rather foolishly not corrected the media when they assumed that the SuperFan was the key factor in building an A340 that would beat the MD-11. When the engine was offered to AI the choice of powerplant enabled AI to offer two versions of the A340, with different range/payload capabilities (the SuperFan version being the greater). According to Heribert Flosdorff, AI Executive V-P, 'We then were able to match the two MD-11 versions . . . which gave airlines the chance for a greater profit potential in a mix of operations than we could provide with the single A340-200 that had been available up to that time'. Loss of the SuperFan put AI very publicly on the spot, and gave McDonnell Douglas a marvellous opportunity to 'knock' what is basically a much newer aircraft. As Douglas President James Worsham put it, 'Airbus may seek a way to continue to present the A340 as an MD-11 competitor . . .' All very galling, because the A340 is so much later in conception that it did not need the SuperFan in order to compete with the MD-11 and everything else.

Before leaving the subject of the SuperFan it should be noted that IAE has reiterated that the viability of the engine is not in question, and long before this book appears some form of IAE 'super fan' is likely to have gone ahead. This merely underscores how foolish it was to let the world's media latch on to what they sensed as a 'great story'. Indeed, Rolls-Royce has never ceased to work on precisely the same kind of SuperFan version of its Tay turbofan, with a similar LP system driving through a reduction gearbox to a v-p fan of 68 in (1,727 mm) diameter, the regular Tay fan being 44 in (1,118 mm). The same company has also been working hard on an unducted RB.509 Contrapropfan, and also on an attractive RB.529 Contrafan, a ducted engine which, if brought down in size to the 30,000 lb class, could admirably suit the A340. Pratt & Whitney has a series of ADP studies (Advanced Ducted Prop) very like the SuperFan. But for the moment AI regrets ever having departed from its rule of using only proven engines.

Indeed, in the author's view it is sad Rolls-Royce failed to sell AI a derated version of the 535E4. Though roughly one *tonne* heavier than the CFM56, it is a basically much more powerful engine, and according to the author's unofficial calculations could save much more than this weight in fuel burn on each A340 full-range trip—which is what airline operation is all about. It would be an engine of incredible reliability, longevity and quietness, and ideally placed to enable the A340 to grow, as do virtually all jetliners. It would also, of course, suit a stretched A320, but not to the same degree on shorter sectors. The point at issue is that, since the Comet 1, the average increase in engine thrust over the life of each type of jetliner has been *32 per cent*. Here was an opportunity to start off nearer the future, and with a totally proven engine, with a 580,000-lb A340 using the fuselage of the A330. But everyone seemed to think the E4 would not be matched to the 330/340 wing.

Fortunately, there is no problem about the A330 itself, which though timed a year later than the A340, for May 1993, does have proven engines. There is a choice between the General Electric CF6-80C2A6 of 64,000 lb (285 kN) thrust, and the planned Pratt & Whitney PW4064 and RB.211-524L of almost the same rating. GE has the edge, and the uprated -80C2 pumps more air through its fan and LP booster stages. Thanks to progressive refinement and clearance to greater weights with more power, the range of the A330 has risen dramatically. Whereas at the 1985 Paris airshow everyone was impressed to discover that the giant twin had become a 3,200 nm vehicle, by 1987 its full-payload range had been increased to 5,000 nm (9,250 km)! There is no doubt the 330 is going to be a winner, and a natural follow-on to the A300-600R as a partner to the A310. AI expect it to sell as well as the A340 in the longer term. Only slightly longer than the A340-200, with a small extra barrel section ahead of the wing and a slightly larger one behind, the 330 does in fact match its designation in being around a 330-seater (typically 328 three-class). It will be recalled that the original A300 designation was meant to denote the number of seats, but the A330 will be the first Airbus actually to fit the numerical scheme.

But what about the ultra-long-haul A340? In the longer term IAE did AI a good turn by making them set their A340 sights a little higher. When the SuperFan vanished in a cloud of recrimination, the marketing and engineering teams at Toulouse were determined not merely to go back to Square One. Instead they worked pretty well round the clock trying to maintain the promised A340 specification by other means, and they have succeeded to an extraordinary degree. Indeed in some respects the A340 programme is now actually superior to what was offered with the SuperFan. There are several reasons for this success. One is the ability of CFM International to offer a further uprated CFM56 engine. Another is AI's ability, using this engine, to stretch the wing and increase fuel capacity and gross weight, which also carries across to the A330 and could upgrade that aircraft even beyond the previously announced 5,100 nm range!

The CFM56, first used by AI as the launch engine for the A320, was originally designed as a conventional turbofan in the 22,000 lb (97.8 kN) class. As it is basically an excellent engine it proved capable of being uprated in the CFM56-5 version to 25,000 lb (111.25 kN). For the A340 CFM pulled out all the stops and offered the CFM56-C2 at 28,600 lb (127.3 kN), an MOU (memorandum of understanding) with AI being signed in October 1986. Sadly, the SuperFan then burst on the scene; CFM International were deeply concerned at this turn of events but did not at that time try to upgrade their own engine still further. It is a pity they didn't, because this is just what they have now accomplished in the refanned CFM56-5C1 (originally designated -5S3 when first offered in April 1987), which is rated at 30,600 lb (136 kN), with a fuel burn four per cent lower than that of the A320's CFM56-5A1. This is a major achievement. In fact a development Dash-5 engine ran at 30,000 lb back in November 1986, but CFM's Ron Welsch said 'We were unwilling to commit formally to this thrust at that time because we wanted to make certain there were no problems'. Had CFM done so, according to AI's Flosdorff, '... we would have handled the whole A340 subject differently'. The new agreement with CFM was signed on 8 April 1987.

Thus the 340 is now to be powered by four engines closely related to those already in production for the A320. Indeed many of the (fairly minor) hardware changes in the -5C1 will in due course be introduced to the A320, and the more powerful engine is a natural for future stretched 320s, giving total powerplant commonality. The pods will be the same, with a Hispano-Suiza quadruple blocker-door reverser. Installed engine weight is roughly one *tonne* (2,205 lb) lighter per engine than the predicted weight for the SuperFan, reducing airframe weight by some 8,820 lb, but AI has modified the A330/340 to increase payload/range and this has added about one *tonne* to the structure.

The fuselage has hardly been altered, but, following further tunnel testing by BAe and MBB, the wing has been increased in span by adding 1.3 m (51 in) at each tip, extending span from 56 to 58.6 m (192 ft 5 in). Wingtip fences similar to the NASA type, 2.9 m (9 ft 6 in) tall have been added, and slightly more aluminium-lithium alloy is used in the skins. This has enabled gross weight to be pushed up from 238 *tonnes* (524,700 lb) to 246 *t* (542,300 lb), resulting in payload/range curves extremely close to those predicted with the SuperFan. Maximum payloads are unchanged but the final sloping line is a little steeper, giving a better range with high payloads but slightly less with low payloads. Figures in May 1987 were: 340-200, 262 passengers (three classes) for 7,700 nm (14,250 km); 340-300, 295 passengers (three classes) for 6,850 nm (12,700 km). Thus, the net result of the SuperFan fiasco was to push AI and CFM into upgrading the 340 with two advanced versions significantly more capable than the aircraft originally offered in 1986, and very close indeed to what was offered with the SuperFan. According to tough customer Abraham, 'Lufthansa considers the new 340 definition very satisfactory. We calculate that its operating economics remain about 9 per cent better than the MD-11, and we are not changing our plans to acquire the 340'. This is especially significant as Lufthansa has a fleet of DC-10s.

In several basic respects the definitive 340 is an enhanced aircraft. Its long-span wing and increased weights facilitate future stretching, both in capacity and (should any operator really need it) in range. Remarkably, CFM International can now see the possibility of getting up to 34,000 lb (154.5 kN), which could be matched with a 340 in the 330-seat or 265-*tonne* class. CFM assured the author there is stretch still left in this remarkable engine, which is worrying to International Aero Engines who believe they have a basically superior product in the V2500. With the launch engine, the -5C1, AI calculate that over a 4,000-nm sector the seat-mile cost of the 340 will be '12 per cent lower than that of all three- or four-engined rivals. Thus, the 340 will save $2 million per year per aircraft'. There is no reason to doubt this claim, which is backed up by the arithmetic done by customer airlines. In the fundamentals the 340 is—naturally—superior to the DC-10 derived MD-11, as a result of which McDonnell Douglas is forced back into concentrating on other aspects such as interior furnishing and earlier availability. In the longer term the MD-11 will probably become more difficult to sell, as its long inheritance tells increasingly against it.

The A340-200 fuselage is 12 frames longer than that of the A300-600, respective lengths being 53.3 m (174 ft 10.5 in) and 59.4 m (194 ft 10.5 in). The Dash-300 is eight frames longer still, at 63.6 m (208 ft 8 in). This is considerably bigger than the 340 originally offered in 1986, and even a little longer than the original TA9. As for the A330, there is no doubt that, without scraping its tail, GE's 64,000 lb engines could allow weight to go up from 198 to 206 *tonnes* (454,145 lb), a good jumping-off point for a further stretched version with about 420 three-class passengers. All fuselages are to be produced in Germany by Deutsche Airbus, as in the other programmes. Features will include aluminium-lithium skins, carbon fibre floor beams and struts, and doors variously of carbon fibre, SPF/DB titanium and one-piece precision castings in light alloy.

In 1986 AI had planned to launch the programme in that year, to achieve entry into service (starting with the 340) in 1991. Unfortunately this timescale was wrecked by the British and German governments showing amazing tenacity in refusing to come to any decision about launch costs, which as in previous programmes are repayable. Pressure was brought to bear on Deutsche Airbus to commit itself to the big fuselages, and to BAe to agree to take on the wing, but newly privatized BAe declined to do so, though it had the money; it said it would wait for the government launch aid. It was tough on BAe, because the wing is the only all-new part, and naturally attracts by far the biggest share of the engineering costs. The actual estimate of the British launch cost was put at £840 million in 1986, and has never altered. Back in the spring of that year Geoffrey Pattie, Minister of State for

Industry, said 'The tenor is optimistic'. But just a year later, in April 1987, *Aviation Week* quoted 'British officials' as saying 'Airline response to the two aircraft has been different from what was anticipated', suggesting that people in Whitehall continued to lack both the ability to look ahead and the courage to believe the evidence, and were concerned instead to drum up some excuse for inaction.

The author often feels like despairing in his own country. As this is written, in June 1987, the popular magazine *Air Pictorial* has run a major leading article questioning the entire Airbus programme, taking the most negative stance conceivable and overlooking the fact that for existing customers alone the twin-aisle total of 451 firm sales will eventually be doubled. It clearly doubted the wisdom of getting involved in such a chancy programme as the A340! At this time AI had signed with ten customers for 130 of the new giants, 89 of them 340s and the other 41 being 330s. Not only is this 130 more than anyone had signed for when Hawker had the guts to put up its own money to build the wing of the original A300 but it is *obviously* just the beginning. In the longer term not even the political clout of the Americans can force airlines to buy a fundamentally old aeroplane when they could buy a new one, and by 2005 even the myopic (or chicken-hearted) British will have realized this.

To be frank, we British hardly deserved this opportunity. Back in 1955 we were building the world's first long-range jetliner, the V.1000—which, unlike the original 707, had true transatlantic capability—but BOAC, the national airline, said it had no interest in such a vehicle and it was cancelled six months from first flight. Within a year BOAC had bought 15 Boeing 707s, saying 'No suitable new British aircraft can be available . . .'!! This took Britain cleanly out of the 'big league' of mainstream long-haul jets. A little later BOAC asked for the British VC10, which was essentially a 707 penalized by having to use short runways (which by this time had been lengthened to match the 707), and then publicly criticized the VC10 for being supposedly economically inferior. With such a crassly inept heritage Britain's 'establishment' does not deserve the chance offered by AI to get right back into the mainstream. But the design engineers and the people on the shop floor *do* deserve it, and at last they will get it because, after months of procrastination, Mr Pattie announced government funding of £450 million, just before Parliament was dissolved in May 1987 ready for a General Election in June.

There was a big sigh of relief from BAe. Previously the British partner had insisted upon a 90 per cent Government share of the launch costs, in other words for £750 million, which according to MD Sir Raymond Lygo would give BAe parity with its major European partners. On the basis that half a loaf is better than none, and because the terms and conditions of the loan had improved, the company said it 'happily agreed' to the lower figure, and would be prepared to find the other £390 million itself. As usual, the £450 million in British launch aid is repayable partly on a fixed timescale at an agreed rate of interest but mainly through funds generated by a levy on all A330/340 aircraft sold, beginning with a specified aircraft some way down the line. The intention is that, again as before, this levy shall continue throughout the life of the programme, so that beyond about aircraft No 600 the Government will be making a profit on its investment. Incidentally, the Department of Trade in London blamed IAE for part of the delay in arranging funding, stating that Rolls-Royce's application for over £1,000 million in launch aid for the SuperFan demanded that they scrap their original calculations on the 330/340 programme and evaluate what had become 'a totally new proposal'.

Britain was, in fact, the first of the major AI shareholders to commit government and industrial funding. In view of the seemingly sincere interest of the US government and aerospace lobby in AI funding, which is traditionally presented as an unfair 'handout' which is denied to the US industry, it is worth emphasizing that European governments do not have such sums to 'give away', and all funding is based on total repayment plus a profit in real terms over the life of the programme. The French have even gone to the banks to help fund the A320, which should prove this assertion! On the A330/340 Aérospatiale wanted a 'repayable advance' of 90 per cent of its share of $1.7 billion. The German government had set up a DM3.1 billion ($1.7 billion) credit, of which DM2.9 billion was used up on earlier programmes. As this was written, in June 1987, there was no doubt this credit would have to be extended, but Bonn has found great difficulty in getting its act together. Fortunately, the engineering design was no longer being held up, so the spring 1992 in-service date is not in peril.

In January 1987 AI entered into an agreement with Fiat Aviazione of Italy covering a 4 per cent share in the 330/340 programme, awarding Fiat responsibility for everything from research right through to production and product support for its assigned parts. A month later a similar agreement was signed with five Australian companies: Aerospace Technologies, British Aerospace (Australia), Dunlop Aviation, Hawker de Havilland and Lucas Aerospace. In each case the arithmetic was based on a run of 800 aircraft, though AI hope the total will reach 1,000.

AI at last was able to announce full go-ahead on 5 June 1987, a week before the Paris airshow. The A330/340 will now complete the entire Airbus family, enabling AI to offer vehicles seating from 140 to 400, tailored to sectors from 300 nm (555 km) to 7,850 nm (14,500 km). Not least of the remarkable features of the family is the close relationship between all the twin-aisle members of it, extending to actual commonality of parts. Even the much smaller A320 has almost exactly the same cockpit as the A330/340, though of course other differences are such as to prohibit a common pilot rating. In early 1987 AI published its forecast market share for the 20 years from 1986. Of 3,298 new narrow-body airliners it expected to sell 756, or a 23 per cent share. Of 2,005 wide-body twins it expected to sell 912 (45 per cent), while of 1,972 three/four-engined wide-bodies it expected to sell 490, or 25 per cent.

From July 1987 AI offered customers an A340-300 Combi. This marked the first time a combined passenger/freight version had been available from the start of a programme, the convertible A300 and 310 having emerged when the basic aircraft were already in service. The 340 Combi differs structurally in having a large cargo door 2.57 m (101 in) high and 3.41 m (134 in) wide located in the left rear fuselage, together with a completely flat floor in this area (in the standard 340 the rear floor slopes very slightly up towards the tail). This version can typically carry 201 passengers in three-class configuration plus six standard 2.44 m/96 in × 3.18 m/125 in cargo pallets. It can also carry the largest turbofans fully assembled, or the outsize AMA containers. Kits will enable each pallet station to be replaced by seats, so that in a few minutes the aircraft can be equipped for 231 passengers and four pallets, or for all-passenger use. MTO weight is unchanged, but MLW is up 3 *tonnes* (6,614 lb) to 183 t/403,400 lb and ZFW to 175 *tonnes*/385,800 lb, giving extra range capability. Several 340 launch customers participated in Combi development.

Another new development aimed especially at the 340 is improved crew rest areas. With these long-range aircraft sector flight times could be as long as 18 hours, and AI has responded by again leading the industry in provision for off-duty flight and cabin crew. The pilots' rest area will be directly behind the cockpit, and the mockup has upper and lower bunk-beds each 1.9 m/75 in long. With the upper bunk hinged upward the lower one converts into two seats, and by sliding aside a panel an immediate full view of the flight deck is obtained, so that an off-duty captain will always be at the nerve-centre of the aircraft. The compartment has stowage for seats and carry-on baggage, inflight entertainment/TV, fresh-air blower, reading light and emergency oxygen. Cabin crew will have a larger five-bed compartment reached by stairs from the main cabin yet quickly removable. It has the size of an LD6 container stretched to 2.44 m/96 in, at the forward end of the underfloor hold. Features include a changing room, refrigerator, interphone and, for each occupant, the same amenities as in the pilots' room. If the crew-rest area is not fitted, the entrance area can be converted into additional storage space. Airlines have not only shown a very positive response to these rest areas but are interested in offering the concept to first-class passengers!

By August 1987 the teams at Hatfield and Filton had virtually finished overall design of the 330/340 wing, though detail engineering design still remained to be done. At that time it was clear that Chester would be responsible for basic manufacture of the giant wing boxes, but it had yet to be agreed whether the equipping of the finished wings with movable surfaces would be done in Britain or by MBB in West Germany. In September British Aerospace hosted bidders' conferences in the USA and Britain to brief potential subcontractors on these wings. Even had BAe received the hoped-for £750 million government loan it would still have wished to farm out about 20 per cent of the work to share risk, share front-end costs and, by requiring subcontractors to enter into dollar contracts, provide a hedge against future growth of the £ against the $. Each wing represents approximately three times the work content of an A320 wing, and even 20 per cent on a run of 1,000-odd aircraft means many thousands of man-years of work; but only the very best suppliers will be picked to receive the carefully structured work-packages. Decisions are due in January 1988.

Quoting the price of a big jetliner is almost meaningless without careful qualification, but AI's Chairman F-J Strauss gave the price of a 747 as $135 million, saying that one-quarter of that was the extra cost to the airlines of a monopoly supplier. AI sources have given the price of an A330 as about $80 million, and a 340 as $84 million, in 1987 currency. As already noted, AI themselves have merely stated that the direct seat-mile operating cost of the 340 will be 'at least 12 per cent lower than that of the latest competing three- and four-engined aircraft (such as the MD-11 and 747-400) on a 4,000 nm (7,400 km) sector, saving roughly $2 million per aircraft per year'. The DOC of the A330 'will not even be approached by any competitor' over sectors around 2,000 nm (3,700 km), with the ability to fly more than twice this sector distance. Lufthansa gets the first delivered A340 in May 1992, and Air Inter gets the first A330 in October 1993.

Only in the market slot occupied by the 747 does AI have no competitor aircraft (neither does anyone else). In all other major jet markets AI will compete very strongly indeed, and in view of the fact that it is a leader in new technology, and in progressive updating of all its aircraft, the production runs look like being unbroken over a period of at least 25 years. As this book has shown repeatedly, AI has an established track record not merely of offering strong competition to the US planemakers but even in beating them in the markets in which it has competed. For example, AI has exported 343 wide-body twins (March 1987) while Boeing has exported 74. This kind of thing disturbs the Americans greatly. When Northwest agreed to buy 20 A340s plus an option for ten A330s, in April 1987, a row naturally broke out in Washington. A US trade official was quoted by *Aviation Week* as saying 'It made some people in this office ricochet off the walls'. He added that the pricing of the $2.5bn order would be 'carefully scrutinized, as will any order of Airbus aircraft'.

The nub of the problem is that the US has little history of fighting against industrial competitors. Its entire heritage is one of industrial supremacy, often so total as to make all opposition ineffectual on the global scale; and this has very much been the case with commercial jetliners. Now, rather suddenly, there are areas of high technology where the competition is powerful, and to some degree even seems to be winning. One such area is integrated circuits, or microchips, where the US giants are struggling to compete with Japan. Amazingly, another area is commercial jets, where all the US worry and anger is polarized against a single dreaded name: Airbus!

To help sell its products the 64-stone giant among planemakers, Boeing, has even been reduced to working out complex deals which result in its ownership of a large chunk of United, the biggest airline in the Western world. As the magazine *Flight International* observed, 'If the Airbus partners had taken up airline-stock purchase, as a step on the route to selling one of their products, the outcry from the US would have oscillated between noisy and deafening. The main benefit may be that complaints about the Airbus partners' governments subsidizing its products might now subside, and a new tune be heard from the marketplace harmoniums'.

With six major US customers already, Airbus is still the proverbial red rag to the bull of the US industry lobby and its friends in Washington. The bone of contention is the supposition that Airbus, instead of being a grouping of commercial companies, is some kind of national government-sponsored outfit which subsidizes its products, dumps everything at below cost and does not need to make a profit. This belief is childish, and insulting to the US airlines. The fact that AI's members are actually commercial companies responsible to shareholders, who expect them to make a profit, has to be ignored for this nonsensical idea to be entertained. Boeing knows better than to suggest that AI is not a commercial outfit; it believes in a head-on assault, and its Thomas Bacher got much publicity by asserting that Europe 'ought not to build commercial jets, but concentrate on those things it does best, like trains'. Apart from the fact that this would hardly go down well with the US trainmakers, it betokens a lack of sensitivity and an un-American wish to dispense with competition as soon as it becomes effective.

In fact, such a publicly expressed suggestion is the best compliment AI could wish for. AI President Jean Pierson was secretly delighted, though he did take the trouble to announce 'We ain't giving up!' This is despite the ongoing hassle of trying to keep those 39 nationalities all pulling in the same direction. One is reminded of an item in Roger Bacon's column in *Flight International* back in 1976: 'Overheard at a meeting on the A300, "Mais on trouve que le shroud box est kaput!"' And of an official report, early in the flight test programme, where Bernard Ziegler wrote 'We have created a most wilful test team'. How can Boeing and McDonnell Douglas ever hope to vanquish such wilful people?

Basic data (US Imperial)

	TWIN-AISLE PRECURSORS						TWIN-		
	Sud Galion	Breguet Br.124	Nord 600	HBN.100	AB300	A300B1	A300B2	A300B4 -100	A300B4 -200
Typical passenger load	241	2490	250	225	267	36+203	26+225	26+225	26+225
Range with these pax (NM)	807	868	809	930	1,200	1,187	1,800	2,098	3,200
First airline delivery	—	—	—	—	—	Nov 74	May 74	May 75	—
Engine choice	RB.178 or JT9D	Four RR Spey 50	Four RR Spey 50	JT9D-1 or RB.178-51	JT9D-3 or RB.207	CF6-50A	CF6-50C	CF6-50C2 or JT9D-59A	CF6-50C2 or JT9D-59A
Engine thrust-class (lb)	40,000	12,830	12,830	41,000	44,000	49,000	51,000	51,000	53,000
Overall length (ft)		147.3	148.7	146.7	159.9	167.2	175.8	175.8	175.8
Fuselage diameter (ft)	20.0	26 × 15		18.8	21.0	18.5	18.5	18.5	18.5
Wingspan (ft)		131.3	118.2	129.0	147.9	147.1	147.1	147.1	147.1
Wing area (sq ft)				2,200	2,800	2,799	2,799	2,800	2,800
Wing sweep (degrees)		30		30	28	28	28	28	28
Overall height (ft)				49.9	52.8	54.3	54.3	54.3	54.3
Max take-off weight (1,000 lb)		209.4	209.4	207.6	264.6	291.0	313.1	330.7	363.8
Max landing weight (1,000 lb)		151.0		189.0	251.3	264.6	286.6	293.2	299.8
Operating weight empty for typical airline (1,000 lb)					153.4	181.3	187.8	192.7	195.1
Max payload (1,000 lb)		55.1	52.9	48.4	59.6	59.0	78.7	77.3	82.7
Max fuel capacity (US gal)				7,506	12,010	11,361	11,361	14,471	16,600
Underfloor container capacity					14 LD3	16 LD3	20 LD3	20 LD3	20 LD3

Basic data (Metric)

	TWIN-AISLE PRECURSORS						TWIN-		
	Sud Galion	Breguet Br.124	Nord 600	HBN.100	AB300	A300B1	A300B2	A300B4 -100	A300B4 -200
Typical passenger load	241	240	250	225 (261)	267	36+203	26+225	26+225	26+225
Range with these pax (km)	1,495	1,600	1,500	1,725	2,225	2,200	3,335	3,890	5,900
First airline delivery	—	—	—	—	—	Nov 74	May 74	May 75	May 75
Engine choice	RB.178 or JT9D	Four RR Spey 50	Four RR Spey 50	JT9D-1 or RB.178-51	CF6-50A or RB.207	CF6-50C	CF6-50C	CF6-50C2 or JT9D-59A	CF6-50C2 or JT9D-59A
Engine thrust-class (kN)	177	56.9	56.9	182	195	217	226	226	235
Overall length (m)	43.0	44.9	45.3	44.7 (48.16)	48.7	51.0	53.6	53.6	53.6
Fuselage diameter (m)	6.1	7.9 × 4.6	—	5.73	6.4	5.64	5.64	5.64	5.64
Wingspan (m)	40.0	40.0	36.0	39.3	45.1	44.8	44.8	44.8	44.8
Wing area (sq m)	—	—	—	204	260	260	260	260	260
Wing sweep (degrees)	30	30	—	30	28	28	28	28	28
Overall height (m)	14.6	—	—	15.2	16.1	16.5	16.5	16.5	16.5
Max take-off weight (tonnes)	95.0	95.0	95.0	94.2 (100.8)	120.0	132.0	142.0	150.0	165.0
Max landing weight (tonnes)	—	68.5	—	85.73	114.0	120.0	130.0	133.0	136.0
Operating weight empty for typical airline (tonnes)	—	—	—	—	69.58	82.24	85.19	87.41	88.5
Max payload (tonnes)	—	25.0	24.0	21.95	27.0	26.76	35.7	35.0	37.5
Max fuel capacity (lit)	—	—	—	28,440	45,500	43,050	43,050	54,830	62,900
Underfloor container capacity	—	—	—	—	14 LD3	16 LD3	20 LD3	20 LD3	20 LD3

Notes
(1) Some figures are rounded (2) Brackets distinguish different aircraft versions
(3) Typical seating is first and economy, except for the A340 which is first, business and economy
(4) Weights and ranges are for aircraft currently on offer, and performance varies slightly between engine types
(5) A320's cargo containers are LD3s with a reduced height of 1.17 m

AISLE TWINS				SINGE-AISLE	PROJECTS (DEC/86)				1987		
					TWIN-AISLE	FOUR-ENGINED		TWIN-AISLE	TWIN-AISLE	FOUR-ENGINED	TWIN-AISLE
A310-200	A310-300	A300-600	A300-600R	A320	A340-300	A340-200	A340-200	A330	A340-300	A340-200	A330
20+198	20+198	28+239	28+239	12+138	18+84+193	18+74+170	18+74+170	30+298	18+84+193	18+74+170	30+298
3,700 (4,000)	4,500 (4,900)	3,700	4,200 (4,350)	3,150	7,000	7,850	7,000	5,100	6,850	7,700	5,000
March 83 Sept 83	Dec 85	March 84	Spring 88	Spring 88	Mid 92	End 92	Late 93	Mid 93	Mid 92	End 92	Mid 93
CF6-80C2 or PW4000 (mid-1987)	CF6-80C2 or PW4000 (mid-1987)	CF6-80C2 or PW4000 (1987)	CF6-80C2 or PW4000	CFM56-5 or V2500 (spring 1989)	V2500SF	V2500SF	CFM56-5-S2	CF6-80C2 or PW4000	CFM56-5C-1	CFM56-5C-1	CF6-80C2 or PW4000
52–53,500	52–53,500	56–59,000	58–61,000	25,000	30,000	30,000	28,600	60–62,500	30,600	30,600	62–64,000
153.1	153.1	177.5	177.5	123.3	208.7	194.8	194.8	205.3	208.7	194.8	205.3
18.5	18.5	18.5	18.5	13.0	18.5	18.5	18.5	18.5	18.5	18.5	18.5
144	144	147.1	147.1	111.3	183.8	183.8	133.8	183.8	192.4	192.4	192.4
2,360	2,360	2,800	2,800	1,320	3,660	3,660	3,660	3,660	3,890	3,890	3,890
28	28	28	28	25	30	30	30	30	30	30	30
51.8	51.8	54.3	54.3	38.6	54.9	54.9	54.9	54.9	54.9	54.9	54.9
305.6 (313.1)	330.7 (337.3) (346.1)	363.8	375.9 (378.5)	158.7	524.7	524.7	511.5	449.7	549.0	549.0	458.6
269.0 (273.4)	271.2 (271.2) (273.4)	304.2	308.6	138.9	392.4	392.4	368.2	368.2	399.0	394.6	377.0
173.4 (173.4)	174.0 (174.0)	194.5	195.1	87.8	268.9	260.4	252.4	243.0	269.9	261.2	252.0
73.4 (73.4)	75.1 (77.4)	92.1	91.5	42.2	97.1	105.6	89.4	103.1	102.7	107.0	102.9
14,500	16,100 (18,000)	16,600	18,000 (19,300)	6,190	33,660	33,660	33,660	23,800	35,670	35,670	24,700
14–15 LD3	14–15 LD3	22–23 LD3	22–23 LD3	7 mini LD3	32 LD3	26 LD3	26 LD3	30 LD3	32 LD3	26 LD3	30 LD3

AISLE TWINS				SINGE-AISLE	PROJECTS (DEC/86)				1987		
					TWIN-AISLE	FOUR-ENGINED		TWIN-AISLE	TWIN-AISLE	FOUR-ENGINED	TWIN-AISLE
A310-200	A310-300	A300-600	A300-600R	A320	A340-300	A340-200	A340-200	A330	A340-300	A340-200	A330
20+198	20+198	28+239	28+239	12+138	18+84+193	18+74+170	18+74+170	30+298	18+84+193	18+74+170	30+298
6,900 (7,400)	8,350 (9,100)	6,800	7,800 (8,050)	5,850	12,900	14,500	13,000	9,400	12,700	14,100	9,250
March 83 March 84	Dec 85	March 84	Spring 88	Spring 88	Mid 92	End 92	Late 93	Mid 93	Mid 92	End 92	Mid 93
CF6-80C2 or PW4000 (mid-1987)	CF6-80C2 or PW4000 (mid-1987)	CF6-80C2 or PW4000 (1987)	CF6-80C2 or PW4000	CFM56-5 or V2500 (spring 1989)	V2500SF	V2500SF	CFM56-5-S2	CF6-80C2 or PW4000	CFM56-5C-1	CFM-5C-1	CF6-80C2 or PW4000
230–240	230–240	250–260	260–270	110	135	135	130	270	136	136	270–290
46.7	46.7	54.1	54.1	37.6	63.6	59.4	59.4	62.6	63.6	59.4	62.6
5.64	5.64	5.64	5.64	3.95	5.64	5.64	5.64	5.64	5.64	5.64	5.64
43.9	43.9	44.8	44.8	33.9	56.0	56.0	56.0	56.0	58.6	58.6	58.6
220	220	260	260	122	340	340	340	340	362	362	362
28	28	28	28	25	30	30	30	30	30	30	30
15.8	15.8	16.5	16.5	11.8	16.7	16.7	16.7	16.7	16.7	16.7	16.7
138.6 (142.0)	153.0 (153.0) (157.0)	165.0	170.5 (171.7)	72.0	238.0	238	232.0	204.0	249.0	249.0	208.0
122.0 (124.0)	123.0 (124.0)	138.0	140.0	63.0	178.0	178.0	167.0	167.0	181.0	179.0	171.0
78.7 (78.7)	78.9 (78.9)	88.2	88.5	39.8	122.0	118.1	114.5	110.2	122.4	118.5	114.3
33.3 (35.3)	34.1 (35.1)	41.8	41.5	19.1	44.0	47.9	40.5	46.8	46.6	48.5	46.7
55,000	61,100 (68,100)	62,000	68,100 (73,000)	23,700	127,400	127,400	127,400	90,100	135,000	135,000	93,500
14–15 LD3	14–15 LD3	22–23 LD3	22–23 LD3	7 mini LD3	32 LD3	26 LD3	26 LD3	30 LD3	32 LD3	26 LD3	30 LD3

(6) The 9,100 km A310-300 and 8,050 km A300-600R options include an additional fuel-cell in the aft cargo-hold
(7) Convertible versions of the A300, A310 and A300-600 are also in service
(8) Last A300B4 version produced in autumn 1984

Airbus Industrie A320-200 Cutaway Drawing Key

1 Radome
2 Weather radar scanner
3 Scanner tracking mechanism
4 VOR localiser aerial
5 Front pressure bulkhead
6 ILS glideslope aerial
7 Forward underfloor electronic equipment bay
8 Rudder pedals
9 Thomson-CSF Electronic Flight Instrument System (EFIS)
10 Instrument panel shroud
11 Windscreen wipers
12 Windscreen panels
13 Overhead systems switch panel
14 First-officer's seat
15 Centre control pedestal
16 Circuit breaker panel
17 Observer's folding seat
18 Captain's seat
19 Direct vision opening side window panel
20 Sidestick controller (fly-by-wire flight control system)
21 Artificial feel and sensor units
22 Crew wardrobe
23 Nose undercarriage wheel bay
24 Nosewheel doors
25 Twin nosewheels
26 Hydraulic steering jacks
27 Messier nose undercarriage leg strut
28 Nosewheel leg pivot fixing
29 Forward toilet compartment
30 Cockpit doorway
31 Galley unit
32 Starboard service door (32 × 72 in/81 × 183 cm)
33 Entry lobby
34 Cabin attendant's folding seats (two)
35 Door latch
36 Forward entry door (32 × 72 in/ 81 × 183 cm)
37 Door mounted escape chute
38 Optional airstairs stowage
39 Underfloor avionics equipment racks
40 Door surround structure
45 VHF communications aerial
46 Overhead stowage bins
47 Curtained cabin divider
48 Cabin wall trim panelling
49 Six-abreast economy-class seating (138 passengers) alternative layout for 164 all economy seats at 32-in pitch
50 Overhead conditioned air delivery ducts
51 Cabin window panel
52 Cabin wall frames
53 Lower lobe frame and stringer construction
54 Wing root leading-edge fillet
55 LD3-46 baggage/cargo container (three forward and four aft)
56 Slat drive shaft gearbox
57 Conditioned air distribution ducting
58 Wing spar centre-section carry-through
59 Fuselage keel assembly
60 Ventral air conditioning packs, port and starboard (Liebherr-Aerotechnik and ABG-Semca)
61 Port overwing emergency exit hatches (20 × 40 in/51 × 102 cm)
62 Wing centre box fuel tank (capacity 1,777 Imp gal/2,135 US gal/8,078 l)
63 Wing front spar/fuselage main frame
64 Centre-section floor beams
65 Starboard emergency exit hatches
66 Centre fuselage frame and stringer construction
68 Wing tank dry bay
69 Inboard leading-edge slat segment
70 Thrust reverser petal door (Rohr Industries)
71 Starboard CFM International CFM56-5 engine nacelle
72 Nacelle pylon
73 Outboard leading-edge slat segments
78 Outboard vent surge tank
79 Starboard navigation lights
80 Wing-tip
81 Tail navigation and strobe lights
82 Starboard aileron
83 Aileron hydraulic actuators
84 Roll control and load alleviation spoilers
85 Spoiler hydraulic jacks
86 Flap rotary actuator and carriage mechanism
87 Starboard single-slotted Fowler-type flaps (down position)
88 Roll control spoilers/speedbrakes
89 Inboard flap segment
90 Inboard speed brake/lift dumper
91 Flap drive shaft and rotary actuator
92 Fuselage skin panelling
93 Cabin wall sound-proofing linings
94 Pressure floor above wheel bay
95 Wing rear spar/fuselage main frame
96 Starboard main undercarriage (stowed position)

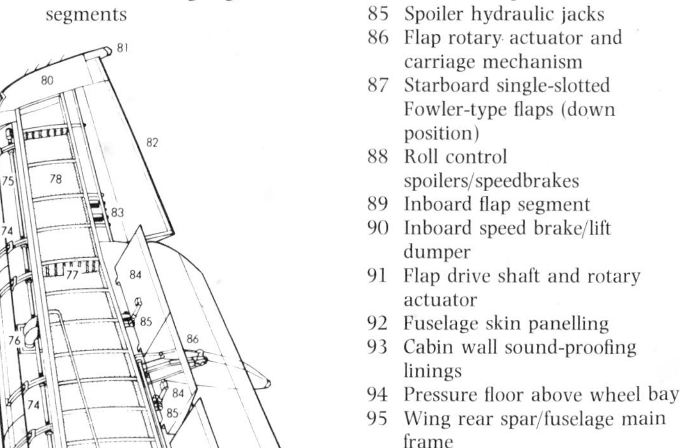

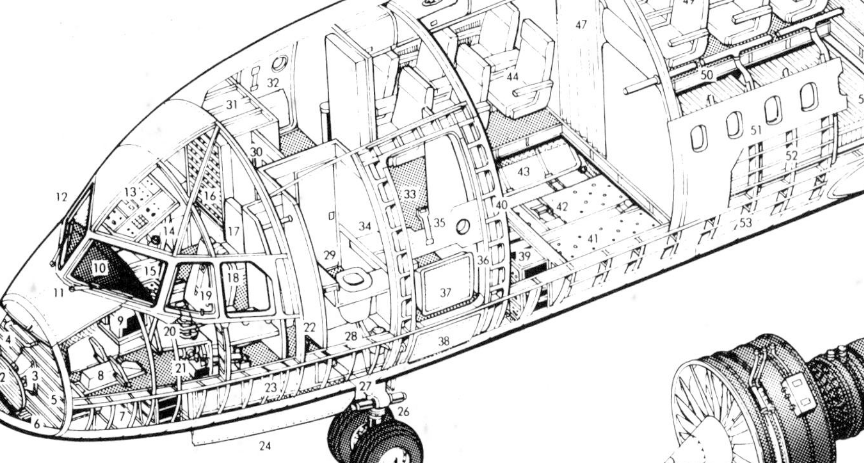

41 Forward underfloor cargo hold (490 cu ft/13.87 m^3)
42 Mechanised cargo handling deck
43 Forward cargo hold door (71.5 × 49 in/182 × 125 cm)
44 Four-abreast first-class passenger seating at 36-in pitch (12 passengers)
67 Starboard wing integral fuel tank (total fuel capacity including centre-section tank, 5,206 Imp gal/6,253 US gal/23,666 l for CFM56-5-powered aircraft and 5,154 Imp. gal/6,191 US gal/23,432 l for V2500-powered aircraft)
74 Slat guide rails
75 Slat drive shaft and rotary actuators
76 Pressure refuelling connections
77 Fuel tank dividing ribs
97 Central flap drive motor and gearbox
98 Undercarriage bay pressure bulkhead
99 Floor beam construction